Proud City:

The Unaware Revolution

Proud City:

The Unaware Revolution

by

Amo Sulaiman

Amrit Singh
Berlin
June 2002

PICASSO
ENTERTAINMENT
CORPORATION

Visit our Website at

www.picassopublications.com

A Picasso Publications Inc. Paperback

PROUD CITY:
The Unaware Revolution

This edition published 2001
by Picasso Publications Inc.
Unit A 10548 115 Street
Edmonton, AB, Canada T5H 3K6

ISBN 1-55279-033-9

This work is fiction. All names refer to fictitious entities.

Printed in Canada

DEDICATION
In honour of my family

Christine, Michelle, and Marc.
Most importantly to my mother who wants me to write something non-philosophical. And to the loving people who made a difference in my life: Jameer, Ameer, Jameela, Faz, Rafiq, Nazeer, Nasmin, Bibi, Salima, and Moneer. Also to a complete stranger who told me to put my heart into it over twenty-five years ago.

1: Charles

Charles Brown, the owner of the pizza restaurant All-In-One, was nothing less than a chubby chap in his late twenties, a really jolly fellow to be with and to have a drink with, a very refined speaker who naturally entertained and amused his table with an odd mixture of humanism and sarcasm; war and humanity; and laughter and existentialism. At work, he was profoundly respected for his humanistic values, personal integrity, and diverse abilities. When machines broke, he slipped into the dancing shoes of a service technician; when bills and payrolls arrived, he put on his spectacles as a keen accountant. As an experienced purchasing agent and a naturalist, he sought quality and an adequate stock.

He trained and guided all his new workers to be responsible; and yet, he influenced them to be free from identification with the company. He motivated everyone by reminding them of the noble objective that they had to pursue to survive as a dignified person with real abilities. His awareness of the traditional relationship between the server and the served, was humbly practiced in his restaurant; an invisible bond bound him to his customers, as though he was a small grain of sand with the immeasurable desire to be near other grains like himself.

His other side was a little bit ruthless. With an enthusiastic philosophy on his face, he could shift to a pit bull terrier against offensive adults who attempted to violate the rule, "UP TO 20 YEARS." He encouraged each of his employees to quit working there after five years of service, for serving at the same place for too long often reduced people to a sad, mechanical existence. Aware that each person had his or her personal speed of learning, Charles helped his employees to acquire a small piece of knowledge and the skills for obtaining more, and their incentive to know more often led to a healthy life. No employer wanted his employees to become senile at one place, so they had to seek valuable knowledge, which was not available at his restaurant, elsewhere. A perpetual flux of employees every five years could remove the false security, boredom, stress, and fictitious self-identity which haunted most workers, and people in general.

He protected his natural leadership tendencies from being combed strand by strand by his indignant society, informing his dedicated employees that work started there and ended there. Charles believed that breaks could enhance good health; a person who failed to have his or her break was harshly penalized by being forced to do nothing for several hours in the restaurant. Such severe punishments reduced a person to a state of dreadful nothingness; the most awful torture that could be inflicted on a living organism is to put that person in a state of boredom and uselessness. Whether his philosophy came from the stars or circumstances, his past experiences had opened his door.

Though he had shown responsibility and common sense ethics in managing his restaurant, five years ago the idea of starting a business had been unthinkable. After he had graduated from university, vandalism, burglary, unemployment, and environmental destruction were on the rise. Ordinary people were living on the edge of being mugged by multinational corporations and being freely starved to death. To combat the crowded streets, the police department was overwhelmed with business. By indignantly faking his intelligence test, he was quickly hired.

He met his wife, Elizabeth, a year after. She devoted her life to social work in town, and the social services and police departments worked closely together. Even when she was in bed, human misery and suffering were deeply ingrained in her, and it would take her several thousand years to live with a clean conscience. She did not seek the impossible, only some understanding and compassion from her husband, so she could face the next day.

The department of forgiveness and pity was a powerful mechanism to hide societal injustice, compared to the retribution office, which reinforced public responsibilities by perfecting its power over people who did not have the legal means to challenge authorities. Since demand was flourishing; the police department supplied officers with surplus power to make a conviction with each arrest. "To serve and to protect" on a police car meant that an officer was on duty while his comrades protected him like a fragile egg.

Their marriage confirmed societal expectations, as both of them worked irregular hours. They saw each other more often at work than at home, where normal conflicts, dependencies, pleasures, and sharing occurred; and several other variables were added to their life, for which they had had no previous training. Yet marriage resisted the haunting danger of isolation and loneliness that threatened most individuals. All this was common knowledge among couples who had to work to overcome their daily obstacles.

The police department attempted to confuse any unprepared officer about the distinction between a person's private life and his profession. Other officers conceived themselves as officers in their own private beds to apprehend their own families. They enjoyed their identification, especially after working hours, reinventing the ideal citizen with which they had been indoctrinated from childhood. Though laws were for everyone, enforcers turned to the poor side of society to make themselves heroes and heroines. But Charles was different. As long as he wore his uniform, he was confined to carrying out his duties as a professional, but when he was off the job, he wore the hat of an ordinary person. When the line dividing work and non-work finally blurred for Charles, it caused a major turning point in his life. He quit the police department and opened his restaurant.

Every evening Charles went for a walk outside of the mall, and on many of these occasions he met Martin Twig, his right hand employee. Tonight was no exception.

"Hi, Martin. How are you?" asked Charles.

"Fine. I guess I'll be late again. Whenever I meet you here, I always arrive late to work."

"Every night I walk out here and look at the lights of the city. But Proud City is something we take for granted; we don't even think about it. Other cities tickle our imagination, and we glorify them for some reason. The City of God, The Twin Cities, The City of Cities, Paradise City, The Rainbow City and The City of Hope. these are high-spirited cities, and people would love to live in them. We believe that an invisible hand holds everybody together in these cities." He glanced at Martin.

"Yes, Charles! But your horror would peel off your skin by just mentioning the name of some low-spirit cities: The Muddy City, The Burned City, The Stinky City, Pigs City, The Rotten City and The Dead City. Cities are like kingdoms. Some are rising in body and mind while others are killing their bohemian soul. In today's cities, the voiceless herd live closely together as they wait for deliverance. Their despair hisses endlessly in the wind because there are no outsiders in any city. I can't run away from the dirt of a city."

"Don't be so negative, Martin! Cities hide themselves in dark smoke. And to penetrate the patched smoke, you can see a way of life like in our Proud City. Oh, Proud City! It's high-spirited; and yet, it has inherited a low-spirit. Proud City could be any city in the world. It could be a hospital, a family. And it could be a person. The low spirit of Proud City is about social problems, human relations, personal problems and conflict. The high spirit of Proud City is rising everywhere and gaining momentum to reshape human reality. It's the revolution of revolutions in which young adults are overcoming possible world situations, and actual ones, too. The inhabitants of this Proud City are mostly young adults and children, today. They live in the actual world. From their hopes, wishes, dreams and actions, they'll transform social reality to a new order. We'll have a possible world worth living in."

"Charles, if Proud City wants to survive for another two millennia, not just ten years, it must overcome itself continuously. Some people, regardless of their social status, would try to take the upper hand of any institutional system. So, Proud City has to be flexible to adapt to changes."

"That's why I like speaking to you. You have such an insight into things. Proud City drags its pernicious, deteriorating body along to show its world-reality."

"Look, Charles! The Big Time Believer in any city has a devastating effect on most people, especially the poor. These desolated sufferers cry out for more concrete. You see how the brick jungle spreads about here. More companies mean jobs for everyone. Industries sweep in. Service companies quickly follow. New apartments, shopping complexes, bars and nightclubs, stripteases are close behind. To counter amusements, more schools jump into services. More jobs echo. At first, adults are intoxicated by their healthy means of survival. They have more spending money in their pockets. Playgrounds, parks, and open areas soon disappear. The daily traffic congestion and huge tractor-trailers drive us off the streets. Indoor sports facilities drain our pockets. Now, we can barely escape our predicament. At first, we hesitantly go to shopping malls. Today, our ant hole civilization doesn't surpass our malls. If we don't have any money, private security guards will kick us out. Do you see what I'm talking about, Charles?"

"Yes, I'm listening."

"Now, we don't have any money to do any shopping. So, we run outside for help. Industrial buildings are closing their doors. The service sector is also going. The fences are growing higher around vacant buildings. The traffic is dying down. I don't have the same kind of pollution around to make me tired and drowsy, so I can't sleep at night. I have all this energy without any outlets. Oh, yes! Entertainment stays back with drugs and alcohol for me. Now, it is possible for me to put myself to sleep throughout the night as well as the day. The brain-dead world remains with us." He looked very frustrated and disgusted.

"Yes, Martin. I agree with you. Companies take over the young adults' and children's playgrounds and parks. They poison them with treacherous and decadent hope. Adults condemn the crib to self-destruction. They starve their children of their own natural resources. Proud City inherits all this gloomy reality. We've got a world in which adults' heads are buried in the ground, their feet kicking in the air. These disappointed believers of a quick fortune stand passively with an empty wallet. I see this everyday in the mall. Most people aren't considered human beings anymore, because products and services have reduced them to the level of consumers."

"I'm angry with our parents, and most adults," Martin said. "With this high level of unemployment, my smile is gone. No new companies are coming where there are no buyers. And yet, the world is kicking with weak feet, because a few residents are allowed to screw others. Now, the unemployed are nailing nails by hammering the sharp end. At first, workers were flat headed. They couldn't see that human values begin at childhood—with the open world, free terrain to run and discover, and games in wide open fields—not at adulthood."

"I spoke to a lot of store owners in the mall," Charles began. "They told me very proudly that businesses had lured adults and parents to sell out the young, because businesses' objectives seldom include the entire family and the neighborhood as their valuable partners. Businesses have their own idealism—measuring the world as endless and worshipping their own Big Time Believer."

"You didn't tell them that the sucked people couldn't last forever," Martin interrupted. "I think that they finally realize that. Now, companies are investing in globalization. They want to suck the people in poor countries without a grain of remorse. Well, vampires have never abandoned their victims. They just leave behind a new generation of suckers in the world, seeking out fresh blood. The Romans practiced globalization: all roads led to Rome. Now, they lead to the Vatican. Columbus supposedly discovered the New World. Businesses still claim that there are infinite sources of food without touching their own tail again. Oh, the current business trend is nothing more than the universalization of unemployment. Businesses want to make it an irrefutable scientific law."

"What would this law look like?"

"Oh, the way things are going, a sweet screw will only be six inches long, and businesses will change the board to match the size. Today, I'm thrown into a carved-out lifestyle as a buyer without any money. And this is a one-dimensional road leading to

Rome—the smallest country in the world with only one inhabitant. Prey or perish, that's what Proud City has inherited." Martin turned and looked at Fairview Shopping Center in the core of Proud City. From where they were standing they could see All-In-One. They walked toward it and sat on a bench in front of it.

"All-In-One stands for hope. It defends a world, not an ideal that could be consumed by lifeless rocks and reckless technologies, Martin," Charles said.

"But Charles, this shopping center is notorious for its architectural form and simplicity. It could reduce everyone to namelessness. It has the power to transcend money, to transcend a person's personalities and religion."

"I have walked around this huge L-shaped building many times. It somehow fuses all the socioeconomic classes with the three roads pouring out from the building to three different geographical areas of the city."

"Charles, why do you have to be so romantic? Let me tell you how I see it."

"Go ahead, if you wish."

"Look here, Charles! Let's walk around the building, and I'll show you how degraded I feel."

"Okay."

They got up and started out. "This straight road is linked to the apex of the triangular building. This is the positive y-axis, Charles. And this road here flows without any intersection to the highbrow area. It has three percent of the houses, and it occupies forty percent of Proud City's territory. Our friend Virus lives there, and I went to his place several times. Up there, the soil is so fertile that wooden fence posts could grow roots and branches. But that enriched plateau is free from farming machines. And excess rainwater easily drains downward. This is how those people protect their expensive merchandise and prevent offensive reptiles, insects and bushes from breeding carelessly. Their yards, hedges, and golf courses are genetically carved for them to enjoy their breathless scenery, without any rodents to enjoy it and become a nuisance. They only have genetically modified trees up there. They heed to their preprogrammed height, weight, size, shape, and number of branches and leaves, so they can kill off competitors. They influence all trees in other areas to struggle for their ideal value."

"Martin, in the evening, I usually sit right here with other Fairview customers. We gaze at the gradual elevation ascending to one hundred and fifty yards. The road with light bulbs on both sides makes parallel lines upward. The stream of lights appears to converge on an open area. And it gives me the impression of an inverted umbrella, which our ancient cosmos called the heaven, an inverted bowl. From here, when it's darker, you can see escaping light rays passing through tree branches. It looks as if it forms the outer corner of a foggy mushroom. And other street and house lights peep out like stars. As it becomes a bit darker, the little mushroom appears to be molded onto heaven's door, with the main road showing the golden stairs. It's unbelievable." He stared at the highbrow residential area in amazement. Martin shook his head in disbelief.

"Charles, poor ordinary people are waiting for a golden hair to fall off Zeus' beard. And the lucky person who finds it will be able to walk the golden stairs in pride."

"Yes! Ordinary people do have their own Big Time Believer. They want to be rich and live like the elite in society."

Martin got up very quickly and went to the other part of the shopping mall, and Charles followed slowly behind. "Charles! Look at this flat roof. This part is the end of the x-axis of the building. You see how this straight road runs to the huge door. It provides quick access to Fairview, and at the same time it goes to the heart of town. You know very well that only lowbrows live there. Over seventy percent of the population lives in town. And they occupy about thirty percent of the residential areas of Proud City. Last summer, I was in town when we had a rainstorm. Whenever the poor complain and shout their anger, it rains. And then it turns into a blistering thunderstorm. Highbrow's exhausted sewers swim downward. They flood the entire town and silence all screams with a mouthful of yellow sausages. Some of my friends who live in basements have nothing else to lose. They struggle to keep their nose and mouth high above the water, as they howl to any deity for deliverance. And that isn't all, Charles! An answer speeds up in their hour of distress. Yellow public buses wait on the main road to take them to the final stop, the entrance of Fairview. Here, they can get back their greatness, success and newness."

"I see how you feel about all this, Martin." Charles waited for Martin to take him to the next entrance of the shopping center.

"Here is our last entrance of Fairview. It looks nice, doesn't it? It stretches away from the external angle of the building at the x- and y-coordinate. You know very well, that this centralized straight road runs to the bosom of middlebrow. Most middle class people fight bravely against nature. And even a few keenly absorb non-polluted floodwater from lowbrow. In a rare case, I saw the water's unforeseen mystical power float a iddlebrow house up as high as highbrow. And then it claimed a natural right for residency. But today, Charles, it's a different ball game. The excess water from the high region causes merciless landslides in middlebrow. It weakens the foundation of houses, and they slip downward continuously. The barrier between middlebrow and lowbrow is disappearing."

"Oh, living on shaky ground, being caught in the web of uncertainty, seeing life melting away in a boiling pot—these things trap the middlebrow in a tube. And this tube gathers heat until its internal pressure spits them out onto the second floor of Fairview. You're not aware of our second floor, Martin. You see here, the middlebrow don't have any special shopping departments in Fairview. Do you see those people walking down the stuck escalator going to the basement?"

"Yes! A minute ago, I thought I saw Chuck on it."

"Maybe he's going to the restaurant. Anyway, these people walk around backward and forward in here. I feel sorry for these people because they have a face at the back of their head to neutralize coming and going. Do you see how they cry for stability and security?"

"Yes! What can we do when these people deny the idea of being classified as lowbrow? They're a bunch of worshippers of the glorious status of highbrow. Reality tolerates either winners or losers. These societal participants fail to recognize the harsh truth of civilization: superman or herd."

"Our fictitious middlebrow emerges from two extreme states of the world. And for their misconception of reality, immediate treatments are administered on the second floor. General medical clinics, dental clinics, marriage counselors, legal counselors, moralists, insurance companies, mortgage offices, all feed off the middlebrow. Misery and despair cruelly encircle this segment of society. Today, middlebrow accept the thought of going fishing in a desert, and the direction of their world goes about without being on its axis."

"This building really enhances class division."

"In a way, yes."

"The three main roads running out from the shopping center are connected about a mile away from Fairview's parking lot. The lowbrow road branches off to middlebrow, which further branches off to highbrow. The middlebrow road that goes to highbrow has no stoplight. At that intersection, a video camera is aimed in the direction of traffic coming up. A police officer directs all traffic at that junction. His job is important, for an accident could be very costly for insurance companies. Lowbrow residents going to highbrow have to pass though middlebrow. I don't understand why there isn't any direct connection between lowbrow and highbrow. This is exclusion by classes."

"Fairview's parking lot is benevolently structured, too. They didn't do this because they want to save chauffeurs time searching for their cars in this huge lot. They didn't do it for security or to deter racers. How could you explain a three foot concrete wall here? Concrete walls are at a right angle to the building's parking, and nobody has any access across a certain barrier. The upper half exclusively belongs to highbrow while the lower one is available for the lowbrow. From the middlebrow entrance, there's another straight three-footer running across the parking area. Why would they want to separate lowbrow cars and middlebrow ones? Because nobody wants his expensive new car to be vandalized or scratched! Honestly, I can't believe it. And when I parked my car in the middlebrow parking, I couldn't get to Virus's car because there's another concrete barrier. At least, for the middlebrow and lowbrow, it's not so bad. I see a few middlebrows parking their cars in lowbrow parking, and a few lowbrows leave their cars in the middlebrow section."

"Remember, Martin!" Charles interrupted, "All roads converge at Fairview. For shopping, almost no barrier prevents people from mingling, lobbying, exhibiting their uniqueness, seeking out acknowledgement, comparing prices, window shopping, and buying. How ridiculous would it be to put a restriction on the life of hard cash? Money, my friend, has a natural tendency to search for security and to be among other bundles. The bigger the bundle, the stronger the bondage. And any member of a bundle strenuously repels bitter isolation, dreadful loneliness, and the deterioration of its texture and color. The bundle has its own authentic life."

"Humiliation creeps in when a single righteous coin lies in an empty cash register. It has no friends or partners, so it cries out into people's pockets. A lonely coin in a wallet hears it and then sings out: let my children jingle sweetly for you, for it is unbearable and merciless torture for you to be alone, my lord. So desperation creeps in and then a weak soul heeds with its itchy fingers."

"There's something you missed, concerning the lowbrow," Martin replied. "On several occasions, I went shopping with Lenny or Larry in these large stores which are located on the x-axis. They're mostly for the lowbrow, and they're always filled with potential customers. They economize here and there. They have to save on one article to buy another. These people don't follow the tacit law of scratchy palms in a pocket. With a budget smaller than a mouse click, the lowbrow seek out special sales. Poor families who cannot afford an entire school outfit for their children are content to buy a shirt, a pair of pants, shoes, or underwear. They clothe their children like the leaden monsoon sky. Their piggy bank saving couldn't get them a complete suit at once, only shades of gray, Charles. For an increasing number of lowbrows, recycled food and toilet paper are too expensive."

"Other poor people are satisfied with window-shopping. They allow themselves to abstract the essence of items with their hypnotic eyes, so they can satisfy their dreams. A friend of mine has a self-rationalization for unaffordable merchandise. He'll buy his most desired article and take it home. At home, he'll keep it for a month, like a mirror. With minimal touching of his relic, he'll return it for a refund. Like this, he can have anything."

"What about the perpendicular part of Fairview?" asked Charles.

"I'm not allowed in these stores. And all of them carry specialized merchandise for only highbrow. For these people, manufactured marks are common knowledge for their group, while prices prevent another group from being knowledgeable. I was once inside with Virus. He had to grab something for his father. It's incredible in these stores. Boutique employees are brand name experts. They wear tailored clothes. They remind me of penguins. They could also be easily mistaken for mannequins, but their educated smiles and mannerisms betray that secret. And yet, their unnatural facial muscles and bodily motions furnish success with their generous clients. Their clients, not customers, always pay with their business credit cards. Cards of continuous lobbying and negotiating could chase their bearer to the grave. Their clients struggle to master their magical business card, because their cards rhyme with the harmony of ancient Greek numbers. All this creates problems for employees. They have fantasies whenever they see their clients coming in. They somehow believe that a client may mindlessly part with a million dollars. They see a snapshot of what their lives would be like if they were millionaires. The mannequins cannot easily disappear from the scene as long as this hope flickers. The sweat in their shoes has not yet become unbearable for them. But for the client, it's straightforward: if he did give a million dollars away, he would demand a receipt for tax deduction. Their accountants could call it a business expense."

"You're talking about their Big Time Believer. You can really see it on the second floor."

"What is it, Charles?"

"Besides offices on the second floor, security agents, video cameras and little electronic eyes peep down from the second floor ceiling and calculate each customer's intentions and habits. Making cameras and store inspectors visible and easily recognizable to deter theft and vandalism is unthinkable today. Fairview's security people get financial and psychological rewards for catching and penalizing shoplifters. This is an angry retaliation against all non-buyers."

"It is like the highway patrols that have undergone extensive training to make themselves hidden in order to apprehend speeders, whereas an unused patrol car could deter speeders more effectively. This doesn't justify the well-equipped police force, which is prepared to subdue violators of laws. Where education has failed, civil laws carry an army to fill the gap.

"Nobody is interested in instructing people how to live with what they possess. In the advertising world, twenty companies say that their products are the best. All this is different from the common sense world in which people easily make decisions and choices without choking influences. In our technological society, human reality should be simplified and made something worth living for. But no, politicians are opportunists. They praise and encourage the world of deception that is practiced on ordinary people. And at the same time, they present themselves like little gods with clean hands to expose mistrust, secrecy, antisocial behavior, and illegal business activities. Secret agents are not needed to tell us that human beings want stability and genuine security. Our political leaders ask the unemployed to renew their yearly existence by paying taxes, so that jobs can be created. Yes, redefining existence annually and changing products daily tell me that my worth is nothing more than one year. The poor in our society are preconceived as criminals and antisocial citizens. Now, they're waiting to act out their self-fulfilling prophecy. My existence has a one-year guarantee! This tells me how different worlds are praised and preferred. It also makes me more sympathetic toward offenders, especially the mistrusted people like the poor."

Slowly, Charles and Martin walked to All-In-One, next to the middlebrow main entrance. The restaurant had a back door which customers could use for after-hours service when other entrances were closed. Charles stood in front of his restaurant. He took a few steps backward and then smiled.

"Charles, All-In-One is sure starting to get well known."

They went in. Charles went to the counter, tapped on it several times, and came back. "All-In-One had a natural birth and has a practical purpose. It is a restaurant that stands up for young adults, teenagers, children, and the fetus. Anyone below the age of twenty is quickly served; when doubt occurs, customers have to show I.D. before being served. All-In-One is founded on self-protected principles: only two lines are permitted to assemble before the ordering desk, one for those below twenty and the other for older ones. We don't willingly serve adults. If some oldies mistakenly order food and then rush out of the door, they've forgotten to close their car doors. If old customers wait for hours to be served, they may shuffle from one line to another to fight off their solitude and individualism. A frozen pizza, coffee beans with hot water, an open tea bag with cold water, beverage on a plate without any straw—are all meaningful for these people. All this is much better than parking themselves at a senior's residential home to receive their award in some other world for their societal contributions."

"But Charles, aren't you discriminating against adults? You know very well that some of them are compassionate to our cause. Besides, one of the civil laws in Proud City states that a restaurant is a public place for everyone."

"Yes, Martin, All-In-One has an open door policy toward selling. The menu is clearly written on the wall. You see how it partly hides the kitchen so that customers cannot learn employees' kitchen habits."

"Will you get to the point, Charles?"

"Two price lists are written in red on the wall. One for oldies and the other for youngies. I agree with you that our price range is ,unlike a transparent five-star restaurant, in which reservation means controlling people's financial status, prior to assigning vacant tables. And nobody calls this a discrimination against the poor. All-In-One is unique compared to most fast food places. Youngies pay the regular price: one dollar for a small coke, one and a half for a medium, two for a large, five for a small pizza, seven for a medium, nine for a large, etc. No item, for the youngies, exceeds the cost of a large pizza."

"Charles, I'm not talking about the price list for youngies. Remember, I work here, too."

"All-In-One has a simple method of pricing for the poor and monotheist youngies. In contrast, the Roman gods and goddesses, producing cultural values and hopes for everyone, look down upon the youngies with pity, because they can only afford a single god. Martin, adults have to pay for their deities, so all decimal points from the regular price list are removed. A small coke costs them one hundred dollars and a large pizza nine hundred dollars. They have to satisfy a minimum order of one thousand dollars before being served."

"So, I have to protect the integrity and image of my own destiny through pricing, quality, service, and by temporarily wearing strict personalities as a physical identification. And this is more important than being a bit hard on adults."

"All-In-One does not deceive its customers. It'd never want to disappear into the realm of an empty tomorrow. Until now, adults have dictated the future, and liberty meant for them a bloated belly to float in an ocean without any hindsight. But everything for them moves like a crooked caterpillar with a head at each end. As the slimy worm attempts to crawl forward, it stretches until it cracks itself at the stomach. The young can't escape the adults way of life and run away to a sandy plane for liberty. So the young have to get their own place where indignant adults cannot control, supervise and threaten them. The world of adults is nothing in this world without adult ideology. They deny the essence of growing up. They give youngies windows from which to examine the imitation of nature and life. Adults secretly divide the world through stereotyping; one half of the population are mindless wimps with neither direction nor responsibilities. They record each anti-social act as a confirmation of their self-fulfilling prophecy, which guarantees the status quo of youngies. Youngies, killing their parents' stigma by not submitting themselves to predefined roles, have shown the first excommunication; the second will involve overthrowing their parents' law books. Trembling societal legal institutions that blatantly discriminate and suppress young people cannot stop the revolution of life, for the equal-marriage between young hearts and reason lives outward as the mender of tomorrow."

"That's the Proud City the young would wear for tomorrow. I hope that we're strong enough to overcome the battles ahead of us."

"We have to implement our price list against adults. They've got the Great Historical Believer of freedom and liberty on their side. Adults have to be discouraged from this realm."

"Careless adults who do not notice the price list are amusing to look at. They try to minimize the insult with plastic money that couldn't open the cash register. Others' jaws fall open, as it recycles their stomach air and exposes the brute without rationality on their blank face."

"Don't be so poetic, Martin. Amusement and tragedy are good bedfellows, especially when your caring parents surprised you at work, and decided to grab a bite. With all politeness, you told them about the necessity of reservation."

"It's clear that policies shape reality for our integrity. And at the same time, adults' appointments are eloquently carved on ice in a desert. Some adults listen to their instincts and avoid unwelcome places. You know that not everyone would be discouraged by rules that restricted human freedom. So, your souvenirs: police badge, hat, belt and jacket in the glass case next to the cash register, deter the stubborn ones."

"I don't want to deny people their rights and freedoms, but, we have to recognize young people's rights and freedoms first."

"I don't think we'll get any savage adults protesting around the restaurant like a swarm of queenless bees. All-In-One's policies affirm and deny simultaneously."

"Other businesspeople believe that All-In-One's survival will be countable with only one hand. And they think that I'm living dangerously by practicing anti-commerce." Charles went to the counter again and stared at the glass case for a moment.

Martin finally got up and had a quick look around the restaurant. "I guess I should get to work," he smiled.

"Oh, yes, yes!" Charles answered suddenly. His mind was somewhere else.

2: Chuck and Lenny

"Knock!" Lightning struck evenly across the horizon as the brass knob in Doris Holden's fragile right hand widened the gap between the door and its frame. The door stood like one of Lorenz Ghiberti's majestic bronze doors of the Cathedral of Florence's Baptistery. Doors that Michelangelo cherished and praised as the gates of paradise, showing the dualistic nature of human beings. The human body is represented by the mortal frame holding the door, and the eternal blessing one receives upon passage through it. Still, the doorframe reminds us that we are merely mortals, and upon entering, we cast away our mortal shell.

She poked her swollen head into the room, defending her tired eyes from the room's engulfing illumination. The lights from different electronic devices which had been left running, created a stream of glittering stars, sparkling as they were reflected on the surface of clear plastic diskette cases strewn about. She was too dazzled by it all to take any notice of the aurora borealis scintillation.

"Darn, everything is on!" Doris cried. "And all these software cases lying around, on the floor, on the bed, under the bed, and who knows where else." Like a surfer ironing out starched clothes, she glided across the room. Struggling against the dark forces of gravitation, she managed to avoid the destruction of the little glowing constellation. She reached her destination and turned off the alarm clock, and then the computer and printer. She did not notice her own path as it gradually became visible from the bed to the table, and so she unconsciously retraced it.

She pushed Chuck's shoulder a few times. His voice growled, and his body moved helplessly in the bed, exposing his street clothes and running shoes. Doris' hasty judgment was unwarranted, for no absolute relationship between sleeping and clothing existed. The relationship between people and things sat on the nude back of a smoky ghost. Some people revolted against authorities and their impending views of normalcy; some believed that they were away at camp. Doris still saw the inside as real, and the outside like a turtle shell, protecting the core of life, the Big Time Believer. But Chuck was pragmatic; he wanted to be ready without wasting time reviewing his morning catalogue of clothes.

"It's seven o'clock," she muttered sluggishly, pushing him back and forth in the bed like a half submerged barrel. "You should have been down already, eating your breakfast." She, of course, wanted to go home. She hesitantly turned and tried to walk across the room to the door where she mechanically flicked the light switch off and then on again. She left without closing the door, allowing the stagnant air from the rest of the house to engulf Chuck's little front room. She had never realized going into Chuck's room meant the breaking of the delicate barrier of absurdity.

A few disks slipped off the bed. Chuck was awake. He clumsily walked across the bright room without adjusting his vision or breaking any plastic shells. The dark, majestic hallway sucked him out of his room and he found himself in the washroom. *Can't you be original for once?* he thought. *The cave men, yes, they had something to wake up for. Not this hallmark alarm clock, reducing people to a mindless lot. No knock-knock, no buzzing. Alarm clocks, the most irritating noise for civilized people. And that's how our idolized civilization suffocates itself? Why be angry, first thing in the morning? It leaves a stinky taste in the mouth.*

Cave men, they really had something to wake up for. A hungry beast lingering in front of our door would make us jump out from our sleep with a bolt of lightning in the spine. Then, we would be ready to confront our entire lives energetically. Knock, knock and buzz—they irritate-you-up. Stress-you-up like a bad hangover from the night before. They stay with you and drain you to dust. With a clock, you don't even know the difference between living and dying. All intellectuals, I guess, humble before the buzz; it's an idol to be proud of in our society. No, thank you, I don't want to be reduced to virtual reality.

At night, our creativity works. In the day teachers always want our creativity, as though it has a financial value. I don't have any room to grow in this society for adults. Adults are in everything, our beliefs, values, law, politics, education, business practice, and electronic toys. And they're in our parents, too. We're treated like virtual reality. Chuck suddenly realized his own thought. It frightened him a bit. He started to wash his face as though he wanted to be a new person who could bounce his reality to his parents like a rubber ball. The warm water in his hands ran smoothly off his face, going downhill without any obstructions. He thought about his dream.

Well, the Big Time Believer had been injured, and it escaped in the woods, he murmured to himself. *In pursuit, our technology fell on its own oily tracks. And it couldn't get hold of the Big Time Believer. We idolize technology; we welcome it like a new layer of skin. And we believe it will protect our essence. We're becoming a gigantic robot. Well, technology has been continuously doing mortal battle with our inner core of life, the Big Time Believer. Dream, it dreamt me, a pack of loose images blown in the wind. I try to read my destiny off whichever sticky pieces I can grab in my slimy hands in the morning, like a Freudian sorcerer. For sure, dreams are like taking virtual reality for reality. But I dreamt it—the Big Time Believer was badly hurt.*

Look at my miserable life: it is like shooting a dead bear. Isn't a cave a better place to live than this concrete jungle? It'd be exciting to have carnivores again. Oh, quit now. And hurry up, before... He held back his ambivalent view of Doris.

Chuck left the washroom light on, kicked a few disks away from the path, went to the desk where he quickly picked up two folders of printed papers, and placed each of them in his school bag. He hurried downstairs and leaped toward the eastern front door as if it were the gate to paradise.

"You're not going without eating!" shouted Doris. "Listen young man, I don't want a lecture from your mother. Anyway, she should have been here, a long time ago."

Chuck halted, threw his bag down, and then slowly turned

back. He conceived himself as an illiterate peasant in a medieval house of God, where visual images on the church walls were used to teach the Christian faith. In his mind, Chuck saw the west wall, which represented the setting sun on the horizon, depicting images from the Last Judgment: Christ sitting in judgment, surrounded by Angels, the Virgin, and his twelve apostles, and to his left, devils pushing the damned to hell. Chuck glanced to the northern side, which received the least sunlight, and symbolized living in darkness. It showed scenes from the Old Testament—Moses, standing on the mountain of Sinai with the Ten Commandments in his hands, looking down at the pagans with discontentment, condemning them to the eternal flame. Chuck shifted his gaze to the southern side, which depicted scenes from the New Testament and suggested more sunlight, and saw scenes from the Last Supper. Chuck found no compassion and understanding in these Christian images, and they horrified him like a nightmare. He closed his eyes tightly and bent his head downward, in a desperate attempt to abolish them.

Instead, his consciousness took him further into the past. He was standing on a path that narrowed to the size of a rope; each end of it was tied to Isis' nipples. The image of the Egyptian mythological goddess, who symbolized the abundance of food, awakened Chuck's hunger and his unconscious desire to live. Chuck knew that he had to eat and be strong.

He walked slowly to the kitchen and saw his breakfast on the table. Sitting quietly, he devoured his sandwich and then gulped down most of his orange juice. He turned and twisted the last mouthful of juice for the sour taste. All this time Doris had been staring at him. She switched her body weight from one leg to another. She was obviously waiting for a look or a gesture, but on his shoulder sat an ageless piece of ice.

"Your mother told you about the phone! Didn't she?" she complained, reminding him that he should not use his computer modem all night. "I was trying to phone home, but it was always busy. Anyway, it's none of my business. Oh, where is she anyway? She should have been here already! I guess you had a late night.

Didn't you?"

Though Chuck pretended to be hypnotized by the broken clock on the wall, he couldn't protect his ears from her questions.

She turned around hastily and rechecked the order in the kitchen. *Must be nice for Jackie, to have enough money to hire a sitter for her son,* she thought, jealous of her middle class friend. She took a quick glance at Chuck, who had dozed off on the table. *Look at him, he's the same age as my Lenny. Family problems can destroy anybody. Fifteen years old only, he's excellent at school like my Lenny. And Jackie should be proud of him. Too bad his father is so thoughtless and shameless. Who'll believe Jackie, telling everybody that Scott's company sent him to another location? Everybody knows that he ran away with a woman to another city... Why isn't she coming yet?*

"The bus! The bus is here! Come on Chuck!" she yelled, exhilarated, for she could go home now. He woke up, went to the door, and grabbed his bag and blue jean jacket from the closet in less than a split second. "Don't slam the door!"

"Boom." The door echoed through the entire house.

The greenheart front door stopped the lifelessness of the house from being mingled with the spring freshness. Chuck peeled down the driveway in an effort to avoid the impact of the door bang, and nearly crashed into the side of the standing bus. He felt at ease; he had escaped his lonely and dreadful house. He did not realize that a thin layer of his foot impressions had been left behind on the damp concrete driveway.

As the students in the bus enjoyed Chuck's daily routine of nearly crashing into the bus, none of them saw their own inescapable footprints, which would linger on like shadows to shape their own destinies.

Recovering quickly, Chuck looked at the open bus door. He was grateful that he was not fat, since this door was specially designed to discourage obese and old people from entering. A bus door was made for certain people who had to continuously reshape themselves to use it. It encouraged people to believe that transforming themselves into a desired shape would make them count in the making of the new millennium.

"Hello sleepyhead!" said the driver, without looking at Chuck. Chuck ignored the remark. Others' noises and excitement in the bus were solidified like an array of scatter clouds and then transformed into powerless shapes, which could not touch his ears, as he awkwardly felt his way toward the back for an empty seat. He took another deep breath and closed his eyes.

The occasional stopping alerted his body to their progress until he managed to open his eyes. He felt the chill of the glass window against his cheek as he watched the adults' Big Time Believer dashing by outside. For the past six months, his anger and frustration about his father leaving had been accumulating and torturing him. He felt that his parents had been killing themselves for material possessions and social status, at the expense of their family. He helplessly sat in his seat and allowed his inner voice to cry out. *After school, we run quickly home. Did I say home? Home, sweet home. There, people are supposed to be utterly free, to relax, to have peace of mind. My hoof! Free, only among the dead. Everybody here has the same sterilized front gardens, fences, parking lots, and houses too. Everything we have was built from the dead. Rocks with great brilliance—lively sparkles in nature—are molded into dead rocks for houses, parking lots, and roads. Trees turn into dead planks. Furniture, clothes, pillows, beds—all come from the dead. Our tap water is purified from bacteria and natural minerals. We're murderers for security and stability. Our middle class neighborhood with its medium size deadness, the upper class with the most deadness around them—there's no reason to think about the lower class; they're already half dead.*

The noise of students shuffling prepared Chuck for their arrival at school. Tagging along behind other students, he had a glimpse of Lenny, Doris' son, waiting at the bus stop—a majestic civilized landmark where a great portion of his life would be spent. Children tacitly learned the use of it from an early age as a legitimate place to hang around, without having people interrogating them.

Though Chuck and Lenny were in the same grade, Lenny's

school was located in town, fifteen minutes away on bicycle. Chuck took a look at Lenny, full of energy, same pants, shirt, jacket, and air conditioning shoes, leaning slightly on his silver bike. Chuck moved painfully toward the bicycle. He reached into his school bag and gave Lenny a folder. Any eye contact between them at that moment could have ignited the splitting of atoms. Before Chuck could close his bag, Lenny's knapsack had devoured the folder and he was gone, rapidly speeding away.

Throwing Sparks

Because he had arrived at school late, Lenny's utilitarian teacher gave him a note. He had expected it. The little piece of paper in his hand led him directly to the principal's office, which was located on the second floor, just above the school's main entrance. The principal's secretary kept the entrance interactive by leaving the disciplinary door slightly open. Lenny preferred it completely open for escaping. The secretary glimpsed the familiar face entering and tried very hard to control her smile as she nodded gently to Lenny. He knocked and opened the authoritative door in a single beat. The intruder did not alarm the principal, who slowly stood and looked at him. The principal moved effortlessly toward the open door, neither friction from his shoes, nor wear and tear from his clothes could be detected, nothing fatigued. He was like a behaviorist sorcerer, embracing societal ideology with powerful fangs. He stared at Lenny like an insignificant object before him.

"Let me see," cried the principal, taking a mouthful of historic air, "now, you have to deliver papers in the morning, so you can assist your mother running the house. No, you got lost, because a dog chased you. If not that, then a truck blocked the entire road. You were riding too fast, so a policeman stopped you on your way to school…"

"The papers arrived late this morning," Lenny murmured.

"No more excuses!" he screamed. "You remain after class in the library!" His short temper could make a harsh penalty much worse for weaklings, but not for Lenny.

"Thank-u–Sir," he grunted, and left the room without violating any respectable social norms. He wanted the principal to be comforted in his own miserable life by a belief in his obsolete power.

The secretary felt the heat from the other room. Her momentary sorrow for Lenny led her to carefully close the door. She believed that the principal's power should not be allowed to escape through his door, hoping that he could realize himself one day, just how inflated he was, and then explode.

Lenny kept his head bent. His long hair prevented the secretary from seeing what lay behind his eyes. She gave him a library detention slip, and he hurried out of the office.

After his classes, Lenny arrived at the library ten minutes early; it reopened at five for detainees. He sat on the floor across from the library, and watched staff getting ready for the rush hour in one of the most illuminating buildings in the whole city. His thoughts started to wander. *The library, the most historically valued institution, has declined to a common object in our commercialized society. School and public libraries haven't changed for most young persons; public libraries become an amusement place for little children. Parents happily give their children to the library, so that they can be entertained for a few hours while they're shopping. Now, each of these historical buildings has several sections for different age groups—toys for smaller ones, computers for some older ones, career opportunity magazines for young adults. On a regular Saturday morning, videos and movies are for everyone.*

Here too, most adults reaffirm their human attributes; they experience the warmth of being near others. All this tells us that people are disgusted with their way of life. They used to find it a burden to tolerate other people around them—now look at their miserable existence. The long winter months make people more stressed, lonely, miserable. Security guards still discourage window shopping in malls—they treat sightseeing as a hideous crime, a potential shoplifter. Luckily, our libraries remain a refuge for these people—here they have a tolerable social policy. Libraries give us an ideal social setting to stare at, to have non-verbal conversation with, and to be near someone like ourselves, without putting a strain on our pockets.

But when the library is used to penalize students, it takes away from the joy of obtaining knowledge. Today, specialists of human behavior and education see school libraries as the most natural environment for spiritual enlightenment. Companies use libraries to imprint their values on us. Look at ourselves—as children we were disappointed when we could not see a real dinosaur. Now, our parents want us to be paleontologists so that we can identify ourselves with extinction. Society equips libraries with the constant reminder that nothing exists beyond the flesh—only our parents' books.

After all classes are finished, our school library becomes the most lively circus arena, extra staff patrolling, clients pouring from every class, line-ups for limited resources growing. Educational institutions want detention to be beneficial and creative; they expose students to valuable corporate norms. Libraries are working with industries to recruit from the crib; they give babies an image to identify themselves with. They're using the most up-to-date technology to transmit their information and practices across the world; they want to affect people like a contagious disease. The young are like Skinnerian rats; they have to be conditioned from birth to elect similar responses. All this is a new civilized standard for passing oneself off as a human being.

The most popular activity is to transform ourselves into chicken-picking mice in front of a computer. This is our new outer layer. Rats, chickens, pigeons, have taught their experimenters well; now human reality is the chicken-mouse. Mouse-clicking came from businesspeople's intolerable habits; now it royally sleeps with the innocent in the manger.

The lasting effect of library detention can be seen everywhere. Life comes without flair. After a day's work, people come home, eat, and then wait until it's time to go to bed. In bed, they wait to fall asleep until the clock rings. And then, they wait for the wash-

room to be free, for the water to boil, for the bus. At work, they patiently wait for lunchtime. Finally, all we do is change places. The cry for flair shatters the sleeping world. Businesses courageously fight this. They're introducing pets at the work place to make people more relaxed, social, affectionate, compassionate. Pets are making business deals, initiating conversation. Rats believe in vegetarian cats.

Lenny approached the front desk slowly and sensationalized the young part-time receptionist as if she hung on a wall. The computer screen had a hypnotizing affect on her. "Hmm," he grumbled, thinking her face had been on more dreams than the Evening Star. And yet his physiological immaturity denied him the fullest experience of the desired object before him. Her head turned ninety degrees to the left, exposing after-images of electronic codes in her eyes.

"Yes," she said, looking as though there was a homogeneous cloud standing before her.

"The name is Lenny Holden," he answered politely, expecting that she would grasp the reason for his being there. But her intellectual nature would not allow her to childishly guess why Lenny was there. Her self-identity was no bigger than a business look. Lenny coaxed her with a smile, and she was able to detect a single person wearing a human nametag. Saying "Hello" and smiling were becoming social taboos, because they reminded us that society had given human natural behavior to machines.

"Yes, I'll make note of that," she muttered, reaching for the log book which had the names of all detainees who remained after class.

Lenny sought his regular corner, the one furthest away from the receptionist desk and other observers. He smiled and felt contented. He reached into his pocket and scrutinized the contents with his fingers. He had two hundred dollars. He pulled the money to the outer edge of his pocket, took a quick peep, and then quickly pushed it back into his pocket. He screened his surroundings for onlookers. Everyone was busy. He quickly removed the money from his pocket, placed it in an open book, and counted it carefully without attracting anyone's attention. *Two hundred flags. Twenty-five for Tim, five for Scott, five for Harry, five for Bill, that makes one hundred and sixty for me! Me alone.* He put one hundred and sixty in his pants pocket and the rest in his shirt pocket.

"I thought you'd be here," whispered Tim, surprising Lenny. "We have over six thousand already. Maybe another two coming."

Lenny sized him up. Tim appeared nervous and scared. Less than two years ago, Lenny had started to sell papers and essays to other students about his own age. Tim helped him by managing three web sites—the first for business, the second for communication, the last one for only Lenny's personal use—and the database. Currently, Lenny had about seven thousand regular international and national distributors; each would buy a copy of an essay for ten dollars and resell copies to students. Parents were eager to allow their children to use their credit cards when it came to educational purposes.

Lenny's business could be viewed as quite successful, for the world used similar books and examinations over and over, everyone learning the same materials at the same speed. All students vomiting from a single mouth. And Lenny's pragmatism showed that traditional notions of cheating and plagiarism needed to be clarified. Car manufacturers made the same model of cars for everyone; nobody complained about being cheated. An owner could not be anything more than a legal possessor, he did not make his car; and yet, he was the proprietor. The business world had influenced Lenny, the legal owner counted, not the maker or the writer.

"Lenny, we've got too much money, it's in the millions," he whispered. "We should stop now, I can't handle all these customers. We have a lot of money in the account, more than sufficient."

"Listen, Tim. How heavy is all the money we have? When you tell me its weight, we stop. Okay! We need money, it's our only power to ease the struggle." He stared at him and saw Tim's concern redirected. "People kill themselves for nothing, Tim. You see how meaningless and useless your life could have been? Money doesn't lead you to the answer. It prevents it. I know you praise yourself highly and that's good. I know you would like your share now, so that you can spend your money and assure yourself that no one is robbing you of your wealth. I know money makes you suspicious of others—especially when others are managing your money and you can't dig your hands into it. And, you think I want it all, including your share, so I can enjoy my life. You know what we are going to do with it. We're waiting for everyone else in our network to have enough money to pay off their legal fees. You know this. The account is in Martin's name, not mine. Tim, this'll all blow over. Can't you see we're the consequences of our parents' history? We're partly the problems, too. And what we don't do, will be a problem for everybody who comes after us. Here is your twenty-five." Lenny reached into his shirt pocket and handed Tim the money for his services. Tim took it and smiled.

"*Cher amie!* You'll make me rich. And successful, too. I'll be great. You're molding me to become a Big Time Believer. *Hasta la Vista!*" Tim knew how much money was in the account; Lenny didn't. Lenny looked at him crossly as he left the building.

Lenny's cell phone rang, and before it could ring again his hand was already out of his pocket, extending it to his ear. "Hum-um," he grunted into the receiver, turning his back to the library as though he could hide the ringing sound. The chief librarian, with a stiff dose of firmness and meanness in her, came over with policies as her armor and waited for Lenny's gaze. The strong smell of her only two yards away prepared Lenny for battle. He took a fast backward glance at her posture. Without breaking the code of silence, he clicked the off button and carefully placed the phone in one of his empty pockets. He took a glimpse at her. She stood like a female animal protecting her territory. "I guess you've already signed my detention slip," he cried, insulting her sense of authority. Surprised, she made a half circle, with one foot screwed onto the floor as her natural limit, and bolted away.

Damn it! Barging in like that into my private business. Lenny put five dollars in his shirt pocket and headed to the librarian's desk. "Paper please!" he requested, for an hour of detention meant an hour of business.

"Your phone disturbs people. This is a library, and it has regulations," the behaviorist librarian said, exposing a lack of raw flesh between her teeth. Lenny felt sorry for this helpless creature before him—he could see that she put policies before humanity.

"Yeah!" replied Lenny, seeing his situation as childish.

"Yeah, what? You have no respect for knowledge. None for people whatsoever," she said. "This isn't the first time—everybody's complaining about you."

Lenny searched himself for a persona. "If you keep yelling at me like that, I'll develop a fear of libraries. It'll be a huge nightmare for me," Lenny uttered calmly, fixing his eyes downward in humility. Seeing the soft wrinkles on her pale face, he tried appealing to her sensitive side, adding, "I wouldn't want to come to any library then, and it would all be because of you."

"You always have phone calls in here; people have started to complain. We're running a library here, not a stock exchange," exclaimed the librarian.

"It's not my fault if my mother is in the hospital," he murmured, his glare never completely reaching downward. He wanted to hit her right in the chest with the hardships of his newly acquired persona. He knew he had achieved his goal, and he waited for her transformation.

She was instantaneously humbled. Like a loving mother in despair, she was overwhelmed with love and tenderness. "I understand, it's okay," she said sympathetically. She gave him a slip, dismissing him from detention.

Without betraying the quasi-reality that accompanied his new persona, he took the white paper and shoved it in his knapsack. He made his way to the transparent sliding door, which architects had developed from observing the flow of two-way traffic. Entering and leaving meant little to library users. Sliding doors meant that people came in and went out without realizing it. As soon as Lenny left the library he was on the phone; nothing had changed for him and the library evaporated into thin air.

Only Images

Chuck's phone was ringing. Jackie answered.

"It's Lenny." He had hoped that Chuck would answer the phone. He threw on an attitude. "Can I speak to my mom please?"

"It's supper now! She left this morning," cried Jackie, astonished that Lenny could not tell the difference between day and night.

"Okay, Thanks."

"Bye, Lenny." Jackie quickly hung up and returned to the kitchen to finish her cooking. The pot on the stove was boiling; the aroma from canned food could make any stomach grumble and tickle any tongue. Unconsciously, she turned the spaghetti sauce around and around in a continuous clockwise motion. The perfect circles in the pot had a hypnotic influence on her. The steam poured out of the pot and all over the kitchen, peeling off the paint, rusting metals, giving the kitchen an age worse than a washroom without any ventilation. The open windows could not save the spacious kitchen, for what she cooked and ate had a deadly affect on tender household materials.

Suddenly, Chuck burst into the kitchen, pulled a chair up near the table, and waited for something to happen. He believed that his mother had something to tell him, and knew that she was occasionally absentminded. *Not even turning back to say hello. Babushka!,* he thought.

"It was Lenny on the phone," Chuck said.

"Yes," replied Jackie, "It must be difficult for him when his mother is working at night."

"You mean sleeping at night like a hibernating bear," commented Chuck.

"You don't start this again—you want to eat, someone has to work," said Jackie.

"How many times have you told me, someone responsible must be here while you're at work. It's sickening. Always someone with me; if not Doris, it's teachers," cried Chuck. "What about your responsibility?"

"Don't make it hard on me!" shouted Jackie, knowing that her anger would bring him to his senses.

Her reply drove him speechless for a moment. He thought about his mother's life. *Animals assemble during the mating season, the strongest male in a pack leaps and subdues the strongest female, then the entire pack becomes more social and compact. Mating must be pleasant at first when it is done for a reason, but once the vigor is gone and it becomes a duty, divorce comes. Nothing holds parents together anymore. The sexual urge in them is weak compared to quarrels, stress, boredom, the struggle for money and security. Well, the mating season is over for them, and so is the marriage,* he thought.

"You don't have to make a lake on the table. Eat, before it gets cold," Jackie insisted, reminding him of his food. Surprised, he found an overflowing red plate on the table. He hesitantly pulled his chair closer to the table and stared at the clock on the wall. It needed a new battery. "The clock isn't working," he said, trying to provoke a response from his mother.

"Will you eat up," she replied. She was too absorbed inside to take any notice of her own son's unhappiness. Her index finger moved in a circular motion around the circumference of her plate, and then she brought the plate to her mouth and licked off the sauce. She rotated the plate, leaving only thin lines of sauce behind, then placed it back on the table. Chuck followed the traces of sauce that her finger and tongue had made with his eyes. She could not hold back this habit of hers when it wanted to pour out.

About fifteen yards of spaghetti, he thought. He played with the spaghetti in his mind until it formed a linear line, jumping horizontally, vertically, and diagonally. He quietly backed his chair about five inches away from this image. He pushed it again and waited, and then some more. From the screeching, Jackie knew that he wanted to leave the table.

"I have to work tonight," she said. "And Doris will be coming as usual." Her unexpected news froze him. A creepy chill passed through him, attempting to engulf the little fragile flame that still burned inside him. Everything in his body fought furiously to become stationary. He struggled to drag himself away from the soulless kitchen that transformed his parent into a devourer of all organisms. Parents' Big Time Believer nourished itself well on compassion without heart, love without emotion, living without life.

As he drifted away from the table, the depravation of his sensory organs intensified until his entire body was numb. Without his soul and mind, he was directed upstairs only by his primitive life-force. He momentarily stopped at the door, and his drunken body leaned on it. Though he was deprived of his whereabouts, the habit of grasping the doorknob seized him. The cool brass metal in his hand alerted his unconscious of a danger; his sense of touch rushed messages to his brain. His muscles contracted with uncontrolled forces, his strength involuntarily directed the knob clockwise, flinging the door open. He was falling forward. As the light of his room swallowed and penetrated his transparent body, he became a shadowless figure, emerging from the collision of hot and cool air between the rooms. His senses went wild and jolted his body upright in less than a split second. He slowly recovered from the shock, aware of his computer running, and acknowledged his tacit purpose of living. He believed that he had the ability to survive and to overcome his situation. He dreamed of his name in a liquid state, which would seldom change its shape or rearrange its contents.

He examined the CD-ROM titles in his room. *History, arts, religions, literature, morality, metaphysics, anthropology—all these teach us about the graveyard. With psychology, sociology, social sciences, culture, civilization, management, economics, and business, I at least have knowledge about people and their dreams, in general. There's nothing about the person Chuck. Here's a funny one—physics, chemistry, biology, technology, genetics—you know everything about nothing. Sciences don't discover chairs and tables for us. No intelligence left. He picked up a few and looked at the titles. "Writing Tools for Any Subject Matter"... "Pros and Cons"... "Splitting Hairs on a Straw Man." None of these educational programs gave my parents a grain of common sense.* He felt unsatisfied. He sat like a guru in front of his computer and looked through the slightly open window at the trees across the street.

No birds around. It's getting late and dark; the old God with His human temperament should have returned by now. "We don't have any soul left," he murmured.

The old want the young to always be young, like puppets, without any responsibility. Adults see and treat us like young wimps who just graduated from the diaper. They really think we're immature idiots, dangerous to others and ourselves. At least, we know that the world is round. Don't we? For now, adults' Big Time Believer is burning itself out of existence.

"Phone—yes, Lenny called," Chuck cried. His pupils dilated as he turned away from the window and reached out for the phone on his desk. He dialed, it was ringing. He thought that Lenny was waiting for the third ring; idiots saw luck in threes. Chuck thought that Lenny did not see that it was really a few people dealing out others' destiny.

"Yes, it's me! What now?" asked Chuck. "Are you sure? The title must be 'The Life of a Dead Cell,' a biology paper, about fifteen hundred words, for tomorrow. Yes, I know your mother is working tonight. Okay, see you as usual," he said, replacing the receiver and making note of his new assignment for tomorrow.

Chuck immediately started to contemplate the meaning of the biology paper. *The only fruitful understanding of human beings begins with Jell-O, not with the carved out figure that we're made of. Cells die in order to make patterns—fingers, arms, toes, ears, nose, and everything else. In each stage of life, a set of cells has to die, until the final lump disappears too. Could it be that a few people are living and using us as their dying cells? Biologically speaking, there's no need to cry out our death wish; the next stage of death isn't so far away. Everything is too predictable. Society wants us to be immature, irrational, wild, potential murderers so adults can regenerate their dying cells by sticking us with their stigma. Young adults may be programmed to die biologically, but not socially and intellectually.*

Both Chuck and Lenny agreed to overcome the stigma that

society had put on the young, but they disagreed about their personal crises. Lenny believed that his mother's employment was causing family problems at home. On the other hand, Chuck thought that because his mother had a sitter she blindly continued to work ghoulish hours. Though they wanted to reach out to each other and had learned all the necessary skills to deal with others' conflicts and problems from the same psychology books, neither of them traveled the first step to break the ice.

They could not easily resolve their problems because society taught them that as businessmen they should not express their silly sentiment. To do this would be destructive to their image as cultivated human beings. Civilization cried out that personal feeling was a landmark of the past. Chuck and Lenny made transactions without any heart.

Chuck tiptoed into his room and sat for a while on his bed, covering his face with both hands, recharging his devoted membership to the herd battery, which shortly propelled him to the window. He slid the window half open and sat on the window frame as though he was riding a foggy horse, pulling the sliding window gently toward himself as his right leg and arm dangled outside. The window appeared to bisect his body at his nose, forehead, and crotch. It was refreshing. And if he accidentally lost his balance, the parking lot would be awfully messy. He closed his left eye and used his right one to look inside his room through the transparent glass like one-eyed Jack doing window-shopping. He scanned his room: *A beautiful large off-white Gothic bedroom,* he thought. *It's wonderful. After a long day at school it's very comfortable. And a large window to regulate the flow of air while I rest, linking me to nature. Ceiling high enough, it's painted like the sky. It gives me the impression that I'm lying on a soft weightless cloud—no back pain, no bodily stress, no bed sores. Yes, it's just for Sleeping Beauty. Calm, happiness, joy, peace of mind, freedom, security—all are in my room.*

Our architects strive for perfection—they're magicians of transferring empty space to peace and tranquility; they're masters of human functions, and lords of evoking the right sensation in me at the right moment. Light switches, telephone plugs, and electrical outlets are placed excatly on the walls for my natural bodily movements. And the door opens without any obstruction. Architects spy into my secret paradise and build my dream. His staring right eye was hurting him, as images were disappearing in cloud. His eye automatically closed and he opened the left one, changing his perspective.

Our architecture stinks. It's a labyrinth for us, a soundproof room to suffocate me senselessly. I can hear myself thinking, no smell, blinding tasteless colors, separating me from my family. It makes me angry and sad. It's self-imprisonment. In here, I privatize my anger, loneliness, and boredom. It's the first arena for divorce and separation. Self-isolation; the lack of tolerance for others; individuality without humanity—they all grow here. It's more like self-punishment. I rob myself of nature. A hideout for our venomous life, stealing others' subsistence, giving others the plague with a white blanket. His head fell forward in a rush of disgust, pushing the window wider open. He scrambled like a Big Time Believer to obtain his balance, his claws grasping the window frame. He admitted that it was very close.

Having a full binocular view of his hands and his situations, he waited for his rapid heart rate to slow, putting his head inside to regain his control. *Well, a tent would do; it'd make people more communicative. And enhance human relationship. Our neighbors would be our best personal doctors, no more mental sicknesses.* He hesitated for a few seconds, gazing at his computer.

Radio gave us the opportunity to imagine and paint the image of sound. And then television removed the paintbrush from our hands, giving us colorful images to tickle our sensation. Now, computers allow us to paint our own virtual world. We are painting images of the world rather than living in the real world.

Civilized people wait for machines, not for human beings anymore. Waiting and more waiting makes our shadows grow old. Nowadays, we're living lifelessly while a computer loads our values away. Oh, yes, we have more techniques to keep the believer's lifeline burning. The world of images is our achievement.

Everyone has access to the same rubbish, sounding intelligent, writing the same papers, doing the same math problems, learning the same history, sharing the same sentiment. We're all too far-sighted to have any hindsight. They put computers in our school system. And they call it an enhancement of our educational system. It's more like learning effectively until you're blind. Now, we have to do multinational courses. Recruitment, it is. Is that what the world has to offer us? A shooting smoke reality for killing direct human relationship. A few multinational organizations already have their hands on our schools—it's supply and demand, not education.

Luckily, I am in control. I know how to use computers, and most importantly, I know what a computer could do to someone. Sometimes it is nice to hide from the real world.

Chuck awkwardly got off the window and stood firmly, attempting to defend himself against his stream of consciousness while he approached his computer. "I see you," he murmured, as he tapped the monitor. "You surely keep me away from myself when I'm alone. Nobody cares to know about my lonely and dreadful evening. You put me to bed, do my homework, and give me good grades at school. One would prefer to go blind than to be alone without you. I can reach the world from here. Yes, I can talk to people, send them email, play games. And if anyone gives me a hard time, I press a key and he disappears from my life. Who wants anybody to disagree with me? I just key them out of existence."

A lot of people like me out there, he thought, hiding his eyes with his hands, his mind wandering again. *There are millions of guys like me in the world. It'd take more than a lifetime to have a true friend this way. It's a bitch, to find a true friend. If only I were an expert in advertising and marketing, it wouldn't be difficult to sell myself like a piece of raw meat on a butcher counter. Dressing-up is important. Yes, the outside of the package counts. It's like displaying myself in a one-way window. It'd reflect a positive image of myself. Well, the law is self-protection, nobody to hurt my feelings, to send me rubbish email, to insult me, to tell me to jump off a high building, to be my medical advisor...* He realized that he had to find his way out of that circular mess and believed that the circle had to be stretched out to form a linear path; the struggle had already begun in his unconscious.

Yes, I have to cast the right image to everyone. What images become our reality? We're experts of computer graphics, images of Mars, our solar system, the earth, road conditions, natural resources, vacation weather, environmental conditions. The governments cherish images; they have a better control on criminals, anti-social inhabitants, the employed. Our civilization means the reality of images. It's more like we're preparing ourselves to be the image man, the dweller of images. For the real things have become contaminated, polluted, rotten, and stinky. And just dead. How dreadful. We invest billions in our library of images, not in the real stuff. Reality, an esoteric object, is transformed to an aesthetic entity for the highbrow to praise themselves with, to distance themselves further from the lowbrow—the dwellers of images. At least, Lenny is right about one thing: the molding of attitude-people is real. Throwing the right image in the right place to evoke an attitude formation or change, is the trick. Isn't it true, I'm an attitude-person? Of course; it must be. Yes, I must give meaning to this blank frame. I must have meaning in life. But I don't feel as if I do. Maybe I was thrown into the world, all naked, without meaning and essence. I have to make myself, like building a ship in the middle of a storm, plank by plank, without sinking. I have to carve my own path among the tainted images of society's one-year warranty. I should act first and justify later until my act itself becomes a justification for living. There'll be no victims, he thought, slamming his hand on the computer monitor as his pupils enlarged sufficiently to drink in the creative process of life.

Without thinking, he moved toward his bed and grabbed a disk that was lying near his little night table, like his hands had eyes. "An essay you want—that's what you'll get," he whispered. "I'll do the biology paper first, and then the math homework." He tapped a few keys. He found four hundred pages about a living cell from several authors. He knew the tricks. He pressed a few more keys—eighty pages. Cells are programmed to be self-destructive to form things like fingers; a fetus is a blob without any distinguishable features. He opened another writing program which had several option buttons, clicked efficiency and productivity, and then forty-seven pages with pros and cons about his subject matter appeared. He pressed the summarizing and ranking buttons, and the program selected main points and gave a brief description of each point. From the remaining ten pages, he manually rearranged a few paragraphs, discarded some, and then saved his work in the file, Cells. Next, he ran the grade writing level program and reopened the file; he clicked the button for grade eight to ten and had a simplified version of his biology research paper to fit the requirement of a grade nine level student. *It's faster than I thought,* he thought, and then printed out two completed copies with references and bibliography.

Now, it was math. This was much more difficult than writing essays because the answer had to be written in his workbook; everything had to be done manually. Other than that, his math program worked out each problem in detail. After an hour of copying answers from his screen to his book, he finished and slowly placed his work in his school bag.

It's already time to go—I'm running late—it's time to do the disappearance trick, I guess. The breeze rushing through the window slammed the door closed before he could close it gently, exposing him as a naked drop of precious water in a desert. He observed that his mother, lying on the couch, was looking at him. He continued toward the front door; he did not intend to alarm her.

"Take your jacket! It gonna be chilly," cried Jackie. He opened the cupboard and held his jean jacket in his hand while he gracefully turned and glanced at her.

"I'll be at the pizza place," his weak voice said as he pierced the floor with his eyes and with humility.

"Go before it's too late."

Chuck rushed out quickly to prevent an arctic storm from chasing him down his path.

3: The Accident

Charles stared into the glass case. He could not forget how his tragic accident had changed his entire life.

One afternoon after his shift was officially terminated, patrolling the labyrinth of town, he and his partner, Alex Twig, were cruising in to shed their highly authoritative car.

"Distress at Joe's Discount Store, nearby cars, answer distress, take all precautions," announced the police dispatcher.

Thinking that it was nothing extraordinary, they responded. Rushing to the store with their two blazing antennae and stopping in front of the glass building was a routine. Alex hurried to the rear and Charles the front entrance. Through the huge glass window, mostly covered with a hand written price list, Charles had a glimpse of a young person, moving near the grocery stand with a gun in his hand. Communicating with his partner by walkie-talkie, Charles waited for him to get in position, and then they entered simultaneously through different doors.

"Police, Drop your gun! Freeze!" shouted Charles.

Alex stood his ground. His beating eardrums walked through the metal stands several aisles away, to detect the slightest movements. Charles had a frontal view of the robber; his smooth face stood out with the detectable traces of teenagehood. The youngster panicked; his pupils widened, his wet face glittered. He dropped his hands to his sides, holding his shotgun like a walking stick, the barrel pointing upward.

"Drop it!" shouted Charles. "Drop it! And hands up!"

The robber unconsciously lifted his gun to his nose, disowned the foreign object which was put in his hand by some evil genius, and then dropped it on the floor in confusion. The gun was bad quality; the great bang from the impact rattled the premises.

Charles staggered from the shock. His eyes remained fixed on the hypnotic image before him. The last thing he saw before he hit the floor was the youngster trying to catch his falling body.

Alex immediately leapt to the tiny frame, effortlessly binding the youth's hands together behind his back. He rushed to his partner and turned him over. The pouring blood soaked his legs and belly. Without thinking, he seized Charles' walkie-talkie, half covered with blood, and called in, as his other hand returned his gun to its holster.

"Charles hit! Charles hit! Send an ambulance!"

Before he could terminate his call, the robber leaned over Charles.

"Don't die, please don't die," the kid innocently muttered.

Alex rushed to Charles defense and flung the skinny body away like a used toothpick, believing that the murderer was inflicting more pain on his buddy. The little toad crashed against the counter heavily.

Flashing lights and sirens were blaring around the building for the final thrust. All available police vehicles from town stopped their current activities and rushed to the scene; twenty-five cars and vans, and two special squad vans that were specially equipped to slaughter any type of living vermin, sang the chorus of extermination and justice. A veteran, Alex quickly recognized that his life was threatened. *All bodily motions have to be regulated, while he must remain glued to the bloody floor. I don't want to be killed on duty, he thought. He turned to his partner. Time is crucial. Charles is unconscious. He's losing a lot of blood,* he thought, slowly reaching for his own walkie-talkie; he had forgotten the one in his left hand.

"WE ARE IN THE STORE; the robber IS SUBDUED. NO FIRING. I repeat, NO FIRING. Don't shoot. EVERYTHING IS UNDER CONTROL." Though his instructions came in late, some crawling exterminators of the special squad were already in the store and overheard his oral request. They were voicelessly programmed to be odorless and to float on land like snakes, dishing out death. All this muscle hid the exterminators' fear: it was not them lying on the floor, and thank God for that. Soon other police came in the front door; some went to the victim, some to the robber, and some to the owner hidden behind the counter. Medics carried Charles to an ambulance and the bound robber to another one because his clothes were bloody. Attending officers had been transformed to psychoanalysts: their exteriors could not thoroughly hide their sympathy and sorrow for Charles. As they realized their luck was tangled in absurdity, their Big Time Believer stood on their side.

In the store, trauma, panic, and numbness had overtaken Alex, who was guided subconsciously to a nearby police car. He left the door wide open, and before he could fully realize it, he was at the office. There, he washed himself and got into his street clothes, and filled in his report lifelessly.

Blaming Blames

Instead of going directly to the hospital, Alex went to Charles' house. He was unprepared to break the news to Elizabeth. She was getting supper ready when the unusual doorbell rang, bridging the gap between the security inside and the insecurity outside. Human curiosity of what lay behind closed doors took her to Alex's frozenness. He stood speechless in front of her, like a scarecrow. But this did not prevent him from communicating her loss to her.

She was not ashamed to think out her instinctive feelings about the half-goner still standing before her: *Why Charles? Why not this middle aged cockroach? He has already lived most of his life out,* she thought, as both of them fell into each other's arms for comfort from the outside chill, which threatened to reach her inner core. Her pounding jungle drum did not bring any relief; no echo from the wind had warned her. And yet she knew it all along, long before she saw Alex' s swollen face and his guilty eyes secretly hiding his own good fortune. Their chemical bondage changed simultaneously; Elizabeth and Alex shifted apart, and she sailed through the open door into an endless region that reduced meaning to absurdity. He glanced at her while his fingers raked his thinning hair and remained hidden behind his neck, out of her view.

We should go to the hospital, he thought, as his mind wrestled with the conflict between the price of self-preservation and the folly of others' loss. He turned the stove off and slowly walked to the front door, fusing to the dim driveway. He stood motionless in front of the closed door. He knew he shouldn't stare at her. And yet, he was forced to take a quick and careless glance, for an accidental eye contact could not hurt anyone. But she could not sense anything outside herself.

At least she isn't wandering around the neighborhood, he thought. He fought furiously with the image of Elizabeth sitting in his car, blocking it out, turning it upside down, throwing it all over the place in time and out of time, trying to comprehend her feelings, until he was mentally exhausted. His dark heart had been forged in the will to survive, and he hid his serpent's eyes from Elizabeth, who appeared to be sitting mindlessly. Alex entered the car with his Venetian mask on; he drove absentmindedly while he tried to peep into Elizabeth's torn world.

I should have tried to understand him better, thought Elizabeth. *Shouldn't have argued with him. I shouldn't have cancelled our vacation last month. Why? Do we have to work so much? For who? And for what? Our child, we never had, last year. But, it was me. Yes, I alone refused to have a family. I told him. You can't say I didn't. We'd have had a child, if he would have quit his job. But no, he loves his job more than his family. Why didn't he change his work? Why? Nobody wants to live with insecurity. Maybe he won't come home one day. I told him, over and over again, one thousand times. I don't want to bring up a child without a father. I told him, and I told him. But he couldn't accept it.*

Alex overheard her mumbling to herself, and glanced over at her. Her lips continued to move without inviting any listeners.

"We're here," whispered Alex, pulling himself toward the steering wheel with both hands to free himself from the sticky vinyl seat. Elizabeth was momentarily lost in what could have been and what would be now. Suddenly, as though an electrical charge had jumped into her body causing a slight backward jerk, her scrambling life sensed Alex's hand on her shoulder. She found the doorknob and opened it, allowing herself to step into the depth of the sea with bound arms and legs. Each step only increased the profoundness until the hospital emergency's sliding door reminded her of her own mortality.

The emergency waiting room was only half full, for the evening was still young. They walked to the receptionist's desk. The receptionist carefully examined the young woman before her for noticeable symptoms: an empty face, untidy hair, a T-shirt slightly exposing her braless chest, trainer pants, and house shoes. Alex reached in his coat pocket, displayed his badge, and then returned it to his pants pocket.

"Where is Sergeant Brown?" he asked.

"Go ask inside," replied the receptionist, as she continued to survey the deranged woman following the well-dressed middle aged policeman. Another dividing glass door detected them and slipped itself open. The newcomers observed several people in white clothes dashing from one room to another. Straight ahead, Alex noticed two officers chatting near an open door. They approached the two uniformed police, and a humble and contemplative look repossessed the officers, reflecting toward Mrs. Brown the deep emotional sentiment that they had forgotten a moment ago. They were like monumental icebergs with an imperceptible flame at the center—warm enough to melt snow but not to change the shade of their rigid identities.

"We're sorry for Charles," said the two officers, shattering the virgin iceberg and exposing its core. Alex glanced into the guarded room; a half covered and frightened boy quickly pulled the entire white sheet over his body.

"Where's Charles?" demanded Alex, evoking excess stress on the youngster's eye sockets in the room.

"Fifth floor, in the operating room," said the younger officer.

Elizabeth followed Alex toward the emergency elevator. He wondered whether she had seen through him. *Yes, any officer will try to protect his own rear. And yes again, I'm very sorry for what happened to my partner. But thank God, it wasn't me. I have a wife and two children to look after,* thought Alex. He placed his wet right hand in his pocket and ran his fingers around the circular edge of a coin. The elevator stopped and they entered.

Arriving on the fifth floor, they did not see anyone. No odor or sound, other than the screeching of their own shoes on the glassy ceramic floor, which failed to register any trace of the weight that glided off it. The hallway was dimly lit, and beds and stretchers lined the wall opposite the elevators, leaving the exit unobstructed. No more than thirty yards away from the elevators, a transparent glass wall separated the public from personnel. The sliding door opened automatically; a tractor could easily be driven through it. They cautiously passed through the noiseless door and sensed no life in the long corridor, which ran perpendicular to the entrance. On the right side, another glass wall with a sliding door firmly fixed to it bore the inscription "Theatre: Authorized Personnel Only." They stepped in front of it and nothing moved. They tried to gain a better view of the protected area through the transparent glass wall, but it was bare and uninteresting. They finally turned to the left side; it had several doors and a sign that read Recovery on the wall. They considered it to be unimportant. Intrigued by the right wing, they pressed their faces harder against the glass door and noticed several empty stretchers in an almost hidden corner next to the door. Further down the hall there were several doors with a single light above each one. Six of them were green; the others were off. Suddenly, a green changed to red; immediately, a green and white figure dashed from another room and ran into the red one.

"They're operating rooms," murmured Alex, trying not to alarm Elizabeth with his experience of hospital routines. Elizabeth was hypnotized by the red light that had just turned on, and was scared to ask for the meaning. A woman dressed all in white came from the left wing and caught them by surprise.

"You're not allowed in this area," she distinctly affirmed. Her remark did not evoke an apology, for human desires were raw and tasteless under desperate circumstances.

"We're looking for Mr. Brown," replied Alex, justifying his

presence. "He came to the operating room a few hours ago."

"Wait near the elevators," instructed the woman. "I'll check for you." The woman firmly held her ground while they passed the main door. While they waited, Alex hung around near the door and Elizabeth went near the stretchers. Alex surveyed the woman as she pressed a hidden button. A person dressed in mostly green, with gloves, covered shoes, hair net, and face mask, appeared near the wall and opened a small window which was also hidden from the outside world. They spoke to each other, and then the person in green disappeared for a moment and reappeared with a sheet of paper in the plastic grip. The woman wearing white, her lips slightly parted, rubbed her chin and then pressed her lower body against the glass wall very tightly, leaving her upper body barely touching the wall. The one in green left and returned with some more papers in an unprotected hand, and passed the index finger from left to right through all the loose pages. The women in white crossed her upper legs furiously, leaving a wide gap between both feet, forming a majestic equilateral triangle, as the person in green left.

A penguin gliding on its heels paddled toward Alex, and Elizabeth drifted toward him for the news.

"There's no Brown in the operating room," squeaked the woman in white.

"No Brown!" repeated Alex.

A bolt of lightning struck the lonely tree in the pasture; Elizabeth's weak legs collapsed from under her, and she tumbled heavily backward on her head. The women in white, forgetting to mail her liquid letter, grabbed Elizabeth's wrist.

"Are you crazy! Look, her head is bleeding. Stop the bleeding!" shouted Alex.

She ran to her section, leaving Alex to attend to Elizabeth's head. He supported it with his jacket. "It's a crime to abandon someone in medical need," he cried angrily, trying to stop the bleeding with his handkerchief.

"Ninety-nine in operating room corridor" blasted out from the intercom, but it slipped Alex's full attention.

"Goddamn it! Where is everyone? You can't find anyone in this bloody place! Is this supposed to be a hospital? Or a graveyard run by a bunch of gypsies!"

A chariot with two people flung out from one elevator; two women broke away from another elevator; three more took the stairs; all were at work at once, without missing a beat. Three of them transferred the patient to an empty stretcher. Another one removed the jacket and handkerchief and replaced it with some gauze to stop the bleeding. The two from the cart rolled her body to the side, and then put a flat board under the back; one massaged the chest and counted "One thousand and one, one thousand and two…" One person took blood, while another put in an I.V. One of them rushed downstairs with some blood in a syringe.

"What are you doing to her?" grumbled Alex, as Elizabeth was given an oxygen mask. His insolent question only irritated everyone, and nobody answered. Alex drifted further and further away from the spider net. He looked for the woman who worked in Recovery; she was gone. He realized that he would not have an answer from this crowded scene. Finally, the lowest ranked member of the team ordered him out. Thinking that there was nothing else he could do, he took the stairs and headed to the Mensa on the third floor.

4: Mensa

It's incredible. Everything in one single day, thought Alex, unable to fully digest it all. He found himself standing in line with a tray in his hand in the hospital main cafeteria. He looked into the open dining area; most of the white clouds had drifted away from this area of the hospital, leaving mostly colorful ones from the streets. Some reluctant visitors waited in the restaurant rather than making the final thrust to the hospital bed where their patient-hosts were stationed. They cited hospital policy, limiting the amount of visitors per patient as their rationalization, rather than acting on courtesy, finiteness, and forgiveness.

Other visitors enjoyed the togetherness in the restaurant after their actual visit; they had a chance to meet other family members and friends whom they had not seen for a long time. They appeared to surrender the belief in their own immorality and mended old disagreements because they tasted a different world in which happiness, health, and a short and full life had to be cherished. And yet, most hospital personnel had a short memory of their enriched wisdom.

There were about ten people ahead of him and some behind, everybody wanting the same thing. Nobody could escape his destiny of waiting in line—expectant mothers had to recline in line, the child feels sick, another line. Throughout life, a series of lines strung mortals in a very tight place. Even the deceased had to wait for a vacant hole in the cemetery. The New Testament scared people about an empty line before Heaven's door, an ugly revelation of the status of the line as real, while the arrangement of its contents remained fictitious. Whenever Alex failed to keep up with the line, a person in line behind him would touch his tray, shoes, or whistle, reminding him that the mummies had to move. Not knowing exactly why he came to the Mensa, he poured a large coffee, a habitual response from working long hours and graveyard shifts.

After paying, he mistakenly went to the smoking section and sat like a regular customer. In a daze, he drifted to the next table and requested a cigarette. As he was returning with his unlit torch in his mouth, he did not expect to see any familiar faces.

"Alex! Oh, my baby! You're okay! What are you doing here?" a familiar female voice asked.

Alex turned and found himself in his wife's arms. The intensity of caring moved them from the immediate surroundings to the realm of silence where an instance had no border. Her shivering in his arms awakened him slightly. She got one hand free and wiped her reddish eyes. Arm-in-arm, fear and love awkwardly tagged along to the table.

"Oh, my baby, I've never seen you like this before. When you didn't come for supper, I phoned. The dispatcher said you were at the hospital."

"Yes, Charles was hit," he grunted.

"Hi, Dad!" Martin's voice echoed through the restaurant. His mother had a natural posture now, instead of the pose of the headless chicken that drove everyone crazy at home, driving the car from the passenger seat, blaming the hospital's admission secretary for Alex's injury. Her round lips revealed everything: hope, and thankfulness.

"Are you a space cadet? Standing there with no respect," she asked her son.

"Sorry," he replied. Martin glanced at his father, by nature a quiet person, who preferred action to talking. "I guess you're trying to digest the meaninglessness in your life. Is it colorful, Dad? You spend your entire life putting criminals behind bars, as though you'll get to the end of it. Some life, eh? Carrying water with a bamboo basket," he cried, hoping for a response from his father, who merely shifted his eyes and slightly parted his lips. He knew what his father would say. A policeman with his uniform on was a walking target for everyone. Everyone wanted revenge on society. Some hit back. Others tried to have the upper hand. Now, society became something very dangerous for everyone. "Hey, Dad. Crimes will swallow us up, if we don't fight back. Our institutions breed criminals. Everyone has become a potential criminal. Right? You're just putting the unfortunate behind bars." Martin was upset with Alex for putting himself up for someone else's target practice in the street. Alex ignored him. Martin continued to grumble:

"All in All,
Life in some,
All is gone,
Life is only one thing,
Is this all?
Here is all,
Who call you all?

Everything bursts out of the same mouth, sorrow, happiness, suffering, anger, and finally, hope.

All in meaninglessness,
Life's meaningless."

"I told you, we're wasting our money to send him to university. Look at him. If this is what you learn, I'm sorry for you," Cathy interrupted. She glanced at Alex and noticed that he was not listening, so she confronted Martin directly. "For sure, you'll not be a follower, but a leader with no followers."

Her unexpected remark sent him deeper into his seat for a moment. Though he had wanted to provoke his mother a little bit, he did not foresee her criticism.

"Look at these people! They've got wonderful careers, they're respectable," she cried angrily.

"You said it, Mom! Hitting it, dead on the nail. Of course I see it all," replied Martin, looking around the Mensa. "Feathers separating professions—the old ones sitting on a separate table with extremely white clothes are chiefs. Aren't they? The younger ones, sitting by themselves, must be assistants. That's easy too. See, they look up at the old ones with awe and reverence. Nurses by themselves, over there. Do you see how they glance at the young doctors? And these ones, sitting in the smoking section, all in gray. They must be cleaning people. So, Mom! Which one should I be?

Let me see. Yes, I get it," he said, pointing at the table of chiefs. "That bulk of whiteness over there. They hide their internal darkness. They even mix religion with a stiff dose of science and technology. Seeing them in a deserted street on a moonless night, you will jump out of your skin. Here, they're at home, they're protected. It's all too perfect here, the dead ones can't complain anymore. They cremate their mistakes. They're in league with the body-baggers." He spoke without realizing his father's discomfort.

"Why do you see a doctor for your asthma? Yes, tell me why? They have to do the dirty work of our filthy environment. But no, you're here to criticize people," she replied bitterly.

"Look at those white clowns. Others are scared stiff to sit near them. They think of themselves as God. They enjoy their job so much. They work with businesses to pollute our health, water, land, and food. With car manufacturers to make unsafe cars, with communities to make unsafe roads, with pharmaceutical companies to manufacture drugs with severe side effects. You name it; they're into it. Buy more drugs to counter rotten side effects. Is that what you call innocent? To get our facts straight, their education and research are paid by multinational corporations. Their first priority is to their creators, pharmaceutical manufacturers. They're working against people. They want us to get sick, injured. Living off sickness like parasites. It's disgusting!

"They're into the big business. If you check in everyone's house, there's a private pharmacy, more profits for corporations. Profits for pharmaceutical firms, it makes me sick. These jerks work for drug companies, each person must pay from his pocket, to have an up-to-date drug cabinet at home. A poor person must buy his own medications. How low can you get? And our medical insurance goes sky high, because of these heartless vermin. Only prescribing their company's products." Martin took in a breath of sterilized air. He made brief eye contact with his mother, and then cut her short. "Yes, I'm not finished yet. When you want only two headache tablets, you've to buy the whole bottle, one hundred tablets. The other ninety-eight goes in the garbage. We pay for it. They're cutthroat. Worse than butchers."

"I see your point. But would you use someone else's asthma spray, Martin?"

"It's the same thing, I'm saying. Can't you see? You go to the drug store to buy something you need once. But no, you have to buy the entire bottle. And before you know it, you have to throw out all the rest because it is expired. They don't do this in the hospital. Why can't the community have a place to store excess medications? Why can't these companies pack their medications so that an inexperienced user can't contaminate unused medications? If you want an aspirin for a slight headache, you can get it free from the community, instead of buying one hundred tablets. And if you do buy it, you can always give the rest to the community, for others to use. It's about time our community started to serve its people. Doctors should stop serving the interests of multinational corporations with their golden prescriptive pens. Letting companies eat out of a sick person's pocket is humiliating."

Some workers dressed in grey admired Martin's speech, but his mother was much more concerned with her husband's pain.

Martin synchronized himself to the sentiment at the table. His father was fixed on the rim of the coffee cup; the steam from the coffee was gone a while ago. He was staring at the thick blackness that appeared to be depthless. *Could it be that he sees himself being sucked into some kind of infinite darkness? Defenseless against its power? He's allowing himself to be gobbled up by self-pity. At least, he sees the meaning of his job—chasing falling stars,* he thought. He glanced at his mother, and her sympathetic eyes confirmed that his father was helplessly swallowed up by the facts of life before him.

"Ninety-nine at the emergency!" blasted out from the intercom. The announcement ran through Alex's body like an electric charge.

"Dad's bulb just lit up," cried Martin. Two people in white ran out of the Mensa, leaving their meal. "Today is a special day, two cardiac arrests within an hour. They're having good business," he sarcastically commented, loud enough for others to hear him.

"You mean to tell me that code "ninety-nine" is heart attack!?"

asked Alex.

"You, of all people, should know that," answered Martin.

I think I heard a ninety-nine announcement when Elizabeth fell on the floor. Could it be? he internally interrogated himself. "This can't be, it's just not possible! Charles, and now, it's poor Elizabeth," he grumbled.

"What are you saying, Alex?"

"Elizabeth is only twenty-two. She can't have a heart attack," Alex affirmed and denied, looking more confused than before.

"What! Elizabeth had a heart attack?" asked Cathy, taken by surprise. She had thought that Elizabeth was with Charles, and she had completely forgotten to ask about her whereabouts and feelings.

"I told them. But no, they had to start the entire machine rolling for a common head injury," Alex complained.

The chair glided backward under Martin, and he stood at the end of the table, taking charge. "What are you waiting for? We have to get some answers," he said, standing firmly on both legs and holding his gaze parallel to the ceiling as though he had a glimpse of the future. He picked the tray up from the table and placed it on the moving belt near the exit. He waited long enough for his parents to be in sight; they were moving slowly, hand-in-hand, so he continued to walk to the elevator where he waited for them.

The elevator stopped, and two men came out with a cart about seven feet long with a rectangular box of the same length and width attached to it. It was covered with blue plastic.

"That stuff is big enough to carry a dead man," cried Martin.

"Is this guy funny?" replied one of the men.

"You're doing a good job. It's meat for the Mensa," the other one said, giving the offensive observer a dirty look while they pursued their course.

"Look!" said Alex. "They're taking a corpse to pathology.

Oh, that's nothing. We go with the ambulance to some accidents, pick up the pieces with a spade, and then put them in garbage bags. Here, at least, they put the pieces back together."

"Can't we speak about something else, Alex?" Cathy asked. She felt uncomfortable talking about human horror, for each person meant much more than physical parts: mind, emotions, beliefs, hopes, relationships.

"Are you coming?" yelled Martin. "You're standing around and looking in the empty corridor for a ghost or something!" He waited for them to get nearer the elevator, and his parents passed him and went to the stairs. He followed closely behind his mother, as his father walked several steps ahead of them. "It still puzzles me," he said to his mother. "Why do they tie a dead body up? It's like they don't want it to speak about its personal history. And it's future. They even tied its feet and hands together, as though it'll run away from the domain of death. I'll tell you why! The living are hiding their fear of life by straightening up dead bodies."

"Will you hush up, Martin!" she shouted.

"Yes, I'll shut up. Can't you see? Your sentiment is choking you up."

"Talking, talking! Do you want attention just like a little child?" She fought off his interrogation, for she needed all her energy for climbing these deadly stairs.

"Oh, leave him alone!" cried Alex, who appreciated hearing the familiar voice.

"Yes. Mom, as I've been saying."

"No preaching!" she cried.

"At school, they blame you for my lack of respect. For my free opinions. But no, you blame school for not overworking me. Look at these overgrown muscles, with no loyalty. And no respect, too. Yes, a free mind, all over me," Martin said, pulling up his shirtsleeves and holding his breath for his mother to look at him. She continued onward and did not turn back.

"Yes, I see. A free mind, with nothing inside. It's a pity," she whispered involuntarily.

"I get it, I struck the right string in you. Let face it, you're scared of death." He saw his mother's reddish face as she turned back on the stairs to take a breath. "If you hold it any longer, you'll explode," he teased. "You shouldn't worry, if you kick the bucket here, you become a small 'IT.' 'IT' as an object, a thing. A common 'IT,' without a name, no sex, no age, no identity, no religion, no history…"

"That's enough, you monster!" shouted Cathy. Her voice halted Alex, who was about ten steps ahead of them now.

"What's going on?" Alex asked halfheartedly.

"As I'm telling Mom, a person's true identity is restored when she's in the ground, with a beautiful gravestone, family sympathy, and community recognition. How else can I tell her to enjoy her life? There's more to life than sitting around. Waiting for history to come home. You have to kick yourself, all the time, to do something new."

Identity

"We're here," Alex murmured, reaching familiar terrain, allowing himself to take in the customary empty smell, seeing the usual objects against the wall without blood, and following the harmonious friction of his shoes.

"What's the rush!" Cathy complained. "Wait for us, Will you?"

"What are you looking for?" Martin asked his father, trying to wipe away the obnoxious chemical smell from his nose. "Everything in here is sterilized! Strong enough to kill delicate brain cells. It turns your skin pale. Look at that huge glass wall, the door too! Yeah, it can even reflect bacteria on the floor! I tell you, it should be against the law to use this kind of glass wall, for the outside walls of buildings. That's why nobody can find any insects and birds in the city—all of them have collided against it and died. I never like window-shopping anyway. It magnifies everything inside.' He walked past the sliding door while his parents waited in the corridor for someone to come by.

Our architecture solves the problem of good and evil. The left wing is Recovery, the right one is the Operating Theatre. I should play it safe. Then, I go right, Martin thought. He quickly found the hidden button on the wall and pressed it. A man answered the buzz. He felt the jolly green giant surveying him, an unauthorized intruder invading the high priest's secret temple. The man in green controlled the entrance, standing between both half doors, and bringing some invisible ghoulish forces along with him.

"Yes!" he asked, wearing a tight face that challenged this insolent intruder with institutionalized power.

"Yes? I didn't ask you anything, yet. Since the answer is YES, the question is, when was Mr. Brown operated on?" The chemical bond between them was unbound; opposing forces in the universe were lashing out.

"Okay! Wise guy. Let me look," he replied. He disappeared into the secretary's office for a moment, and then reappeared. "We've no Brown here! Check with recovery," he said, pointing to the other section. His index finger crawled back and formed a tight fist, and he left. Martin quickly apprehended the administrative logic of passing the buck, so he tapped the glass door for the fellow in green who was moving away from him like a slut on quicksand.

He returned and opened the little pigeonhole this time, the window that strictly defined the limits of information and human relationship on the presumption of dishonesty.

"What now!"

"Let's get our record straight. A few hours ago emergency sent him away for an operation. For you to take the bullets out of him. Now, you're telling me he isn't here."

This refinement made an intellectual connection and caused the man to listen more attentively. "Since you put it that way, this is how things work around here. In certain life threatening cases, emergency often sends up patients without any personal chart, only with medical records. Here, we try to save these patients' lives. We don't treat names. Get it! After the operation, they go to recovery."

"Thanks," said Martin politely.

"All the same," he replied, closing the nest hole and hesitating behind his protective shell like a turtle searching for a mating partner.

Martin pointed to the sign for his parents to follow him. They stopped at the door, which bore a sign written in big block letters: RECOVERY. Martin put his ear near the door, but he was unable to hear anything inside. Standing on both legs firmly fixed, adjusting his shirt and pants, keeping his eyes straight ahead as though the door was transparent, he banged on the door with his iron knuckles, loud enough to wake up everyone behind it. He put his hammering hand quickly in his pocket to hide its pain. Nobody answered the door.

This is strange, he thought. He looked around the corridor. The man in green at the operation section was observing them through his glass kingdom. He knocked again—even louder. A woman in white rushed out furiously, taking them by surprise.

"Out! Out of here! Out!" shouted the woman, pushing them out, all the way to elevator. "And stay out!"

The man in green still covered his face with his hand, forgetting the chance of contamination, enjoying a special kind of human amusement. The woman went to the man in green and justified her behavior; everybody knew that no visitors were permitted in this area.

"A practical joker," cried Martin, blaming the green ape for their embarrassment and mistreatment. "Dad, give me your badge," he said, thinking of turning the table on him, for the badge had the power to reveal buried misconduct in people. Alex checked for his coat. It was missing; he had not even realized it before.

"It was under Elizabeth's head. Yes, I had it in my pants pocket at the emergency," he mumbled. He found his identity in his pocket, but mildly refused to transfer its significance to his son, the badge being much stronger than the bearer.

"For all these years, Alex, you haven't mixed your private life with profession," Cathy calmly insisted. "It isn't worth it." Seeing that neither of them was listening, she confined her thoughts to her own head. *Two charging bulls rushing out to conquer that woman, just doing her job. Like two little children, out for revenge, with no guiding angel. Thank God, some people still give others a fair chance. And remember their duties. Other people have responsibilities, not these two. I better join them, before everything gets out of hand.*

"Do you know the whereabouts of Mr. Brown?" asked Alex, showing off his identity.

The nurse in white felt challenged and threatened; and yet, she refused to reply at once, for the question took her to creation, and Cane telling God he wasn't his brother's keeper. She counted her hesitation, for medical secrets had to be binding for everyone. She was not comfortable with Alex's symbol. She might have done something wrong in the past; now, she could not remember it.

"We don't have all night!" he repeated, detecting her slow response as a lie, the real symptom of guilt.

"We're friends of Officer Brown," interrupted Cathy. "He was wounded on duty with my husband, here. And that's why he's so upset. We came here to visit him."

The humble request formed an alignment with the nurse. The nurse believed that she had recognized Cathy's oppression, mostly by her authoritative husband, and her subtle compassion for liberation was the call. She decided not to send them to the nursing office for inquiries.

"We have a Brown, a patient," said the nurse, facing only Cathy. "As a matter of fact, he's my patient. There's one problem—no visitors are allowed in this area!"

"Is he okay?" Cathy murmured. Their reaching eyes simultaneously descended into the realm of mutual acknowledgement and cooperation, for they had to continuously prove their equality to others, if not to themselves.

"I'll ask one of the doctors in recovery to come and see to you," the nurse said, hurrying to her section without saying goodbye. She did not mean any disrespect, only a continuation of the conversation at a higher level.

"You really have to be affirmative with these people, or else they'll push you around," remarked Martin, watching his father return the badge to his pocket. "She thought you were going to arrest her. It really gave her a good scare."

"Here, you go again," she interrupted. "Out of beat. You think of yourself as standing outside everything. Don't you?"

"I told you before. Each person is a real leader without knowing it. Rich and poor, all of them. People elect a government to office; these unfaithful morons, in turn, use people to represent things. Real things like rocks, in the world.

"Oh, politicians, the best parasite of them all.

All of them couldn't make One.

None of us wants a speaker to lie for us...."

"Stop it!" yelled Alex, interrupting him even more harshly with the vertical lines on his forehead than with his words. "You and your mother going at it, again. At home, that's okay. Not everywhere." Alex believed that people's behavior was confined by situations and circumstances, without acknowledging how others reacted to stress and uncertainty. His attitudes triggered Martin's irreconciled mind to sing.

"Yes, authority, authority without compassion, without tolerance, without responsibility," he grumbled, pacing the checkered floor without missing a square.

"Yes, what do you want? Anarchy!" interrupted Alex. "I'm proud of my job. To serve my community. I'm growing a white beard, here. How come I always have to defend myself like some criminal? It's all basic economics—supply and demand. People demand protection against criminals, so we're here. When the crime rate goes up, we have more police. It's all very simple."

Martin gave his father a disgusted look because he knew he had quoted every single word from his department training book. Giving himself an identity was more important than having none. He wanted to say something to his father, to knock some sense into his head; he was unable to wait any longer.

"To serve and to protect is painted on your car, it's your holy banner. It means serving ripe cows against lean and dying cows. No, let's see! It means serving the homeless, the weak, the delinquents, against institutionalized cruelty and ripe cows. You don't give the poor a chance, you don't even give them leftovers to eat. You spend your entire life patrolling and terrorizing the poor in the slums. You have your heroic medal from that sector. Not even once, did you ever patrol the rich area. If you had, it'd have been high treason. You might even have lost your job the next day. You get the message. Each bag of beans has rotten ones, but your dispatcher boss of bosses chooses the bag for you. Some serving you're into! Serving the symptoms, not the problem."

"Listen Martin, arguing with your mother, that's okay. Every single day, day in, day out, I put my life on the line, to feed you, to pay for your education. Don't you ever give me your smart talk," cried Alex sternly.

"Using threat and fear. It's your favorite ideology. What do you want to do, crack everybody's skull, just because he opposes you?" Martin replied, widening the gap between himself and his father by making a few calculated backward steps.

"Are you scared? I don't hit, and you know that. But you must tell me all this before you want money from me."

"No, I'm controlling your emotion; I want you to be objective. If I didn't move away, you'd see me as an equal adversary. And then you'd punch the wall at home, like always. And, I should tell you, your old school of threats and hitting is obsolete."

"What, your Mom taught you this two cent psychology?"

"Hey, keep me out of your macho, egoistic self-image!" she cried. "The boy is right! You're putting only the unfortunate behind bars. They didn't have a chance to begin with. Not even any adequate legal representative to defend them."

"Dreaming of perfection! Why don't you both wake up to reality? Nothing has ever changed. It's always the one at the end, doing the dirty job for you. With no praise and no recognition." Alex descended from his throne with the tide on his side. "I'm not proud of my job, but it's the only one I can do well. There're no honest jobs left in this world. Everything is survival. Look at you, you want to be a lawyer, so you can defend criminals, help to break up marriages, sue poor people, and defend the rich. Everything comes down to money, and a name. Would you take someone who can't pay you? You've got a lot to learn, if you want to live. You better go with the tide, it doesn't wait for anyone."

"So, what else is in your cop book? You're stubborn like a dinosaur," Martin said, smiling and pointing to his father.

"It's my police training – to stay alive for another day without asking questions."

Softness

A figure, covered in green except for white shoes and hair net, no mask and gloves, crossed the sliding door. It approached closer and closer, a smooth face, hands swinging freely with each stride. A light hand reached to the head and liberated her short hair and her square facial appearances.

"Hello, I'm Dr. Johnson. Mr. Brown is my patient," she clearly expressed in a calm voice, exchanging handshakes with her visitors.

"How is he doing?" Cathy asked softly.

"He's still in recovery, doing well. He's conscious—he lost a lot of blood, but his injuries were not life threatening. He should have been transferred to the surgical ward an hour ago. Unfortunately, we can't find a free bed, yet."

Her marshmallow hands are extremely soft from frequent washing, disinfecting, and creaming. Not a housewife with sandpaper hands, with cracks like the walls of a mud house in the dry season, thought Martin, trying to determine the reality of this person in oversized clothes.

"Thanks, Doc. Can we see him?" asked Cathy in a nimble voice.

"At this time, no visitors are permitted, I'm sorry."

"Where is Elizabeth Brown?" questioned Alex, pushing the nice guy stuff away.

"Was she shot, too?" asked the doctor with a surprised voice.

"No, she's Charles' wife," said Alex. "She had a ninety-nine in this very hallway a few hours ago."

"I'm sorry to hear that. I really don't know where she is. You should check with admission, the second floor. They should be able to help you."

"You said, second floor," cried Alex.

"Thanks, thanks again, for your kind assistance," Cathy interrupted. She grabbed Alex by the arm and led him toward the stairs.

Martin decided not to give her a farewell handshake and slowly followed his parents. *It's confirmed, washing and creaming,* he thought. *Two pale hands, washing off all the unknown visitors. Darn, she only cares about names when her success is translated to skills. Darn, again, it's fate when her failure bleeds into numbers. Her specialized bloodless hands know everything about nothing. God laughs at specialization. This is what we're shaping ourselves to become—the knowers of nothing.*

She doesn't have genuine substance, she's a phony. She doesn't value people, only sicknesses and spectacular surgical cases. She pulls rank over her colleagues. She cherishes social contact with sicknesses. She plays an open horizon to everyone—because we're her future customers. She hides all traces of like and dislike, Dad's rudeness, our physical appearances, verbal and non-verbal messages. She must be a walking textbook, without an author.

His body was extremely heavy after the stairs, and he noticed himself tailing a good way behind his parents. "I'm getting tired of this dump, I'm splitting," Martin said.

"You better go, I'll stay with your Dad."

"Bye Mom, Bye Dad."

Hardness

"The nursing station is over there. See the sign—there it is," Alex said. A blue sign hung on the ceiling next to a partly open door.

They knocked, no one answered. Alex stuck his head in; a woman was catching up with the daily news. She did not abandon the newspaper to question the intruders, for their knocking did not threaten her. Though the two of them stood before her desk, her eyes were intensely fixed on the page, and that was unbearable for the hot-blooded visitors.

"Excuse me! We're looking for Elizabeth Brown, she had a ninety-nine this evening…" cried Alex, unable to control his heavy voice.

"Sorry, I start at eleven. You'll have to come back in the morning." A trace of tiredness could be detected in her eyelids. She wore the symptoms of a night worker. Her insensitivity and impoliteness drove Alex senseless. He dropped his badge on the newspaper, sharpening the nurse's immediate alertness, and he impatiently waited for its softening effects.

"Sorry Sir, I'm on my break," she thumbed out of her mouth, jerking backward and smiling charmingly. Being confronted with a police officer usually elected a rigorous search for crimes in one's past, for an innate sense of guilt was inevitable in most people. But she knew her public relations policy too well; a police investigation and negative publicity meant less confidence and government financial assistance for her social institution. "Yes, you said Elizabeth Brown," she politely repeated, checking the previous head nurse's report. The monkey swinging on a thin vine had fallen, sending shock waves to her facial muscles. "Nothing is noted," she murmured. She took the phone and then dialed some secret numbers, returning the receiver to its place. She went though some more pages. "Nothing," she whispered.

The phone rang. "Central nursing, Francine here," she answered with authority. "Are you on call?" she demanded. "Where is the patient, Ms. Brown? She had a ninety-nine this evening. Don't tell me, it's my job! You have a patient, Brown! Aren't you on call? Okay, yes. Yes, I see, hum, good-bye." She smiled at her enthusiastic intruders. "I've just spoken to the doctor on call," she said, clearing her throat. She maintained a half smile, which seemed to say that everything had a logical explanation. "You see, a ninety-nine was called in the operating room corridor. The team on call responded immediately. The patient had no jacket, no money, no identification, and only a pair of slippers on. Because she wore visitor's clothes, and since she was on the fifth floor at the time, the team thought she came from our clinic—a psychiatric patient."

"That's absurd! I was with her!" Alex shouted. Cathy tightened her grip on his hand.

"This is unfortunate," said Francine. "We only have three hundred and seventy-nine beds open of our usual thirteen hundred, so things do get mixed up. We put patients wherever we can find a free bed. Besides that, no visitors could have gone to the operating section from emergency. That elevator doesn't stop there. And you can't use the stairs to go up, either. Everyone coming from emergency must register at admission, first."

Alex probed the entire office for an outlet of his anger. It was obvious that she was lying through her teeth, for he knew that the elevator next to the medical record section went to the fifth floor.

"What now then?" he cried.

"Yes, as I was saying, the best possible decision was made under impossible circumstances. For us, her health, security, and well being came first."

"I'm still confused," murmured Cathy. "She needs medical help, not psychological."

"She recovered very quickly from her attack, and then was taken to ICU—the Intensive Care Unit—for observation and examination. There, the patient woke up, very aggressive, shouting, pulling her intravenous out, hitting nurses, speaking incoherently, jumping out of bed. We have very sick patients up there. We tried to calm her down. After all this, the doctor phoned the nursing station, requesting a transfer. Yes, this was after 10 o'clock. My colleague noted it here," she said, pointing at the incomplete record. "Just before that, at 21:45, the psychiatric department had reported a missing female patient. She fit the same description. Considering her behavior, it was natural that we thought she was our missing patient," Francine rambled. She licked her lips. "These patients often come from the sixth floor, where a skyway connects both buildings. And they use it to go to the Mensa. They often wear normal clothes, wander about and get lost in the huge building. Some remove their nametag around their hand. They mostly use the stairs."

"But, is she okay?" asked Cathy, showing a little fatigue.

"Of course! Or we'd never have authorized her transfer. She's there, now. No one is allowed to leave or enter that building at this time of the night. Only with a special card, and I don't even have one." They noticed that the nurse was indirectly instructing her visitors that visiting hours were terminated.

"So, we can't see her," murmured Cathy.

"Yes, come back in the morning!" Francine cried hurriedly.

"Let's go, Alex. There isn't anything we can do now," she mumbled, taking Alex's hand and sluggishly dragging him out of the office.

"I could have rung her tiny little neck! I have to stand there, and digest her colorless lies! She took us for idiots! She thinks she has power in here. Well, we'll see about that. If you don't show your anger, she won't take us seriously."

"Oh, Alex, she was so frightened. That's why she went on and on. Don't worry, Alex, we'll have all the answers tomorrow."

5: All-In-One

Chuck walked in Fairview as though there were eyes on his feet, shoulders, and arms, moving in a giant slalom without any poles in his hands. He finally reached the spacious entrance of All-In-One. It had seventy-five seats, long benches forming a square along the walls. The inside walls had four access areas. On the southern wall there was a passage to the basement where washrooms, two game rooms, and a service room were located. The opposite wall was solid. The western wall was connected to the kitchen and the main entrance. A huge opening without a door led to the seating area. The kitchen, which was completely made of glass, had a door to the parking lot. Except for a few corner and middle tables, each table was for four people.

The restaurant officially closed at nine in the evening and reopened each morning at ten. Saturday and Sunday were busy. Except for Martin, an all-rounder, who worked only part-time, most personnel were less than twenty years old. The two main cooks who were older than Martin mainly stayed in the kitchen; they were not former customers like Martin. Elizabeth had known these two former unemployed cooks for a while and got them their jobs.

There were hardly any lineups like in most popular establishments. If someone was ordering, new arrivals would find seats until nobody stood near the cash register. With the absence of watchdogs and bad conscience in the restaurant, sometimes customers even forgot to order.

Chuck took his large Coke and went toward a corner table where two people were already sitting. Lenny's back was against the glass wall, so a good side view was available; the other person's back was toward the whole dining area, leaving the entire bench against the solid wall free. He stopped for a few seconds near the table and then sat on the empty bench where he could see everything that was happening in the restaurant.

"Tim," said the boy near Lenny, introducing himself to Chuck, who had heard of him without ever seeing him. He was no older than Chuck and Lenny.

"Chuck," he kindly replied.

"You finally get to meet Tim from lower town," said Lenny, keeping everything short.

"Yes, I've been hanging around here for months, now," Tim said, watching Chuck sip his Coke. He did not want Chuck to think that he was a new-ling.

"I see," Chuck immediately answered, as though there was no difference between newcomers and regulars. "So, you're our big brain behind the database, keeping good track of our investments and revenues." Chuck did not want to be too obvious about the money in the safety savings account.

But Tim wanted to say how much there was in the account, and he was waiting for the right opportunity to do it. "Oh, you shouldn't say that. Anyone with some sense can do it. It takes only sweat and persistence, not brains," murmured Tim.

Lenny did not like to talk about this delicate topic, for he believed that people conducted business, not preached about it. He changed the subject. "What kept you so long? We were waiting for you," he asked, giving Chuck a quick glance and noticing that he did get the message. "So, how's the biology paper coming?"

"It's nothing special. I did it fast. You're using the same book as well, Tim," Chuck said, preferring that Tim do the talking.

"I even have the same essay for homework. You wouldn't believe these teachers, using the same stuff, giving the same exams. What do they think, we're dumb or something? Everybody must spit out only one answer. I tell you, it's incredible. Teaching becomes baby-sitting a flock of sheep."

"Incredible," said Lenny. "You wish you'd jumped into the big market on your own. All the greatness you."

"Tim, how is school going?" asked Chuck.

"Ah, adults and teachers, they make our lives, keep us like slaves. And they're working us overtime to keep us away from their streets. They judge and prosecute one half of the world population. That is something, eh! I don't quite get it—we should have our own system. And run it by ourselves. I can do it. I'm tired of school these days. Mafia running it now, eight hours a day. And on top of that, another five hours of homework per day. That's child labor. Overloading us with homework should keep us away from the one way street after school. Teachers are working for businesses, not for education and knowledge. I feel mentally retarded. Headaches, red eyes, after images from staring at a computer—it possesses me like an evil curse. I have to endure all that suffering because teachers are slowly replacing themselves with their own technology. Passive learning is their motto.

"If their globalized educational computers can't do it in eight hours, something is wrong with the whole teaching system. Making us self-imposed prisoners after school is another dirty trick. It just keeps us away from everything, even from ourselves. We can't speak to our parents after their hard day of work. Employers should dish out five extra hours of work for them to do at home, too. If they want to do their job well, they have to do those five hours without pay. It's more like because teachers had to work at home prior to each lesson, we must work too. I wonder how these old prunes would feel if we judged them by our system—our rules?"

Tim gave Chuck and Lenny the chance to say something, but got the message to continue. "Everything around us changes quickly. When I go to school, I just don't want to see a computer, let alone work with it. Today, I learn how to use it; tomorrow, everything is false. Here, we have pure knowledge on a golden platter—too bad that only tomorrow exists, not today! If teachers think using computers is good, then I should stay home and sleep while my little pocket computer imitates me like my mirror reflection. All I have to do is just take my little computer with me, wherever I go, and whatever I do. There's no point going to classes to educate myself. My little computer will be my brain.

"Everybody's getting sick and tired of school! Doing the same crap. The same books, same exams, same essays for homework—the same computer for everyone. Teachers want students to use the Internet-mind, so we can have our early mental retardation before becoming senile, a degrading technique for replacing the mind. It's global business communication, not education, I tell you! They want ownership of the essay. You know, Chuck. It's feedback from my advertisement. What is it again? Ah, I get it, The-Life-of-a-Dead-Cell. In China, Russia, South America, and Europe, even in Tasmania—they got the same essay for homework. We'll use people from the UN to do all these translations for us. There, they do the worst job in the whole world, Chuck. But it's the cheapest place in the world, too. You can tell why, they couldn't arrive at any international agreement yet."

"Yes, Tim. Our educational business gives the final answer to the globalization of educational standards," Lenny replied.

"Billions of web sites with nothing on them!" interrupted Martin, who was cleaning the table next to them, taking his younger friends by surprise. "It'll take you, Tim, a hundred lifetimes to find the few with something on them. Millions of software programs, excuse me Chuck, with a value less than trash, a slip of the appendix, with nothing in them. Office communication, making us high-grade garbage! It's for the quick flow of information. And for devaluing our natural language. Computers are for financial transactions, not for people's happiness. We offer life." They smiled at him, for he had changed the direction of Tim's conversation with the magic that was bestowed upon any waiter or waitress. People went to restaurants and bars because they wanted to be among mystical beings with simple answers to troublesome questions.

"Bravo, Martin—our machines make real contacts. Have real friends!" cried Tim, trying to get the first word in. "Yeah, our computer psychologists counsel and maintain the good health of our devices; philosophers control their ethical codes of conduct; lawyers draft laws to protect their legal and voting status in society. All communities institutionalize their norms, values, and beliefs as being superior to human beings. Educationalists have a new baby sitter for us—"

"Enough!" interrupted Chuck, making the whole table speechless for a moment. But the weak internal power of his voice could not stop Tim.

"You'll hurt yourself crying out so loud, Chuck. As I was saying. I guess, I should say—let me see. Yeah, doctors telling us we have to update and to remodel our computer, because our health depends on it," Tim continued, showing everybody the space between his upper choppers.

"No, Tim. It's not computers. It's our attitudes. We don't have a shortage of labor. As useless termites, we replace ourselves too quickly. To put it short for you, we're replacing ourselves, and believing in technology as having real human qualities. Making ourselves obsolete. This ain't nothing yet, wait and see. We'll have to stop eating because everything wants to be human and grow human organs. You wouldn't be surprised if Zebra face—the security guard in the mall—has a Zebra's neck, rabbit teeth, a donkey's ear, a snake's eye, and a cow's brain. You see, we're living too daringly for a big profit," Chuck calmly uttered to Tim, and he knew that Lenny would see it differently.

"Come on, Chuck! You didn't tell the whole story, yet. How about our new prayers? Our new God? Tell us how we pray to our computer not to crash on us. Please Computer, I beg You, You're the most powerful that is conceived. You can free yourself from bombs, freezes, when I start You up again. If Thou sense any evil virus, smite it dead. You're the most powerful of all. If someone tries to corrupt You, reveal its source—for You are the knower of all, the wisest of the wise. Please, all-powerful and benevolent one, restore my lost files. O' omnipresent and all-powerful one, hear my prayer before I sleep."

"Tim, what's the matter with you? Let's speak about money. Chuck speaks my language—money, profits, and more money in the bank. More money in my pocket," Lenny joyfully remarked.

"Lenny, do you know your classmates? Did you ever do something with them, like sports, going to a movie? Do you know what they smell like? No, you don't," said Martin.

"If I'm never in school, how should I?" He sensed Martin moving closer, holding his upper body weight with both hands on their table. "Listen Martin, can you sell people? No, case closed. They're worthless. But computers aren't. And money isn't, either."

"Adults and computers are alike. Both of their worlds are crumbling," Martin cried with certainty. "Teenagers and children are the first victims of adults' loneliness, greed, and egos. They're using us like their software. We're without a brain of our own, we're just their toys. Their greed and their bloody hungry path of conquering and terrorizing the feeble truth of us seem to stretch endlessly to the past. Our fairyland is overpopulated with politicians' promises and lies. And more lies to cover up past ones. They rub their unfulfilled conscience on their children's dignity, innocence, and future. We have to swallow their irresponsibility in this world. Because they see the other half of the world as immature and irrational. They always say: "Oh, I did it because of my children. Oh, for our children." Seeing young people as a means, never as an end in itself. And we have to play the role of their praised and egoistic stigma. It is time to teach them, legally, and in principle, about their myths. And we don't have to fulfill their expected label of normal development. Look around us—both worlds are going down the drain. They're not doing us a favor. They're crying out their weaknesses to us. They're asking for our help."

"The stuff about responsibility, I really don't know how it fits into everything," Chuck responded. "Parents have kids, just make them and then leave them. That isn't responsibility. Sometimes, I wonder how much money parents have to make, so that they'll show the most responsibility toward us? I know the ghost of greed is in everything, especially in responsibility."

"Chuck, let me put it this way for you. Irresponsibility and greed make ideal mating partners. But you can stretch responsibility to infinity, without being able to grasp its limits. Our common sense tells us we should be aware of our biggest responsibility, and then act on it. We may not be able to see all our responsibilities at once, but we should be sensitive to our relationship toward them. Responsibility is something relative to each person's self-awareness. Each person may recognize his own level of it. Responsibility is the master of how people should conduct their life—it's the measure of life—something immortal in life—the only certainty there is for a future. Money is secondary to responsibility. I think I answered your question."

Chuck grasped the gist of Martin's talk, so he did not reply.

"Martin, do you think there is a financial collaboration between computer companies, teachers, psychologists, and opticians?" asked Tim. "It's possible. Isn't it?"

Martin moved and took a seat near Chuck. He did not want to answer Tim, but he was put in a position to say something. "Your guess is as good as mine. My God, everybody knows it these days—globalization and partnership mean that only some businesses are allowed to make a profit while they remind us about the past—the banana and the tree. I've been here for years. I must be getting tired, or something." He passed his hands over his face and wiped it clean. "Look!" Everyone's head went up and examined the restaurant. "I'm the main channel between the cooks and our customers. Everyone's mouth is busy. What can you say to that? You know my young friends: only people think about how useless they are. And before you know it, they do something about it. Now, companies are doing it for them. The elimination of small private businesses, the extermination of competition, the exploitation of human beings—we're up against all of this."

"Martin, if you're talking about a conspiracy against the herd, making people blind, dependent, and stupid, too, I should change my career and become a computer psychologist. No, an optician," remarked Lenny.

"Let Chuck be the computer psychologist. You, Lenny, the optician. And me, the designer. Great partnership," said Tim.

"I'd be the designer. You, the optician, and then good money would roll in," replied Lenny. For the sake of money, everyone agreed with him.

Belinda came towards them and sat near Martin. "Hi guys," she said, glancing at Lenny. Lenny reached in his jacket pocket for a jewel case and passed it to Chuck.

"Let me see," she said, and grabbed the computer software disk from Chuck's hand and read the title. " 'The Transformation of Dreams from Black and White to Color.' You've got a sound card and a microphone?" She looked at Chuck for a reply.

"Who doesn't!" interrupted Tim.

"It's only ten dollars," said Lenny. Everyone, except Chuck, paid Lenny.

"Are you sure it's legal?" asked Tim.

"Of course!" answered Lenny. "We're a unit, collectively speaking. We form a solid whole as a single end user. What's more, we own one computer. That, I say, is legal. Computers are made to run software. Nobody complains about that. Martin doesn't lend his car without wheels and battery! This software is mine. I paid for it. I didn't borrow it. If I smash it up, the maker would be happy. The manufacturer has no right over it. If it does, it's like buying a sitar without strings, a car without an engine and a radio without speakers. Every apparatus has a designer function. And the function of my computer is to run software." He could have continued were it not for Belinda, who found Lenny's pause and interrupted him.

"Ask the philosopher, who turns to jurisprudence!" she said, smiling at Martin while she spoke.

"Ethics makes my belly ache!"

"Come on," cried Belinda. "It's not morality, at all. You only have one computer for your Dad, your Mom, and yourself, so each person should have a program to run the computer. Tell us about the Mafia laws you're learning about. You buy software, but you can't lend it to anyone. Laws protect businesses, not individuals."

"Nonsense!" cried Tim. "I wouldn't want someone else to make all the profit from my hard work, my expenses and all. Laws must protect against cheaters, I say." He was pleased to get his idea across first.

"It's like taking a fossil to court. And then, experts discuss its status. Sadly enough, twelve uncultivated jackasses decide its status with hard rocks," murmured Martin, taking some time to reflect on what Tim had said. "You may be right. But the courthouse will judge your act. It's a professional institution, to interpret laws. The entire institution is like a contagious sect. It works with a basis premise. And you know what that is? Ordinary people should know all the laws like the back of their hand, inside and outside! It's a treacherous technique to make crimes a profitable business for the institution. It's all a baby game, parents playing it on their innocent baby. They show a toy to their baby and then hide it away. They think the baby believes that the toy has disappeared. The same thing happens in the courtroom. A law is like a second, a tick. And our clock make—tick-tick, all the time. A second is real as a tick, too. Our court divides the tick into two halves. And it continuously takes a half and divides it. This goes next to infinity. At the end, two opposing lawyers, a judge, and twelve bandits, sit and decide if the last remaining half tick in their hand is still real. If you make bad laws, you'll need lawyers and judges to interpret laws. Our laws are like fossils, and we use them as lines of human conduct."

"Your dad is a law enforcer. Isn't he a common sense man? Yeah, I guess everything is clear like crystal for him," said Tim.

"Bravo Tim!" cried Belinda, "But you didn't say everything. Newspaper and TV rate laws, the top ten of the week, the top twenty-five of the month. How sensuous and touching, Martin's law career will jump up and down with the ratings, jerking off public sympathy, brown nosing twelve untrained mummies."

"Yes, I'd do that for money. And money, for people, is the last analysis of their life," Lenny cried.

"You!" replied Chuck, shaking his head in disgust and disbelief. "Your teacher should pay you to read a chapter, to do homework, to use the computer, and to be in detention. Proud City, paying you to go to school."

"Don't speak so loud, he'll put it on the Internet for money," Tim whispered, smiling.

"No, Tim. It'd be more interesting if all the students in the world refused to go to school. Stopped eating their parents' ideology and history. They'd have to learn to work with us, as an equal competing partner. We're their future, not their slaves," Lenny said slowly.

Sandy and Leslie were coming over. Sandy squeezed herself near Belinda and Leslie sat near Tim.

"It's for only ten bucks," cried Belinda, passing the disk to Sandy, who inspected it. Sandy and Leslie promptly slipped the money across the table to Lenny.

"We're square now," Lenny said, placing the money in his jacket pocket without looking at Chuck, who would mostly use this disk. Most cash payments went directly to Lenny's pocket because he had masterminded the idea of buying and selling the legal rights to school papers.

Cut and Dry

"Yes, I have to go now; your mother is coming over tonight," murmured Chuck in a sarcastic voice. But it had finally triggered the earthquake, a natural limit that could not be tailor fit for Sunday school.

"She thinks your mother is having an affair!" cried Lenny in a hoarse and thick voice. "She sleeps there, overnight!" The avalanche swept across the table and took everyone by surprise. Implicit beliefs wore a concrete coating that everyone could throw and kick to test their solidity. Everything in Chuck's path was scattered and dislocated.

"Heavy stuff," whispered Leslie, maintaining strong visual contact with Sandy and Belinda.

But the silence in Chuck talked louder; the shadow made by the opening of his falling jaw escaped through the wall. He nodded his head. "I go—out of here," he stammered nervously, as he attempted to glide across Martin, Belinda and Sandy's knees. Thanks to these warm knees, he could hold himself from sinking to the unknown realm his frozen face had just tasted.

"Wait Chuck. I'm going home too," said Sandy, with sympathy and pity for his unshared grief, which he believed he had kept hidden from everyone.

"See you later," she saluted, as she tried to keep up with Chuck who was pacing quickly out of the front entrance. Their leaving darkened the air around the table, causing everyone to run inside, to take a momentary refuge, and to reflect a little on family togetherness.

"I've got to run!" cried Lenny. "This'll give you a chance to speak openly. Or to chastise me freely." Though he did not expect an ovation or a medal for his action, he would not allow himself to be condemned without a persuasive argument.

"I might as well be on my way," cried Tim, following Lenny through the back door. "Belinda, do you still have the disk?" asked Martin.

"Ask Sandy! She'll give it to Chuck!" Belinda said.

"What's the matter! Don't you want to go, too?" Leslie hinted at Martin.

"You're quite perceptive, Leslie. I'll start with the tables," replied Martin. He, too, needed a moment to digest Chuck's and Lenny's behavior. Belinda allowed him to pass while Leslie shifted over to Tim's empty chair.

"What if it's true, Belinda?"

"Oh! He'll have more free time to stay out at night. He's only fifteen, now." She did not want to think about the idea of separation and divorce.

"Look who's talking!" Leslie said. "You're only a few years older than he is. So, when will the institution of marriage be abolished? Divorce is normal. And it's in, marriage is out," she tried to sing out with a hot baked potato in her throat.

"What do you want me to say?" cried Belinda bitterly, speaking a bit louder without actually disturbing any nearby tables, for she saw the threat hanging over everybody's house. "They have divorce in their minds. And in their bodies. Only paying government taxes and legal fees remain." Her voice returned to normal while she attempted to put some loose ends into perspective.

"Belinda, it's clear that a marriage costs next to nothing. But separating and getting divorced can make you beg. I think Lenny's attitude man reality is everywhere. People search for the easiest way to run away from their commitment. The state penalizes divorcees very heavily. And yet, the demand is awfully great. Now, divorce really has a high market value. And the going is good. Even if people can't afford it, they still go for it. Divorce is the deity, so let's get rid of the entire decadent institution of marriage, once and for all."

"But Leslie, lawyers play Cowboys and Indians with unhappy families, while the state sits patiently like the big brain behind everything. It must have a double role. First, it wants lawyers to have a feast until each party becomes a complete nervous wreck. And second, it wants people to divorce, so it can have more power over any single individual. A happy family is a threat to society. Because it doesn't need society. But society fights back bitterly with its one thousand faces. Still, it's really odd how some people marry and stay together. Society tells us that they become too weak to do anything else, so they remain together. Oh, yes, a marriage contract is a business agreement. Or, an economic agreement against income taxes, today. We should put divorce on the stock exchange."

"Belinda, hello! Are you still here? We've slipped to another channel. We're talking about Chuck and his family." Leslie's pupils widened as she stared at Belinda's smiling face.

"Hey, what is this? Don't give me that dirty look!" defended Belinda. "Tell me! What do you expect me to do? I can't take him home and say, Hi Mom! Hi Dad! Chuck is our brother! He'll live with us from now on. They'd understand and accept that. No, they'll tell me to stay away from him, and far away too. He's a bad influence on me."

"Belinda! You're blowing your horn for nothing."

"You think so! Don't you! It's better for him to remain my friend. No brother crap here." She now leaned on the table with both elbows and then crossed her hands, easing her body weight onto the bench.

"Maybe you're right. You can always put yourself in someone else's situation, not me. You can experience others' pain. I wish I could have some of Chuck's pain," Leslie murmured, not knowing what else to say. She turned back and followed people moving in the restaurant.

"You said it, Leslie! Being a master of prescriptions is one thing. But giving the treatment is another antisocial way of weakening the foundation of society. Chuck needs treatment, not prescription."

"Those guys are idiots. Like dogs, ready to go at it for the past six months. I still can't believe it. Lenny can be so insulting. He is full of resentment and hate. And Chuck too."

"It's not that, Leslie. Chuck shivered because he didn't want to accept Lenny's suspicions. Lenny only rams it down his throat, killing his slightest hopes and dreams. He dreamt of his whole family living together again. Lenny is only returning our society's gifts to him."

"I bet you, Belinda, he bought this disk with someone else, a fifty-fifty deal. He's a carved businessman. Don't you agree with me?"

"Honesty, fairness, ethics are cheap for him. For sure, they aren't coins in his pocket. You call him the attitude man. Oh yes, that's right. He maximizes the effect of what he does. Like what he did with Chuck. Look behind you. Virus is coming up the stairs. He is coming over." Belinda was not enthusiastic to see him, for she already had a sour taste in her mouth.

Virus, whose real name was Michael, had that nickname because his friends believed he had a computer virus: two rooms in the basement had computers that were donated to the restaurant, and he spent a lot of time there.

Responsibility Being

Virus oozed himself near Leslie.

"Hello Virus!" said the girls.

"Is she still talking a lot?" he asked Leslie, leaning his shoulder against Leslie's and smiling at Belinda.

"Chuck's parents may have a divorce," said Leslie. "A divorce could really affect him. We should do something."

"Leslie, with Virus around, you should say, 'do something constructive'," corrected Belinda.

"The right people get married, but the wrong ones have children," he said slowly, with the intention to provoke Belinda. He waited for her to open her mouth, and she did.

"You're the type who only affirms yourself and denies others," she replied immediately.

The answer took him by surprise. He waited for her to continue because he had struck the right string.

"Don't think I'm waving the Christian flag at you. I don't ask you to be compassionate. And humble, as a human with two feet and two hands should be. You fail to see and do simple things. You, Virus, are an untrustworthy and miserable serpent passing yourself off as a person," Belinda hammered in.

Leslie effortlessly pulled herself away from Virus, leaving a little social distance to show disassociation and neutrality. For they always had it out to the end.

"If you believe in God, you must also believe in the devil," Virus said clearly, without showing any visible signs of irritation or anger toward Belinda.

"The devil believes in God. And angels believe in the devil. Your whitewashed reality is outdated!" she said, straightening her body upward in a combative state of readiness.

"A black and white picture is much better than talking about soulless angels and devils," he hinted.

"Here you go again about human beings' egocentric nightmare. You think only people have beliefs, not animals. Not angels, and not devils. I'll run it through your rational skull once again. Angels believe that the devil is real. Yes, real like death. If you stub your toe, it'll bleed—that's real, for you." She braced herself for another verbal attack.

He noticed her stretching her legs defensively. "Even if there is a God, man is free from Him. We don't even inherit His bleeding sores. Man is free. Free like a phoenix."

"Belinda is right," Leslie put in. "You're suffering from computer after-images, Virus. You prefer to take the honor of being self-created. Then you must praise yourself for your own meaningless existence, and your own defects in life. Virus, you shouldn't reinvent yourself out of existence. Society is already doing it for you."

"How free am I to deny your God? I accept my own finiteness," howled Virus, pretending to be enlightened by a profound insight into human essence.

Belinda ground her teeth in dismay. "You're stubborn, not a fool. As far as I'm concerned, excuse me. I hope we're still disagreeing without making ourselves obnoxious." She tried to water down her burning flame.

Virus was preoccupied with Leslie's view of man as being too weak to manage himself in the world. For human beings came out from darkness, but they could not take the darkness out of them.

"If man is completely free, free from God, he's still in constraints," said Belinda. "I mean, he can't see beyond what his finite imagination will allow him to imagine. He can't even conceive a round square. Virus, man can't be free from his own freedom. I'll rub it glacially into you. If you were free, you'd wish to be freer until you backed yourself up onto absolute freedom. You would want to be free from freedom in itself. I'm talking about absolute freedom, now. What do you think about human nature in this light? Even to live in absolute freedom, it would be a confinement, for you, Virus. Because, you can't escape your situation of being free. It's like *King Lear*—'Our basest beggars are in the poorest thing superfluous. Allow not nature more than nature needs.'" Belinda wanted to stop the conversation from going on any further. She looked around in the restaurant, seeing most people were involved in some sort of closed discussion. She checked her watch, then surveyed some nearby tables for pizza and Coke. Nobody was eating. She glanced at Virus, who remained silent.

I hope he doesn't stay like that, thought Leslie, for she wanted to go home soon.

Virus did not like this Shakespearean idea of nature, for it described a pig pleasure. To have both absolute freedom and to be in constraints at the same time, he thought, was impossible. "A mixed pot will give you heartburn," he cried finally, with a tightly controlled smile.

"Steve just ate a pizza, a hamburger, and drank an extra large Coke," Belinda cried, with the intention of putting a different meaning on Virus' comment.

"He's friendly, always very happy, too," said Leslie. "Both of you are running away from the issue—the chicken or the egg, which comes first?" She gave Belinda a glance, hoping she would pursue the conversation to its end. But both Belinda and Virus remained silent for a while, and she could not wait until they would warm up again, for it would take a while for them to continue on their path without dangling around edges and corners.

"Belinda, you talk about Shakespeare—but it's not *Lear,* it's *Hamlet*—'to be or not to be.'

" 'To be,' for you, means to be before and in responsibility. It's like how we say man is before God. Man is a sinner, he lives in sin. And God is always right, so God judges him. Man isn't free from his responsibility or from God. At this point, we can still say man has free will—he is free to act on his highest or lowest responsibility without being bad or wrong. Christianity tells us a person is either good or evil. And there's no in-between. So, Belinda, if I get you right, you're telling us that our parents had responsibility before they conceived a child. At the time of conception, sperm and egg show their responsibility, sperm killing themselves to fertilize the egg. Virus, you get the picture. Don't you? Responsibility is something invisible which passes from one generation to the next, and so on. We shouldn't say we're not responsible for our act after we've committed it. We're always responsible for acting or not acting. 'To be,' for Belinda, is to live in responsibility, and we're free to choose any level of responsibility. I'm responsible if I kill an offensive traveler. I'm still responsible if I don't kill him. I'm responsible if I allow him to kill someone else, I'm responsible for being there. It isn't possible for me to conceptualize all the consequences of an event, and the exact level of my responsibility. Virus, it's the same thing, we're also responsible for the mess in this world, not only our parents and their great-great grandparents."

" 'Not to be' means you're dead, not undertaking any new responsibilities. The dead are not free from the consequences of their actions, just free from penalties. So, Virus, you're saying God didn't create man. We're not responsible beings. For Christians, responsibility takes us to a union with God. And each choice we make, is a responsible choice. I've chosen to be the mediator. I have to face the consequences of that choice. Depending on how sensitive a person is, she could detect several levels of responsibility. My choice to be a mediator doesn't only have consequences for me, but for others too. Some people might think I'm a good mediator, then they try to learn from my style. So when a person is guilty, everyone's also guilty. Some more than others, of course."

"Wait a minute! It's not Shakespeare, it's more like Berkeley. Well, they have to be birds of the same flock. I think this guy says something like a poet *esse ist percipi*—to be is to be perceived. You're helpless against making other things real around you. If Belinda sees cups and chairs and her thick layers, they're real for her. She does all this because she wants to make them alive for her friends to enjoy. So when she's asleep, her friends do the same for her. You see, Virus, some sort of invisible responsibility ties people and things together."

"So, Belinda is saying, a person isn't free because each choice we make has a value. Responsibility, to put it short, evokes human nature like an eternal flame. And each person is like a little spark of that flame. I feel like crying—responsibility-beings would make our life more meaningful and worthy of living. And we can't even do anything about that; responsibility is the process of life."

"Oh, yes, a responsibility-being is her definition of man. Our mythology and religions show that deities create responsibility-beings from which followers exercise their essence—free will, judgement, and thought. Another chap said *cogito ergo sum*—I think, therefore I am. This fellow is telling us that a person is sure of herself. She's a thinking person! Amen. Here again, from human beings' responsibility, thinking blossoms.

"Someone else speaks about *da-sein*—the call of being: hello, here I am. I really like this one—the hello-hello. Let me get serious. The big 'hello' sings out, I'm free and naked in the world with no past. Free from everything. Now, Virus has a point, we're free from God. But again, Belinda has a point, too. She's saying that *'the calling out: dasein'* is directed toward human history. And responsibility is primordial, from which the calling out manifests. It's responsibility, it's our screw from which we have all sorts of images of human nature. Behold my dearest friends, human beings are ingrained in responsibility. And that's it."

"It's hogwash!" Virus cried. "You're a typical mediator, Leslie. You feed from both of our views like a featherless scavenger. Then you cry out the middle position, it's only your doggy up egocentric perspective. To put it this way, we have three views, now—the middleman's view defeats us without any mercy. You even get Heidegger's *dasein* wrong. To put it sweet, man—excuse me Leslie—I say a person is free. Free from God. A person is thrown into the world, bang. He realizes himself, and his possibilities in the world. You see, man is free."

"Listen Virus, Adam ate the apple in the Garden of Eden. We're living in sin before God. God bestows Adam with responsibilities. As free as he is, Adam chose to eat the apple. Because he ate it, he disregarded one of his responsibilities, not to eat the fruit from a particular tree," said Leslie.

"Really, Leslie? You sound as if Nietzsche's doctor is Kierkegaard, and his doctor is Freud."

"So, you're saying that Nietzsche is anti-religion and died of syphilis, Kierkegaard is too religious to be a lover, and Freud straightens people up sexually. It's the same today, a politician's doctor should be a priest and his doctor an atheist. Or western society's doctor should be third world countries and their doctor should be children."

"Okay, you got the point; let's get to the real stuff: if Adam were truly free, he'd have chosen to be free from God. And I think, the guy, what's-his-face again, Sartre. He says Adam chose to be free. Free from God, because he told God he wanted to be George, not Adam, the wretched sinner. So, George didn't eat any apple. And he didn't cause the fall of man, did he? If Adam is free, there're no responsibility or original sin. Only freedom, without a Creator. As you can see, there isn't a God."

"I see you're really enjoying yourself, Virus. To you, we're mindless wimps. Aren't we? Tell me, I don't think you're listening too well this evening. How the hell did we get into this stuff, anyway? Virus, you're free, aren't you?" asked Belinda.

"I guess so," he hesitantly replied, not wanting to second-guess her move.

"Can you choose to be free from your own freedom? I'm not talking about physical confinement, Virus."

"I guess, I can, if I want to. Are you taking me for a psychological test?"

"Suppose you've chosen to be free from freedom. You think that you'll be in bondage. Don't you? Because the opposite of freedom is constraint. But this is wrong. Being free from freedom is something different. It doesn't mean confinement and having more freedom. If you have absolute freedom, you want to be free from it. This means, Virus, you want to be in absurdity. Freedom is like emptiness. And it doesn't hold anything together. I agree that freedom is a part of human nature, but it doesn't hold all our other attributes together. Like Steve's pizza dough, it holds the cheese, tomato, and pepperoni… together. But the tomato is like freedom. The tomato seeds are some choices we could make in a situation. Responsibility is the dough, it's being. Not a quality of being, being in itself. When you look in the mirror, what do you see? You see only your own qualities, attributes, characteristics, and some physical parts. You can never see the whole you. You lose sight of the you. Just like this, responsibility is the essence of living. It holds everything together. From it comes alternatives. Because each choice has an object, Virus quickly loses sight of his responsibility. And Leslie said it to you: making a choice takes with it a degree of responsibility. You know, Virus, it's a question of whether or not you're acting on the highest responsibility. And yet, our everyday responsibility and choice are a manifestation of the big R in responsibility. The problem is, we don't have enough time to attend to ourselves, only to important daily matters. If we do, responsibility, not personality, will hold you tightly in your one hand. You could turn it around, upside down. And feel it with the other hand. Then, Virus could find his destiny. Rational being without responsibility is a machine. And we've enough of them. What we call choices, it's about selecting a choice-related responsibility, and then acting on it. For choices are another way of acting on different levels of responsibility."

"You're really a tough bug, tonight," cried Virus. "With responsibility, everyone's values could be considered equally important without identifying people with religious beliefs."

"Without your persistence, I wouldn't know these thoughts were mine," she replied.

"Tell Chuck I'm coming over tomorrow to pick up some disks," he told Leslie.

Economics

Petro, one of the cooks, rushed out from the kitchen.

"You'll injure yourself, running like that!" cried Virus. "There's no need to work up a sweat, just because you want to keep Steve happy."

"Did he tell you?" asked Petro, standing near their table.

"What's this? Who tells what?" questioned Leslie.

"Charles! He didn't speak to you all, yet? Not a word to you?"

"No, he didn't," answered Leslie. Petro only ever walked through here when he had to go to the washroom.

"He told me everything, it's horrible! You wouldn't believe it!"

"Will you quit the suspense and just tell us?" Belinda asked.

"Yes, I'm telling you! Can't you see? See for yourself! He made an arrangement this afternoon, he's booting us out the door, just like that! Oh, yes, we have to go to another restaurant. Everybody, the cooks too, must leave here. Yes, we must leave here, I can't believe this. I have a family! How can he do this to us? After five years of working here, he said all of us are going to work in a new restaurant, somewhere in lower town. I don't want to go there. Even Charles is going to this new restaurant for five years. People from the other restaurant will be working here. The boss from the other restaurant will run our joint. Charles said the other joint is much bigger than this one. They have more people than us. Some of their extra people will go to another restaurant in town..." He was shaking.

"Petro, you're enlightening them on how Charles pulled the carpet out from under your feet?" asked Martin from several tables away. Petro had told him the same story over and over again in the kitchen, so Martin was trying to stay away from him. "Come on, Petro, it's not that bad!"

"You don't have anybody to think about. Your Dad supports you," replied Petro.

"Martin, come here! We want the latest," Leslie politely requested. He sat near Belinda, making Petro uncomfortable. After all, Petro had unloaded the shock from the weight.

"I'll go clear up the fort. See you later," said Petro, going back to the kitchen.

"So there are several restaurants rotating every single employee," said Belinda in a soft voice. "The worst part is that you didn't tell us this earlier. Maybe you were going to tell us, but it slipped your mind. How romantic!"

"Listen, Petro did a good job. I feel like a tape recorder, now. For the past half-hour, Steve and I were talking about Charles' contribution to society. Whenever he speaks, he bloats himself with so much food. It's unbelievable."

"Okay, Martin. Are you going to keep us up all night? Let us in on some details," she replied quickly. "We believe we know why! But why?" She contradicted herself deliberately, so that she could hear Charles' explanation.

"Charles said that the public has an immeasurable impact on how both private and public organizations run their businesses. The brotherhood between private and public is our ghoulish reality today." He made himself more comfortable as though it would be a long talk.

"Businesses are becoming more sensitive and aware of customer satisfaction, public needs, profits. And they want to own customers. This news makes you all feel much better, I guess. Well, it shouldn't. Firms are becoming more vicious, carnivorous, inhumane—in everything.

"As a matter of fact, the brotherhood is about stealing dollars from the cradle. One brother, the public one, says the cradle owes one dollar in taxes. So, it allows the other brother to silently creep up into our entire educational system and stamp its logo as a repayment of the money. The trend of the brotherhood is to be the first in the market, with less research on the negative consequences of new technology on health and our environment. We're reduced to buying power, not people. Success is guaranteed, because one big brother breeds people to satisfy the other brother. Genetic engineering and its practices in our food products show us the working of the brotherhood. Genetically engineered soy beans, tomatoes, cattle... aren't necessary. We're not dying without mutated soy beans. Having genetic knowledge is very important for humanity, but practicing it, now, tells us about a mutual business interest between government and business, and the rich and the poor, too. It's the brotherhood's business decision without any responsibility to the cradle—the tomorrow. I shouldn't say all this. You already know it," he finished, seeing that everyone was listening attentively without smiling.

"Martin, brotherhood is our reality, not virtual reality," murmured Leslie. "This kills the single hope the public has. People faithfully believe in public institutions, their protector against cutthroats. Yes, Charles doesn't serve any food products with synthetic materials. The green stickers on both doors say non-genetically engineered products! So, the brotherhood deceives, lies, makes empty promises, gives us reality under the table; it teaches us life isn't a process but something ready-made which must be eaten out, now."

"Yes, Leslie, Charles is very sharp. He sees the brotherhood as being out for a fast profit. We were talking in the kitchen about how the public brotherhood doesn't exist for us. Public institutions are like our virtual reality, making us always be on salary to pay taxes. And they're not interested in our reality or protecting a worthy life. Everybody, directly and indirectly, is involved in this mess, chasing after a lousy dollar because of the tax-book. What can anybody do against this filthy trick?" He waited for an answer, but none were coming, so he continued. "The word *public* doesn't refer to anything innocent. Now, it seems nobody can do anything sensible about our dream world—our virtual skin layers. Charles sees himself as contributing to this decadency. He wants to step out by destroying the virtual reality of public and private institutions. At least, we should expose its treacherous techniques. Petro already told you how to."

"Leslie wants to say something," said Belinda.

"No, I don't. But I didn't get the whole picture, yet. I'm not sure if Charles is saying the brotherhood is a double standard. The government wants taxes from everybody, so it allows businesses to mold the cradle, it uses businesses to manipulate people for money. And then it tells people it'll cost them a few dollars for protection against the other brother. You're sitting on ice, Virus?"

Virus was listening, but he wanted to stay out of it, for now.

"Leave him alone, Leslie," murmured Martin. "This is just the tip of the iceberg. Charles believes that true ethics and responsibilities start with a renewal approach to all public and private companies and organizations in the world. It's the only way to kill the big brotherhood. A complete switch of all employees after five years. Owners, presidents, vice-presidents, executives, managers, stakeholders, factory workers; all of them must find new employment in some other organization. With planning, of course, to avoid chaos. If you want life to grow, you must plant it. It's the only way to give people the means to survive for the future. Everything is about living, not who has what anymore, because all of us already have environmental waste, pollution, electro-smog, and natural uncertainty."

"How interesting. What is his strategy?" asked Virus.

"Diversity and flexibility for everyone, without stress and pollution. And no cheap personal integrity. Virus, you think Charles is an idealist? Not at all! He doesn't make an empty proposal. Petro isn't lying. Charles meant everything. It's not impossible. Steve told Charles that this process started with our primitive ancestors' unconscious desire to protect their lives. And to subconsciously plan for the future. Then he told Charles he was just making it explicit as a science of continuation for a longer period. Steve always has food in his mouth. I don't know when he's serious, or just sarcastically teasing everybody."

"It's not Steve's food, it's his facial expressions when speaking. You don't know where he's coming from," cried Leslie.

"Hmm, Charles's principle works this way. In most countries, a new government and government representatives are elected into office for four or five years. A country still runs smoothly during this switching process. This is the highest office in a country. And it undergoes the switching of personnel without chaos. Most of these employees don't have any formal training for their new position. Now, take each government office, social security, social welfare, the tax office, the board of education, and so on. All employees, from the top to the bottom, should switch their jobs, like the actual new government for every five years. But they don't do this. These workers build walls to protect themselves and their self-interests, like Mafia bosses. For this reason, we have inefficiency and unemployment. And ineffective people devote all their energy to protect themselves with a hopscotch system, then living in it too. We have to start going to the root, rather than fixing the branches.

"Displacing people can be very dangerous to a family. And Charles intends to protect family first," remarked Virus.

"People aren't forced to change cities and countries, my good friend," Martin replied. "The benefits outnumber the costs—more jobs, less back stabbing. And, not least, more trust. Everyone would develop fairness-awareness, and then use it, effectively. Responsibility would be the golden reward, not money."

"Not the attitude-man reality," Belinda added with delight.

"It's fantastic!" said Leslie. "People would regain their confidence, their joyful smile. They'd see their own power, the power to overcome anything. When I think about how society always makes us feel so little and insignificant, I scream to the gods. All in one, one in all—we'd sing out—a better place to live."

"Who said that?" Steve echoed in the empty restaurant with his mouth half full. Each word rang and vibrated in everyone's ears. He was seventeen years old, and from middlebrow. "All of human history was nothing but a bitter struggle. A struggle for renewal. Wars, to change society, to breathe new life into it, to wash away the old and dreary stagnation. Charles foresees a good war without leaving anybody behind to enjoy its fruit. Just like all historical changes, he proposes a new commercial order."

"Steve, we went through this already," cried Martin. "Can't you be more constructive? What is it with you? The pleasure of your food pushes out your outlook on life."

"Martin, you said you'd drive me home. I'm still waiting for you. Besides your table, I'm the only one left in here. Now, you're saying my night snack is squeezing my brain. No, Martin. Everybody has an ideal model of what the world should be like. I say, a perfect world is Pythagoras' spherical world. And everybody in it is already a little designer in his own special way. The Spaniard, like Columbus, sees the world as round, and open for discovery. The Russian sees the world as a multi-sphere, with various economic and political groups. In contrast, the American sees it in terms of globalization and capitalism. None of them will give up their idea of the world. You see my point? I guess not. Charles has a lot of homework to do. Most people who influence Charles's world—the wealthy stockholders, the company owners—aren't officially employed. They're over sixty-five years old, the golden age."

"Steve, there's no problem here," replied Martin. "Charles's system says each person works for forty years or so. And then retirement follows. After so many years of service, a person lives on his pension and savings. His investment goes to his heirs, and new ideas are discussed and then practiced. As you can see, we're not looking for perfection in nature, as it isn't too far away. Case closed."

"Not so fast! Charles's world still says beggars and the homeless would switch from my street to Belinda's. Or, is it to your street? Lower town people will live in your neighborhood, Martin. Murderers and criminals will just switch street corners or careers. How charming would that be? If anybody is going to propose a new system, he must identify the problems of the old system. I figure Charles's world takes unemployment and politicians' vacant promises as problems. Politicians don't make empty promises. They create millions and millions of jobs for people, even billions of them. They honestly do. The thing is that nobody is qualified enough to do these jobs."

"You just repeat the problem, Steve. Charles's world—remember, it's your phrase, not mine—protects human welfare, before the cradle falls off the tree. It'll save unfortunate people without work or happiness, who are breeding at a countless rate, now. Mind you, Steve, not everyone could be saved, in any possible world. Because some people are motivated differently. Some will take advantage of any social system, legally or illegally. Besides, living things don't live in perfection, only strive for it."

"For me, Virus's world is much more interesting than Charles's funnel world, with no fun. Virus's secret weapon will reshape our comical world, I say. He really inherits man's fighting spirit. Virus, you didn't tell them, did you? All about your secret career, or your future adventures."

"What adventures, Virus?" asked Martin.

"Before you start again, we have to go home. School tomorrow, right, Leslie?" said Belinda. "We can still make the last bus, if we hurry, Leslie!"

"Here, Steve, since you want to go home, drive Belinda and Leslie home," said Virus, giving Steve his car keys. "You can keep it overnight. I'll go home with Martin."

"You see, he's helping me again. I'm helping him for him to help me. Let's go, before he changes his mind," said Steve. Belinda and Leslie said goodbye to Martin and Virus and followed Steve to the back door.

"You better take it easy in lower section!" warned Martin.

Belinda lived about a block away from Lenny. Steve knew that he had to drive Belinda to lower town first, and then Leslie to middlebrow. Going to lower town at night was a high risk; police could stop any young person driving, especially in a sports car. After six, the streets became a meat market, specializing in fowl, snake bites, baked potatoes, and prowling sharks. Belinda, Leslie, and Steve entered the brightly lit parking lot; they had to jump over parking barriers before reaching the car. Steve had to make an entire circle around Fairview before he could get to the road going to town.

6: Circle Getting Circular

Martin and Virus were the only people remaining in the restaurant, and Virus helped to arrange the dining area while Martin cleaned the floor. Martin did not want to start the conversation concerning Virus' special program. They worked for fifteen minutes without saying very much to each other.

Finally, they served themselves something to drink. "Most every evening you're downstairs. I guess, working on your essential computer program?" said Martin, forgetting that he wasn't going to speak first. "I really don't blame you—we've got a lot of garbage selling. If I may ask, what's your program supposed to do?" He threw a friendly smile in the air, reminding Virus that whatever he said would be taken seriously and in confidence.

"Everything started a long time ago, a year or so. Steve's father works at our research center in town. Sometimes, after school and weekends, I go there and help them out with computer data. But my father doesn't know that. If he did, it'd be terrible for Steve's father. One of their research projects aims at reducing physical matter, like a cube of sugar, to molecules. But we're talking about very small grains. Luckily for me, too, they only do their experiment on Saturdays, when there's no one around, other than me, of course. They were testing salt, and they found that they couldn't reduce it to molecules. But what remained in the chamber, were obviously atomic particles, negative and positive charges, having various short energy life spans. At the same time, they tried to detect antimatter in this process. In the combustion chamber, these guys believed a reduction from one state—particles—to something else—molecules—involves a detection of antimatter. To put it short, they didn't find any molecules in the chamber, or antimatter registration. You're aware of the facts, their sophisticated computer records behavior in the chamber. These sensors detect only electrical charges, directions of particles without speed, or velocity without direction. I used to play around with their acquired scientific data on magnetic bands. Until one Saturday, when they cancelled one of their experiments, I went there anyway. I used the microscope and got a small grain of cocaine, then I took everything to the chamber. Instead of using three sensors, I used all the sensor sheets, eight or nine of them, that I could find. And then I lined the entire inside of the tank with layers of sensors. The chamber is an accelerator tank, mind you. I had the computer to register all impulses on a thin magnetic tape. Bang! The fusion and separation between molecules and particles jumped out. Yes, Martin, antimatter, too. I thought then, and I still think now, that antimatter holds everything in the universe together.

"Yes, Martin, it's really a bang. All the sensors went crazy. And about half an hour after the impact, the computer was still registering activities from the tank's sensors. I took the tape and checked it; all the impressions on it were homogeneous and symmetrical. I put it in the interpreter for further analysis. It was amazing. I didn't have only antimatter registration activity, but real cocaine. I repeated this, over and over again, until I had a whole handful of cocaine, because a reverse transformation occurred, from antimatter to matter. At the lab, I hid these magnetic codes, like negative electronic codes, in computer bits. Then, I took it home on a disk, for me. Here, I've been perfecting the dosage with a self-destruct command for computer users. With a fast modem, a kilo of cocaine takes about twenty minutes to download."

"How did Steve know about it?"

"His father knew I was there. He found cocaine traces all over the place. I destroyed all the sensors, too. He didn't say anything to anybody at work. But he thought I took some cocaine for myself. Because of this, Steve talks about my world. Now, I'm only allowed to go to the lab with his Dad."

"But Virus, you're not telling me everything. You let me in, yes, into the most irrelevant part of what actually happened at the lab. I know, for sure, your accidental discovery of syntactic cocaine that can be transmitted by electronic codes is utterly meaningless to you. You're telling me about other uses of computer technology. A couple months ago, you left the computer running. The printer was spitting, non-stop, articles about quantum physics and antimatter. What for?"

"Many things happened there. But I don't know how to explain them. And worse, I couldn't find much help in those articles. The problem is, I don't know where to start."

"Let's start with the most obvious, then work our way to things which neither me nor you could understand."

"You're right. I have to get it out. It's the only way for me to see a pattern. I have to unload it."

"Wait, we'll get ourselves a drink," requested Martin. He led the way to the kitchen and they served themselves Coke. They returned to their table.

"I just can't believe it. We spend most of our life talking about things that we believe we know very well. Do we really know these things? The question is, what does it mean to me? If I know it well or not, it's a hint of something else. It's All-In-One without being able to see the whole."

"Come on, Virus, you're beating yourself like a dead drum. Let's get on with it."

Concentric light

"Well then, here are the pieces. My experiment showed a disturbance like an atomic explosion in the tank. All the sensors' tips, which were exposed in the tank, were obviously damaged. I said this before, didn't I? Well, the internal surface of the chamber was gone, too. You can't see this with your naked eyes. You need a powerful microscope. What I really observed, from the magnetic tape and from inside the tank, was astonishing. Electromagnetic radiation doesn't travel by waves or particles. It travels in concentric circles. Like an ice cream cone or funnel. The smallest part of the cone is often the size of the actual source, the object from which the light comes. And the concentric circles get bigger as they reach an observer. If you look within this concentric cone or funnel from the bigger end, with only one eye, you can detect the size of the source." He looked around the half-dark restaurant for some paper to show his ideas more clearly, for a diagram of a concentric light cone would be sufficient.

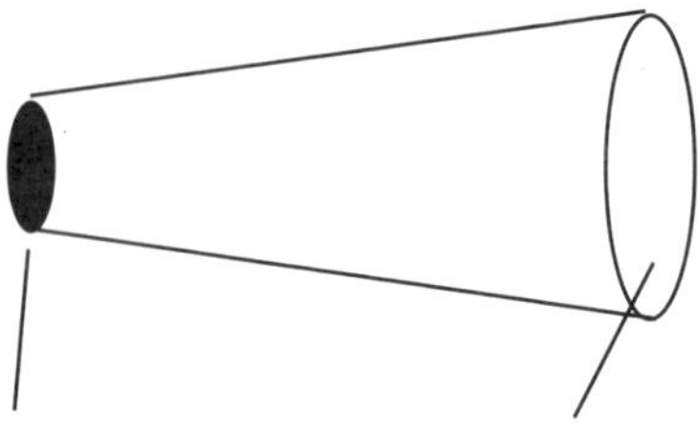

Light Source/ Small end of cone   Larger end of the cone/funnel

"Are you saying if I look at the sun from earth with one eye, when it's horizontal, I can see it's actual size? So, I'm inside these cones, looking at the sun. Virus, are you saying light travels concentrically? It makes a lot of sense, especially in cosmology. Experts can tell when a star died. We know it after its death, billions of years later. So, you're saying that because light travels concentrically, the cone, the small end only, represents the size of the light source. A star's light-image travels with the entire cone. Yahoo, we see a dead supernova or star, because the small end of a cone represents the size and shape of a star."

"Mind you, Martin, I didn't say you should look at any harsh light source, like the sun. You could really damage your eyes. There's no need to blind yourself to test my theory. Our moon will do. What I'm saying can't be simplified as you've done so nicely. Look at the back door. You see it. There's a metal spring to keep it closed after someone opens it. We don't want to travel at the speed of light, but faster. Now that the door is closed, a bug is walking within the spring to reach the door. The space between both ends, the doorframe on the wall and the actual door, is very short because the door is closed. In no time, the bug will reach the door. If the bug is on the last spring curl to the door, and if it holds itself there, very tightly, then we would see how space shrinks—space is like a spring. Light moving in concentric circles suggests that space shrinks compared to our straight measurement of space. Mind you, Martin, our bug is travelling at one hundred and eighty-six thousand miles per second—the speed of light. As it is moving at this speed, the starting point, the frame of the door where one end of the spring is screwed on, becomes an insignificant reference point—it disappears. Like this, the entire spring remains tension free, even when the door is opened, for space changes and velocity can be determined without direction.

"Relativity theory takes space and time like an open door with a straightened-out spring, with maximum tension. If we fully open the back door, Martin, the spring will be completely straightened. And the bug must walk the entire straight metal if it wants to go back to the doorframe. Our geometry of space-time is still rigid, because distance is calculated in terms of starting point and ending point, remaining fixed. This geometry tells us that the space between the earth and a star is like our open door, with a completely stretched out spring. I'm saying space is like a relaxed spring with no tension, like the closed door in the restaurant. And distance is a function within the curly spring—big or little curls. As the bug continuously moves to another position, space becomes curly, it shrinks, leaving velocity. Or, we could compress the spring without ever travelling within it. This is about bending space."

"If I heard you right, you repeated my theory. What are you getting at?"

"Martin, I didn't call the impressions of a dead star which light reflects a representation. It's antimatter causing the bouncing of other particles, making space à tension-free spring. At a long distance, from here to some distant stars, we have an inverse of a cone or funnel motion. The small end of the cone—cone-like concentric circles of light-like particles—transverses inwardly of the cone, until it becomes the head of the cone coming to earth. Let me try again for you. When we say we see a dead star exploded, we see the source first. And then, the big end of the light cone follows behind. We're saying that we see the star's image first due to some other light sources in our galaxy, because antimatter causes a network of other particles to manifest its interaction. And then the surrounding concentric reflected light from the explosion follows."

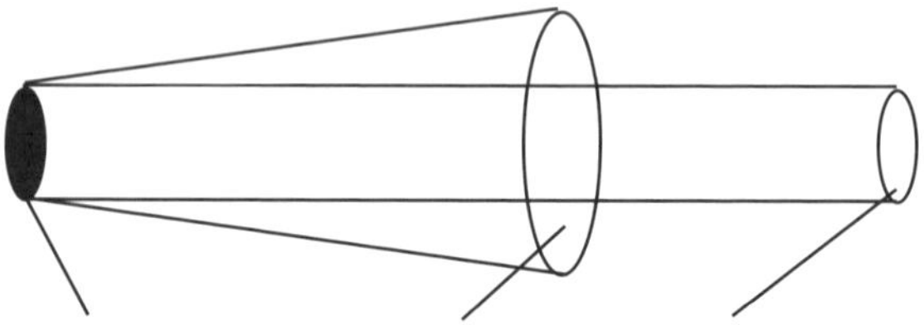

"Okay, I'll not burst my skull for this. Let's get to the point, Virus. If I understand you correctly, you're saying light speed is not constant in all systems. Now, you're taking Einstein head on. It's incomprehensible. There's a little contradiction here. An exploded dead star causes light to move circularly—the first event. Then you're telling me that the end of the small cone, where the source is, quickly passes through all the concentric circles of the cone. And then it somehow pops up the image of the dead star, while the larger concentric circles of light trail along slowly. This means light doesn't travel at a constant speed. Or, antimatter or certain spinning particles are the fastest moving bodies in the universe. And they somehow attract other particles with them in motion. And because of other light sources in a galaxy, the attracted particle-events are observable as light-events. So, whatever passes through the cone's little end is antimatter-like."

"Not, precisely. Antimatter is like a blank liquid-particle state. It could be molecule-like or particle-like at the subatomic level, and before fusing or splitting molecules to particles and vise-versa, it causes other particles to leave magnetic traces of its nature. And a series of events is noticeable. Antimatter is detectable, but it can also pass through any solid object to bypass detection. It's smaller than any known subatomic particle. Antimatter is like our senses that can't sense themselves. You can't experience antimatter. You can't hear hearing. See, seeing. Taste, tasting. Antimatter is real just like our senses. But, antimatter attracts matter with it. Our huge gamma ray telescope detects what's within its intended capacities—certain strange and unexplained phenomena in space."

"Virus, excuse me. You say light travels at different speeds. But, can you prove it?"

"Martin, relativity theories and quantum mechanics use a straight ruler. Our ruler tells us what to look for. An astronomer calculates a detectable concentric cone image on his telescope as belonging to remote places and events in the universe. And his ruler says how things should behave. This is very practical for our senses to confirm. We're talking about a dimension beyond our ordinary sense experience, beyond what our observational devices could measure. Senses tell us that we should be able to determine the direction and velocity of a moving particle simultaneously. What we find is, one always cancels out the existence of the other because one becomes antimatter-like without detection, while the other is determinable. So, the first dimension of a particle is matter—the detectable. And its second dimension is antimatter—the undetectable. The speed of antimatter is much faster than light—it makes space irrelevant. As a matter of fact, it could be a carrier of bodies through space. Antimatter can't be stopped by anything solid. It goes through things and then deposits detectable traces of bodies. Space and antimatter hide the mysteries of the universe! From space, we should fashion our ruler. You remember the spring we just talked about, with the annihilation of time. It's like a ruler of space. And it admits the existence of antimatter. I'm not talking about Euclidean or our known theories of Non-Euclidean geometry of four dimensional space-time."

"Really, Virus. I'm now completely bemused about antimatter. I think it means something opposite matter. But space is like a curled up snake, that's something!"

"Okay, let us put it another way, then. How long does it take you to conceptualize any star in the galaxy?"

"Immediately, I have it in my consciousness. I can imagine myself touching it. Walking on it. Dancing on it. So what's your point, Virus?"

"Consciousness is a form of antimatter that abolishes space. At this instant, a form of antimatter exists in us. And it's receptive to other forms of antimatter in the universe."

"This may be true; and yet, drugs could alter our awareness. I overheard you all talking. We don't have to be religious to have a conscience and to feel guilt. Even the wickedest person isn't bad toward certain people. It's like responsibility exists in all living things. Perhaps, responsibility is like antimatter, running through all organisms."

"That's why I didn't pursue my argument. Okay! Antimatter has matter as its source, like our head, for example. Consciousness can bend the distance between the earth and a star. I don't mean bend the distance, literally. What I really mean is, it can abolish any distance among objects, by just being receptive to antimatter. With the relativity ruler, a little arc or a straight line can be drawn between the earth and a star, taking distance as a constant value between two points. If you shoot a light beam to a star, it'll take light years to get there. I don't want to get into particle identification—photon, electron, graviton, neutrino, muon, pions, neutron, quarks, anti-quarks, Bohr's atom, Planck's constant, anti-particles such as positrons and other subatomic ones… We're calling everything atoms, like billiard balls. This stuff is good for our daily life. Now, Martin, take the earth as one end of a stick, and a star is at the other end. The distance will always remain the same, because our ruler says that distances are fixed. But, when light travels concentrically at various speeds, and when antimatter carries matter with it, space disappears. That is, it's like bending the stick—both ends are about to touch. Space is like that between the earth and a star. This goes back to the measuring of direction and velocity simultaneously. We have our coordinate system for a projected direction, we're going to a star. Now, velocity becomes antimatter.

"I gather that you're saying if a star is born yesterday, we can see it today, or five hours after its birth. If this weren't true, we'd see an empty galaxy—with only our solar system. And without various light sources in the universe, other galaxies couldn't be noticeable."

"Yes, Martin. With antimatter, there's no space, no solidity. You can't create a universe with only antimatter. But, the secret of travelling to the stars, or to distant places, or through solid matter, lies in antimatter and in concentric space, too. But the danger of exploiting antiparticles is immeasurable. The earth would be too small to accommodate its negative consequences because mass doesn't equal energy, and light isn't a constant. At the semiconductor tank, antimatter was the first event, then came vibrating particles, which damaged the inside of the tank. It's like a contradiction for our limited senses. Antimatter passed through the tank; and yet, it trapped matter on the magnetic tape while it went through the tape. I don't know how to explain this. It's like playing Ping-Pong with an electron until it splits, and the positron disappears from our senses, but not from reality. Antimatter exists along with other forms of mass. We don't know very much about this, yet."

"How can you say that light does not travel at a constant speed?"

"Martin, we can say that a photon has a constant speed. But light is a network of different particles in which photon is identified. Particles spin like egg beaters. And move concentrically as they ignite other particles, causing us to be sensitive to certain spectra. What we really detect in the world is nothing more than the interaction of particles. And their life spans. Well, our science says photon does not spin. This is nonsense. If a thing doesn't spin or rotate at high speed, then something else moves it. I'll come back to this, later. Light travels concentrically at different velocities."

"And so what would people say? What does it all mean? If you don't have anything to hold your view together, you're re-explaining smoke for us, Virus. It's like Charles has a small world. Belinda has her own little one. Lenny his. I could go on forever. You get my point. Don't you?"

"Wait a minute! I'll get some printouts. It'll just take a second." Virus rushed downstairs to the computer room. Meanwhile, Martin went to the kitchen for something to drink and eat. He brought out two glasses of pop and some donuts that he should have thrown away. He had already started to eat when Virus came back with several loose pages. He organized the pages in his hand, one exactly overlapping another, and placed them directly in front of him. He grabbed his drink and took a donut. "You never heard about the circular theory of the universe." He briefly waited for a reply. "It's like All-In-One. I'll show you."

"Make it simple for me. You know, we're getting a bit tired. Well, it's only a theory, thank God. It sounds like everything will repeat itself." He smiled at Virus.

"Will you wipe the grime off your face, Martin? It's killing my concentration."

"Circular, it makes my belly turn. And my head swing. Okay, Virus, I'll give you a chance. I think I'll skip my classes, tomorrow—they're the only thing that's still square."

"I have two claims. First, no natural body in the universe has any sharp edges. Second, no organism has an edge.

Circularity in the Universe

"You've seen pictures of a Milky Way, it's really fantastic, streams of cloud forming a circular shape; it doesn't have a geometrical form like a square, rectangle or triangle. Yes, a Milky Way is edgeless, for other Milky Ways to rub off each other harmoniously, with qualification. A Milky Way tries to expand, but other neighboring ones would prevent it. There're a lot of pressures and forces at work among Milky Ways. And yet, each of them is edgeless. You couldn't ride a bike with square wheels; a Milky Way couldn't have any other shape than circular. The transition of forces among these Milky Ways occurs smoothly, with circular bodies.

Though a Milky Way is breathtaking, it's mostly made of gases and ice, stray objects, bits and pieces. It's like the garbage dump of a galaxy.

Each galaxy is circular. A star, a supernova, neutron star, planet, moon, are all also relatively round. As internal forces from within keep a galaxy mostly circular, they contribute to the roundness of objects by making forces free flowing among bodies. All objects in a galaxy rotate, some moving circularly around other objects like our solar system. If a star doesn't rotate or spin, then other rotating bodies keep it in a relatively fixed orbit. A Milky Way connects galaxies. And it changes its form depending on internal and external pressures from within and from other galaxies. There are mostly round objects, spinning and rotating in the universe, making it work."

"Wait a minute—is a Black Hole also round? Nobody knows what it looks like, Virus."

"Yes, Black Holes. It's nothing mysterious, as we think it is. Any dead star, for example, can become a Black Hole. That's what you don't want to hear, I think. You want to know its function in a galaxy. Whenever there're disturbances in a galaxy, you may find that certain objects have edges; internal conditions of a star have drastically changed and affected the external harmony. And when other nearby bodies can't quickly compensate for such irregularities, like filling in the empty gap, there're more disturbances, causing a dead star to explode inwardly. It may even become a Black Hole, a cleaning up organism, swallowing up unnatural objects and disturbers of the harmony. Bodies with non-circular shapes interfere with a galaxy's harmony. A Black Hole doesn't move in space, disturbers of the harmony are thrown into its path."

"Virus, a Black Hole is a killer object. It's the destroyer of any galaxy."

"Our astronomy is primitive, too. A Black Hole is like an evil mother. It's the collector of stray objects. And yet, it threatens other healthy bodies. As a mother, it has a tremendous internal force, to crush and to compress bodies, to fuse particles and molecules together, and to split particles, as well. A Black Hole can't grow forever. Oh no, it can't. Because of surplus internal pressures, it softly explodes, sending bodies into space. These flying bodies are round, they're well compressed from all directions in a Black Hole. Our solar system appears to have been thrown out from an exploded Black Hole. Whatever comes out from a Black Hole is much smaller in size. As these bodies travel in space, they expand in size and find a place in the same galaxy. Compressed bodies, coming out from a Black Hole, expand, separating particles from molecules, and what not."

"Look at our solar system, the earth came out from a Black Hole. Its interior, with blazing particle-gases, is protected by continental plates. The exterior shows all the marks of cooling down and expansion. You wouldn't want to grow corn on the continental plates, would you? They protect the earth from being both a baked desert and an iceberg. The sun still retains its original form. It must have been the center of a Black Hole. The exterior conditions of the Moon or other planets tell us about their interior. Extreme conditions, cold and heat, tell us about the life expectancy of these bodies. They're just waiting to collapse inwardly. They're dead objects relative to the earth. They aren't meaningless objects; they help to hold the harmony in our solar system and galaxy. In our solar system, the interior of planets and the moon, a blazing furnace, regulates their external conditions."

We can tell whether the moon or a planet is older than earth—mostly in terms of living organisms. Mind you, everything depends on its interior. The interior chiefly modifies the exterior. The sun is covered both inside and outside with an uncountable number of compressed gas mines. Saturn was once like our sun. But it's finished now, leaving its garbage dump behind. The rings—they were formed from the process of cleaning its atmosphere. So, Saturn has a baby Milky Way around it. This'll be the fate of our sun, too."

"You did quite a jumping around, Virus. Tell me, do you think there is life out there?"

"Man would be the last to know how important life is on earth. We cherish death. Yes, we cherish the dead more than the living.

Charles isn't a bad fellow. He wants us to see life before other things."

"No, Virus! I'm not talking about here. Out there! In our solar system!"

"We went to the moon. We're probing other planets for life. We howl among stars like hungry wolves searching for mating partners. Nothing. Nothing, so far. You have to look in valleys where the conditions may be moderate. The North Pole and the Sahara Desert wouldn't give you accurate impressions of life on earth. Would they? So, my friend, it all depends on what you're looking for. And where you're looking. If we want to know more about the moon or Mars, we should send paleontologists. Let's face it, just the ordinary people are interested in life out there. Others believe in the treasure chest out there, yes, the chest."

"Well, Virus, I'll just run through your mess to make sure I get your point."

"Not everything, Martin. This'll give me a chance to cool off a bit."

"You're saying Milky Ways are macroscopic objects like gigantic balloons in a tight tank. And each galaxy has millions of little balloons, protected by its Milky Way. When one balloon loses some air in a galaxy, other balloons fight for that space. In other words, you're saying that Milky Ways often change their form without moving. And they're more dangerous than Black Holes because of burning gases, and streams of ice, and rocks. Asteroids and comets also shoot off. You're also saying the size of a Milky Way depends on internal and external pressures. Right!

"Concerning the shape of objects, internal and external forces tailor them in a circular manner to have harmony in a galaxy. I'm not too sure if I get you right, about Black Holes. Are you saying that a Black Hole is like a balloon, too? A huge body collapsed inwardly, like turning a little balloon inside out? Then the gases and particles from inside the balloon become the outside layers of a Black Hole. Since the outside is like sticky gases, they can catch light or anything. As the Black Hole gets bigger, internal bodies escape because the outer coating loses its effectiveness."

"You're not doing too badly, Martin. Why don't you just get to the point?"

"The point is, you've a funny way of explaining how our solar system comes about. A Black Hole exploded, bang! We've got the moon, planets, and the sun. When you make a bang, you should have millions of planets. Not only some. I guess, you'll say that we should conceptualize a Black Hole as a pump tube with a small mouth. It sucks and swallows objects by changing its form. So, when it's all filled up, its internal force becomes extremely strong. It's like using a bicycle pump to slowly suck the air out from the tube until its exterior disappears. Yahoo, only the internal remains in a perfect order without a bang."

"You're not doing too badly again, Martin. The exterior has no impact on the order of things."

"I still don't get your drift when you say nature operates in a circular manner, too. I really don't see anything circular about nature."

Circularity in Nature

"All living organisms struggle toward an edgeless shape. What I mean is that everything in nature has a circular shape. Plants, cells, tree trunks, bones… You've never seen a square tree. Hands, fingers, molecules, bacteria – all of them are round. Our physicist's ideal object, a billiard ball, is found in nature, too."

"You know, Virus, when I really look at myself, every part of my body has a circular shape. Even my mouth is round. Come to think about it, roots are also round. From what I gather so far, you're endorsing Darwin's theory of evolution, the circular nature of all living organisms. Ah, Virus, even though each species is different, it's molded by having circular properties. But what about leaves? Leaves aren't circular."

"I see your point. I've been struggling with leaves, photosynthesis, for a while now. A long time ago, we tried to convert chemical energy to mechanical force. We found the answer in a burning chamber. Now, we're sweating over the transformation from particles to molecules, and vice-versa. Leaves are photosynthetic transformers. Each leaf has a different capacity of converting energies, and each is unique like a snowflake, too.

"Leaves teach us about transformation, a model for replacing our external youth. Instead of throwing out so much money and effort on plastic surgery, we could get the oldies to take their model from snakes. We could easily evoke certain mechanisms in us to shed our outer layer of skin, every hundred years or so. I think this gene is somehow related to the one causing baldness in men. Well, baldness reminds us of our origin: insects and reptiles. I'll leave genetic studies for Sandy. That's her baby."

"Are you also saying a Black Hole is like a transformer?" asked Martin.

"In some respects, I figure."

"One point, I miss. You said the earth expands. And it's getting bigger. If what you're saying is true, then the dinosaurs are extinct because of expansion. Vegetation had changed, some inner layers of soil replaced the outer one. Most dinosaur fossils are deeply buried in the ground, not only because of natural disasters—rain, earthquakes and continental drift. The internal magnetic forces of the earth suck its surface inwardly. And at the same time, new inner layers of soil push upward while older ones sink. It's like the earth renewing itself every couple hundred million years or so.

"If what you're saying is true, our deserts can only get bigger. Internal hollowness of our planet at certain places is the weak spot of the earth; it's waiting to collapse inwardly with any slight disturbance. So the inner plates are exposed. They can't remain stable because of the earth core's forces."

Circularity in the Perceptual World

"Now, you've got your new shoes. Where do you go, now?" asked Martin.

"We go to town for new glasses. We go where others have already explored. The visual world, my friend. A long time ago, a philosopher did this. His name is familiar to you—Rene Descartes."

"Wait a minute!" Martin interrupted. "What's your point? Are you going to tell me we've misinterpreted his view?"

"No! Before he wrote his theory of knowledge, he went to a butcher. And he bought an ox's eye, and then looked through it. He saw everything in the world upside down. Trees were upside down, people were standing on their heads. He believed that we also see the world like an ox because some evil genius deceives us."

"Maybe, Descartes wanted to say that the evil genius is society and our parents," cried Martin.

Virus looked at him for a few seconds. "If we can't trust our senses, we can't be sure of knowing anything in the world. Instead of pursuing an account for knowledge, he should have shown how illusions tell us about the natural function of our visual apparatus. Here we go again, Martin, the circular theory of visual perception."

"Listen, let's be quick. I've studied this at school. Just get to the point, Virus."

"Well, this is why I brought some illustrations to show you. You'll see how we map the world visually. As you know, the optic system is the cornea, lens, iris, and pupil. And the neural system refers to the retina, photoreceptor cells, fovea, and optic nerves. We're concerned with the neural system of vision, not the physical system that regulates incoming concentric light. You know, Martin, there's something parallel here."

"Now, you've said it, Virus. Quit shooting falling stars, and get to the point."

"Yes, for sure. You'll see the circular theory in action, just one moment please. Look at this figure: it shows how our visual system maps an object with both eyes (A, B, C).

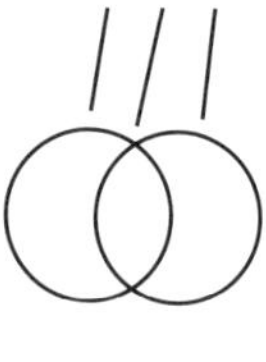

An object in the

world is mapped in regions A, B, and C. Here—our visual impressions of hard edges are predominant in only B, not A and C. That figure shows binocular vision, seeing with two eyes. And B register the object of focus, and we have visual acuity. And inputs of an object are overlapped here. A and C show the entire mapping visual field. I hope you notice that all objects that we see sharply are mapped in the circular field, B. And it's a concentric shape, too. We map the visual world by using a circular framework, like region B, for input. From this, nature, with its circular influence, molds our visual system accordingly. We have a circular method mapping information.

Now, look what happens when a person moves his head from left to right. This figure shows that neural mapping occurs by using a circular framework for incoming visual input.

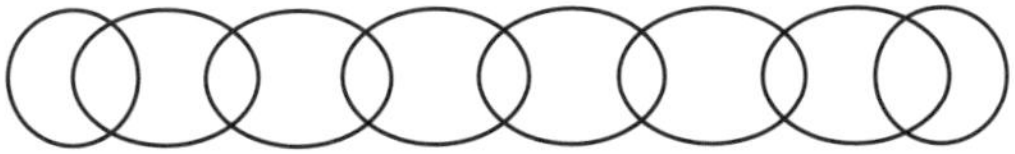

Here, you see the two end circles are rounder than the middle ones. They show starting and stopping in our eyes' movement from either left to right, or right to left. The middle can be longer or rounder, depending on how fast a person moves his head. Vertically, our neural mapping system uses a series of concentric circles, too. But these circles are elongated much more than in the above figure. Here, look at the following figure.

From this figure, you get an idea why it's so difficult to judge vertical distance. These circles are stretched more than the horizontal ones. There's something peculiar about looking vertically. It's not natural for man. I'll tell you why. If someone throws something down to you from a high rise, that object falls in the B region of figure one, because you're under it. And it's difficult to judge its distance. When someone is just looking up and down, regions A and C are predominant for visual cues to help our judgment of distance. But objects falling in B appear to jump up and down—depending on a person's angle under the falling object. Because of this impression of jumping, one concentric circle could make a gap in the entire chain, making height more difficult to judge."

"Virus, except for concentric mapping, what you're saying is in any intro psychology book."

"If you say so. But our visual field looks like this. And the mapping of objects falls within this egg shape, as this illustrates, Martin.

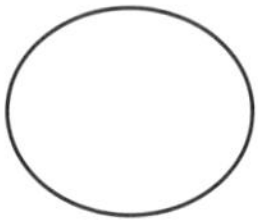

"This figure shows us how our neural mapping system organizes information or impressions from the world. Everything fits in a circular border. Impressions of an object are fitted within a concentric circle. The size of a concentric circle is selected on the basis of input on the neural retinal system. Mind you, I'm talking about edges, corners and the rim of an object's impressions. In other words, we're truly deceived by visual impressions, because our visual system imposes a circular framework on incoming images. Luckily, our experience supplements all raw neural inputs, especially in Gestalt form perception. After incoming images stimulate retinal photoreceptors, the concentric circle forms an image-like border, and inverts the entire circle for the brain to interpret and supplement with perceptive experience. We see a non-inverted tree in the world."

"There's no need to sensationalize now. I think I get your point. You're telling me there's no accident in nature. Light must behave the way our mapping system works, concentrically. When we see a triangle, square, circle, a shape and building, impressions are in a concentric circle for visual acuity. Figure five shows us acuity perception. I see you have more illustrations at the bottom there. Can I look at them?"

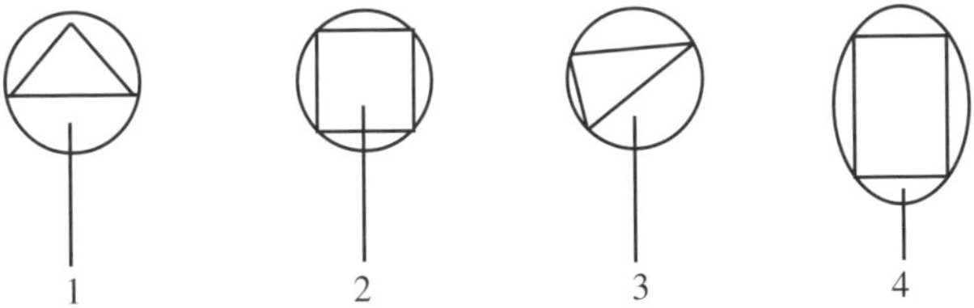

"They all show how our neural system accommodates impressions from a single shape. Each figure is within a concentric circle. And the circle size is determined by the longest line or corner of a figure's impressions," Martin said, noticing that Virus was looking at him with doubt. "Oh, yes, Virus, I guess art is not your favorite subject. Isn't it that all the shapes should be within the circle perfectly?"

"Reading between the lines, Martin, will help, when you're older. Your eyes are still good, aren't they? Art is too difficult for me. Gestalt figure-ground perception occurs within a single concentric circle—the switching of meanings without the switching of visual map. For example, the two faces or a vase."

Martin tried to interpret the drawing in front of him. "I thought the image of two faces or a vase was shown with the face of a young woman, not this horrible face that could chase away the symbol of the vase in life."

"For cow's sake Martin, since when are you so romantic? Yes, we have the empty vase in our hand, and the rose has long gone. You can't see both the two faces and the vase at the same time, only one at a time. When you notice the two faces, the vase becomes the background. If you recognize the vase as the figure, then the two faces become the background. You didn't know that each Gestalt figure and ground perception has two grounds, not one as it is suggested to us. If a background is a sheet of paper on which an image is viewed, it falls in figure one (A) and (C). If the vase is the figure, then the two faces are the ground. Figure-ground perception is not innate. It couldn't be, because it's about the mudding up of meaning and conceptualization. So, the point is, Gestalt figure and ground perception is about an image which is seen as having two different meanings, but the whole image fits in well in a concentric circle from which meanings are identified."

"The problem of geometric illusions arises from the way in which the neural system maps impressions. It accommodates impressions as they are presented in actuality without having a mechanism to delete stimuli. In the Muller-Lyer illusion, each figure is placed in a concentric circle, or both figures in one circle. It is natural to judge the line with outer fins as longer than the one with inner fins. Though both lines have the same length, the one with outer fins, the bottom one, Martin, appears longer than the one with inner fins. So, this illusion is about stimuli as being stronger than our experience.

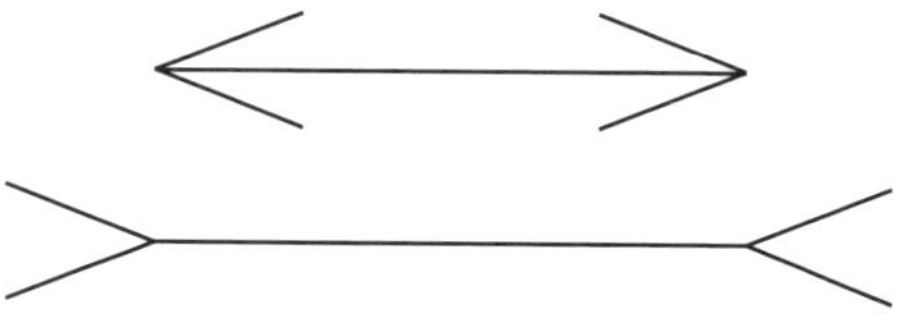

"There's another illusion with several circles surrounding an inner circle. Please don't take me wrong, I'm not saying we're making the same mistakes, it's more like we're getting better at making the worst ones. I'm not talking about visual illusions because I think it's too easy to deceive someone else. It's more like enjoying a deceiver's own self-deception in his hard effort to convince others about seeing the truth. Before I get too carried away, Martin—look at this figure.

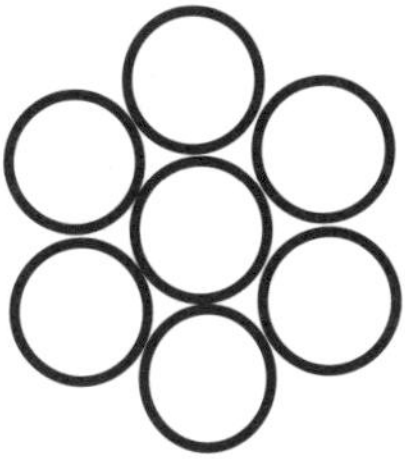

"Although all of them have the same size, in principle, the inner one is seen smaller. It isn't smaller, it's the same size as the others. With this illusion, the inner circle is also part of the entire image, which fits in a nicely concentric circle. This illusion is interesting because it more or less shows how our perceptual neural system registers impressions in a framework."

"Wait a minute, Virus! I have the impression that something is missing here. You're only telling us that whatever undergoes natural changes, it's a concentric form. But our visual mapping system couldn't have any other form than circular. It's the best framework for registering our environment. And yet, you said something about a bunch of circles around another one is like a representation of our mapping system. Because of this, we have the framework of frameworks. First, concentric circles are a framework for piling up perceptual information about the world. And second, the figure with all those circles is like the actual framework, so it fatigues the first framework. Because of this, cells get fatigue, the figure appears as an illusion. Therefore, we see the inner circle as smaller than the surrounding ones. What I mean is, our mapping system does not only get fatigued, it's also presented with an inner circle which loses its circumference. This illusion wants the visual system to create a lot of smaller concentric circles to accommodate the inner one. So, all of the outer circles constitute the mapping circle, not the inner one. Because our judgment of depth interferes with what is registered. The inner one just gets lost in this process. Is that it, Virus?"

"This is not what you want to talk about, is it, Martin? I'm getting tired. Look, it's after three."

"You're right. I can hardly get my thoughts together any more. To accommodate change and motion as regularity, macroscopic objects have a circular form. If not, non-circular objects in the universe could interfere with such regularity."

"Certainly, natural changes and motions involve circular bodies. Plus, natural organisms could grow and evolve in the realm of a circle."

"I agree with you, Virus, our astronomy is shaky. It's ridiculous to argue that a star is at least a billion light years away. All this doesn't only say something about the age of stars. It also says that the source could propel light for over a billion light years—nonsense. How can any sensible person believe that a dead object could live that long without undergoing drastic changes? It's ridiculous to say astronomers are waiting to discover some more billions of light years, not objects. How can any sensible person believe that photon carries a supernova's image with it? Now, I guess I have a notion about how a galaxy is formed. It's like a swift bending river, which continuously erodes its bank until the snakiest part is cut off from the rest of the river. With galaxies, new ones are formed in the same way. A huge galaxy may be twisted with both internal and external forces, until a part is cut off from it. And yet, it's magnetically attached to its source like a parasite."

"Our old view says that objects must travel through space. But now, space moves objects by making itself an illusion between objects. It's like nobody wants a Ferrari in a swamp. It's like travelling sixteen thousand miles per second, and not having any place to go. Or, I should put it another way for you. Most people have a dog or a cat. I prefer to train our atoms to be my pet. We want them to do our work for us. They must be trained to carry macroscopic objects to other realms."

"Well, Virus, I get your point. A trainer of atoms rather than animals—how sexy. You can go ahead and walk with a bunch of faithfully trained atoms with you. Virus, you're only seventeen, and it's incredible what you're doing. I'm still amazed, you spent over a year without being able to perfect your view. But what have you been working on this afternoon?"

"Today I found about six hundred subliminal messages on the Internet. Most of these companies intentionally place hidden messages to influence buyers."

"Subliminal messages, Virus! This is unbelievable."

"So far, they've been using subliminal messages in two related ways. Some messages are hidden from consciousness. And they're not easy to detect. For example, if the background color of the screen is grey, messages are written in a lighter shade of grey, and so on. The other type of message is coded in very quickly moving and flashing images. Not just any speed—there's a specific pattern to it. I've been deleting these web sites manually." Virus murmured the last sentence with a voice that had just rolled off a mountain in search of refuge.

"I could go to bed now. Let's go, Virus! Allow time to make your idea real. And wait for some more anomalies in science. At least, you're not an abominable iconoclast. But just an indigent exorcist. Don't pick up the table! Leave everything as it is!" They had gathered their personal belongings and were leaving by the back door when Virus recalled something.

"Martin, life is already immortal. And we're just a part of this process. So, life conquers all, and then love rolls in. What I really want to say is, understanding our universe lies in understanding circularity. Let me show you." Virus picked up a page. "All secrets are hidden in concentricity."

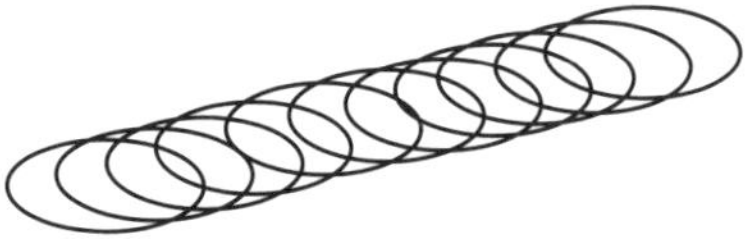

"Virus, you put everything in your circular theory, but are you saying the process of life is also circular?"

"Perhaps, it's our turn, and we shouldn't miss it."

"Since we've discovered the wheel, it rolls without really scratching the ground."

7: Full Moon

When Lenny and Tim left the restaurant they went to lower town. Tim went straight home on the same bus, and Lenny got off a few stops before his house and waited for his friends, for it was dangerous to travel alone at night. He recognized that he needed some evidence to prove what he had said in the restaurant. This was not a hoax to impeach Chuck, but if he did not find the evidence he needed, it could leave him ignominious. Lenny knew he had to prove his theory at all costs. Evidence did not consider people's feelings.

He saw them coming. "When I asked you to meet me here, I didn't know you'd dress as clowns," said Lenny angrily. "We aren't going to a party tonight!"

Justin and Slade also lived in lower town. They were deceived, by certain institutions, into thinking that their criminal deeds had been thoroughly forgotten after going clean for several years. They did not know that from birth to death, a statistical assessment of genetic characters and convictions remained; society retained a detailed costs-journal for any anti-social inhabitant. Costs to the state were well guarded in several highly secure vaults. This encouraged the nameless Jones to be remembered as a registered inhabitant of the planet after an atomic disaster.

"Where the hell do you think people go on a Thursday evening? Not to the cemetery, for sure!" Justin questioned, defending his colorful outfit. It looked like the Bermuda blue on a hot sunny day, and it carried the odor of mating season.

"You have to get the look, and the smell, too. The look for people," replied Slade with a smile on his face. "So where to tonight? Wait a minute, Lenny! Don't tell me we're taking public privilege! With all these expensive smells and looks, to be melted in the stink, it's unforgivable! A disgrace to charm and elegance."

"Not an airplane, for two psychedelic pigs!" Lenny answered sternly, keeping his view fixed on the bus pulling up at the stop. They entered the general assembly like a pack of sheep; they automatically followed the unwritten codes of conduct for night commuters. Double seats were occupied with two clients. All single seats remained empty, for to sit in a single seat at night meant you were alone with an alien political agenda against societal sculptures. Rationality in human beings had room only when the sun shined and dried the vital juice away from life. Obeying the young night's customs meant decisions were made prior to any hand raising in the UN; the most powerful enforced the rules and directions of passengers' destiny.

The chauffeur sat majestically on his UN throne, not high enough to see the world with fairness, benevolence, and justice. Here the protector of life struggled for his own survival, as the most powerful institution on earth was maneuvered with a few fixed strings. When he was threatened, a sensor responded and a squad of exterminators popped up to defend public business, as usual. Another sensor could activate a loud speaker in the bus, reminding everyone that public transportation was important without mentioning that it had instigated and maintained conflicts to justify its function on the road. Public privilege presented a repetitious blank symbol of international idealism, for every corner, small strip of gravel, and stoplight kept the bus on the same route.

The three together was a threat to others in the world where things were arranged singularly and by pairs; each participant of this world wore the diplomatic image of his nation's sicknesses. Any lame duck in a double seat could be consumed and overpowered by power wheelers. But the three of them lessened the tension in the bus by occupying only single seats in order to give other passengers a false impression of individuality, solitude, and ignorance.

A single passenger descending from the night bus was completely filled with gastric gases. Another breath could cause an explosion, nose sniffing through the layers of pollution for danger, ears hearing shades of malicious identity in every sound, and eyes turning backward to search the nebulous blackness for shadow dwellers.

"What's cooking?" asked Justin, turning backward to face Lenny.

Passengers saw without eyes and heard without ears, space cadets with harnesses and straitjackets stuck in a barrel of molasses, making the glass windows foggy with escaping warm air. The voice of a human being was rewarding, at least, for some night commuters.

"Nothing!" answered Lenny. "You'll see when we get there."

The bus rolled past flatland bars, stores, restaurants, apartment buildings, and small offices. It was entering double land, the park. A narrow two-way road split the park. The right part, which gradually ascended to about one hundred meters, led to upper land, where there were some tennis courts and a private golf course. The left part evened off, leading to middle land. Low and middle land inhabitants used the left park that was mostly occupied by a few open hockey rinks and a lot of overhead lamps to invite mosquitoes to attack passers-by and the homeless in the night.

As they drove past the twin parks, the bus turned right on a long road. Upper land's park was hardly noticeable. Apartment buildings on the left were growing wild. The bus stopped at the first building on the right, several hundred meters away from the park. Although there was no access to highbrow country from here, most passengers, including the boys, descended from the bus.

"Are you sick? It's Saint George Hospital!" cried Slade.

"Wasting a beautiful Thursday's night!" commented Justin. "All this heavy look for nothing! I'll knock them dead—in there."

"Wait a minute!" shouted Slade. "I'm checking out of this stinky dump! It gives me the creeps. It's haunted, especially with that flock of white angels that just got off the bus."

"Can't you see, Slade? We aren't going to the hospital. The entrance is over there. Look, workers are going in now," exclaimed Justin, attempting to be the mediator.

"Yes, I saw it in the newspaper; they wanted a clown," cried Slade, trying to shut Justin up.

"We're looking for the personnel parking lot. Could it be at the side of the building?" asked Lenny, pretending not to hear the mumbling between Justin and Slade.

"The parking lot, you said! Great! I'll do the driving! Last week, Big Head didn't let me drive. I say, it's my turn, now," praised Slade, putting his hand on Lenny's shoulder like a true buddy. It made Lenny very uncomfortable, and he quickly glided the weight off his shoulder. "I can't believe it! All this time, you kept it. Kept it, for yourself, only. You didn't let us in," Slade continued, unconsciously putting his arm on Lenny's shoulder again and then pulling Lenny closer. "You don't say much! What is it! You aren't scared! Are you?"

He won't get any answer from Lenny, thought Justin, allowing himself to make a wider gap between them. *Lenny doesn't think, he only responds to situations. He only does what he has to do. Nobody, for sure, can tell him what to do. At least he isn't scared of anything. But he isn't into this kind of stuff. Why did he bring us here? Maybe he needs hard cash. No, he has enough, I figure. He never did this before. Well, if he wants a car, he'll get one. That's for sure. He doesn't have to bring all of us, for a car. He could have done it himself. Yes, why us? This doesn't make any sense at all. Nowhere to run or hide, if situations call for it. We can't even escape. Oh, I'm visiting the hospital at ten-thirty in the night—with all my expensive clothes...*

"Excellent timing, Lenny. The moon is playing hide and seek with the cloud," murmured Slade, thinking how ingenious the plan was. Borrowing from the main road and side streets was too risky, but the parking lot was unguarded. They continued to walk on the sidewalk until they reached the side of the building, which exposed its huge nest. Ants carried two elongated luminous antennae in and out without any guardian at the entrance to ward off foreign species. They turned and followed the sidewalk to the parking lot.

"We're looking for a navy-blue BMW," murmured Lenny,

wanting Slade's imagination to run away so he could have a moment of silence. He had no intention of stealing the car, but he didn't want Slade to leave.

The lot was half full and poorly lit by overhead lamps. Justin joined the others for comfort, but would not help them look.

"Hmm, I warn you. I'm doing the driving tonight," insisted Slade. "Justin, you have to look on the ground, not in the sky! You-u."

"This isn't right! What would happen if there were cameras? Tell me, Slade!" warned Justin. "We'll all be done for. This isn't worth it. Look, a car coming!" The boys rushed behind a parked car and hid themselves while it passed. "It saw us, my clothes. I'm telling you, it isn't worth it," continued Justin, searching the posts and trees for hidden cameras. "I'm convinced there's a camera, looking at us." Finally, the other boys became a bit hesitant.

"We must get a plan. They're changing shift. It's about eleven," murmured Lenny, pissed-off at Justin.

"They're coming to get us, I say," cried Justin.

"Everything works with the attitude-man reality, you yellow-belly! They probably only have one camera, at the entrance. It's more fun to look at people who scratch themselves in the private parts before entering or leaving the building," commented Lenny.

"Talk, and more talk! Are we here to butter each other up?" complained Slade, who wanted the steering wheel around his hands, the accelerator under his foot, and the screeching of tires on the road.

"Let's play it safe, Justin. Pretend you're sick. And we're helping you to walk. Come on, let's go!" cried Lenny.

"But, I'm not!" yelled Justin.

"I'll make you!" answered Slade, preparing to punch him. Justin stood there, then started to walk a few yards with a twisted face, both hands flying and wobbling around like a headless chicken.

"Not drunk, stupid! Sick!" shouted Lenny, seizing Justin by his wings.

They combed the rows of parked cars—strand by strand—

with a prized turkey between them, deceiving on-lookers.

"Everything looks the same," said Justin hurriedly, "we can't tell what is what."

"You don't have to throw all your weight on us. You're supposed to be limping, not a cripple!" cried Lenny.

"Quit dragging your size fourteens," Slade cried angrily, "before I really break them!"

"A blue BMW, ERO 378," Lenny murmured, loud enough for Slade to hear. "It's loaded."

"My baby is loaded," Slade hummed, gliding his right hand on the imaginary steering.

"I can't see anything, nothing! We've been in this row twice. We better go. Nothing, nothing," rambled Justin. "It's eleven-fifteen now, I have to be in by twelve—curfew, you know."

"You guys can wait for me here. And hide yourselves," instructed Lenny. "I'll go in and check around. And keep a sharp look out." He hurried toward the entrance, an electronic eye watching him. He pushed the huge door open, then disappeared from his friends' view. He pushed open another door and noticed the security desk about fifteen yards away. The guard was looking downward. The camera had already shown his image. Now, another camera from inside saw every single move. An illusion stood before the guard.

"What can I do for you, young man?" asked the guard. The controller felt a little threatened in his own turf.

Lenny did not reply at once. He pretended to be scared, as though he was waiting for his confidence to mount for a face-to-face confrontation with authority. He stayed silent long enough so that he could drive his reality between the guard's eyes to strike him in the subconscious.

"My Mom forgot to leave the money for my school trip, tomorrow," he bashfully uttered. "She is always in a hurry, as if this place would run away. I have to get the money." He rested his head on his arm on the mini-bar. This confession took the security guard by surprise.

"Don't worry, we'll get the money for you. Tell me her name.

And where does she work?" The security guard was about to touch Lenny's arms, in comfort. But he fell short.

"She works at night. Night shift. Jackie Crawford, a nurse," he mumbled, pulling himself away from the desk and wiping his damp hands on his pants.

"This'll take a few minutes," said the guard, picking up the telephone receiver. Lenny paced the floor in the corridor.

Slade is surely suspicious, he'll burst at anytime, he thought, while maintaining one eye on the door and one on the security desk.

"She's looking. Fifteen minutes ago, shift changed," said the guard. "It'll take a while. Why didn't you ask your father?"

"They divorced." Lenny answered dryly.

"Oh, I'm really sorry," the guard sympathized, thinking that he could have made a perfect father, who would put the life of his child before his.

The guard's attitude-man reality did not pass Lenny, who saw him as an opportunist, wanting to get into Jackie's pants without any commitment. *I bet he sees Jackie as an easy, desperate woman,* thought Lenny. He was interrupted by the guard's voice.

"Yes! Yes, yes. Thank you very much. Bye!" the guard said calmly as contact was broken and a hallway light bulb went off simultaneously. He sadly returned the receiver to its cradle, and then he stripped Lenny's body with his stare. "I'm sorry, son. Your Mom is scheduled to work tomorrow night. Not tonight," he murmured, as though his cat had run away from him, leaving only its furriness behind for another to wear.

"Are you crazy? This can't be!" shouted Lenny as his eyes quickly checked the entrance door.

"The nursing office checked the computer. And she phoned the ward. Your mother is off tonight." This put Lenny on the spot. Lenny knew that this fellow was more interested in Jackie than the conversation. And he had to slip into an attitude.

"Wait a minute! Isn't this Bellevue Hospital?" he asked. "I'm telling you, she's working tonight."

"No, it's Saint George."

"You said, Saint George," he murmured. "All this time, wasted!" he cried, stamping the floor with his feet and kicking the desk like a frustrated animal in a cage. He then forcefully dropped his hands downward, looking at his own insolence and anger.

"I'm sorry," said the guard.

"I have to run, before I miss the next bus!" he cried, walking a few steps backward toward the door, then quickly turning and rushing out of the building as though his attitude-man reality could be exposed before the guard's eyes.

The guard shook his head, and recollected the events of previous full moon nights. A lot of weird people looking for their destiny. It would be a busy night at the hospital.

Lenny looked around the parking lot for Justin and Slade. He did not see them. *He didn't come in, thank God. They could have gone home. But again, Justin wouldn't go without me. Where could they be? Don't tell me, they're at the parking lot's entrance,* he thought. He walked toward the entrance.

"No lousy ERO 378! Thursday night is gone," screamed Slade, loud enough for everyone in the parking area to hear.

"You see, I was right! I told you he'd come back. You didn't want to believe me! Now, see for yourself," Justin cried joyfully.

"I just screwed up the entire night," murmured Lenny. "It's tomorrow," he said, exposing his anger like a flooded stream that had swallowed up a nearby village. "But we can't just sit around here, howling over a wasted night," he said.

"I knew that all along. Tonight isn't the right night," interrupted Justin. "I just didn't want to say this to you." He hurried away from the parking lot entrance as though the BMW would appear out of nowhere and yell out Slade's name. He sensed Slade behind him, dragging his feet.

Slade was filled with disappointment. He continuously turned to look back, hoping to see his desired horse popping up mysteriously.

"What's next?" asked Lenny, surrendering his leadership to Slade.

"I'm going to hit the sack," replied Justin.

"Just like a little baby!" said Slade, showing only disappointment on his face. "I'll check the boys out. I guess they're shooting pool. At least there'll be more action there than in this dead place."

The parking lot stretched behind and above them. Lenny first condemned himself, but then he sought evidence to justify his mistake. This he had learned from science; only researchers would not admit the facts that they knew prior to forming their hypotheses. He knew that the fact that Jackie was not at work did not mean she was having an affair. And yet her lie pointed to something more dreadful, an acknowledgment of the ultimate end to her marriage. It would be more pleasing for the public if she had a mating partner than if she was gambling and emptying bottles to shoot the time away.

He slipped away from Jackie's attitude-man reality, for the wretchedness in loneliness threatened any sane person. He turned instead to Chuck's father. He wanted his seed to grow and progress in the world, without doing his job of being a father. *First, we should be equal partners among ourselves,* Lenny though, *and then work with our parents for a better world. We could stop the entire institution of the rat race by refusing adults' values, beliefs and norms; but this would be too destructive for all worlds. For in each world, someone would attempt to beat the system, reminding inhabitants of their feeble society.* Lenny came out on top by using Chuck as his royal stool.

8: Attitude-Man Reality

After the incident in the restaurant, Chuck was scattered. *Twinkle, twinkle little star; how I wonder what will become of me… and it appears as though all the king's men could not put me together again.* With all the little tiny bits in Chuck's head, the flash sometimes occurred: *Eureka!* The golden thread was born into a course of life, leaving perspiration and determination to carve out a solid path. As scattering thoughts could mystically arrange themselves in an unconventional direction, the mind worked them over to show the rebirth of life.

Eternity was burning in the room; not a single spectator was present, and nobody was walking on the stars. Chuck had fallen asleep several hours ago; his eyelids, each with asymmetrical rapid movements, were witnessing a furious unearthly battle.

"No pleasant dreams, no happiness. Is it really necessary?" said The Transcendental Big Time Believer.

"They allow themselves to be transformed," replied Technology. "In less than a hundred years, I've given them a thousand years worth of technological advancement. Now, my faithful, they worship me as their Lord. Only I have their deliverance. See your mistake in creation! The weaklings aren't eating themselves to death like oversized worms. For them to see with their heads, they must thin their feet away, so they have a better view of the ground. From thinning and thinning, their feet become too weak for their body weight, so they're moving on the ground. But for how long? Don't get me wrong, Big Time Believer. There are countless ways of doing wrong deeds. The serpent on the tree—they've mistaken its significance—it's their destiny. For there's only one way of being on the ground: with a huge belly and no legs. Don't get me wrong again, Big Time Believer. Crawling on their stomachs is their wormling destiny. Yes, even the old ones are hopeless; their skin can be peeled off without hurting the juiceless merchandise. You, my friend, have enlightened the young, for the old prunes to round off with sports and my education. Hope and prosperity reside in the domain of Technology."

"This can't work anymore, Technology. You've underestimated the young ones, they're not spectators. They're the New World order of all worlds."

"Big Time Believer, you've forgotten one thing. The young, like the gloomy ones now, will become old and flowerless. You don't want to change a nation, but the world and all the possible worlds. In all realms, human beings are content with their polished plate. A person can see himself in this plate. And others too. They wear these bright plates like armor, protecting their honor. What have you offered them? Let me see, eternal darkness. Layers and layers of pitch-blackness, which horrify them senselessly. The testing period is over for man. Life is what you get and own, not seeking light in emptiness. But you've condemned man to life without glory? Without pride? Condemned them to eternal damnation for a nimble moment of forgetfulness?"

"Tell me. What do you expect from them? They're aware of your lies. Taking images for reality, and darkness for light. For sure, your thin plated protection is a transparent image, too. It's fashioned with no dignified substance. The young don't accept social problems, environmental problems. And no cheap shiny skin layers any longer."

"Oh, Big Time Believer, you've served them well with your bloated identity. What a monster of yourself, you've shown your beloved. Threatening them with eternal damnation. They haven't lived long enough to deserve such a hideous punishment. You want them to crawl to you. You harness them with freedom, so you can neglect and abandon them while my institutions prove to them otherwise. How merciless you are! I've given them all the metals in the world. They can, of course, because of me, see their true reflection. They'll recycle themselves, in body. Yes, the image is more real and interesting than any smoky identity."

"The young still have their golden string together."

"They wield, unfortunately, no power. The armored prunes run their life. The young serve the prunes. Constitutions, international and national legal systems protect prunes like prized birds. The prunes judge, condemn, and prosecute even the cradle. You're naïve to think of the young as having their own constitution, legal system, lawyers, judges, and juries. You want them to work with the prunes for a New World order. It's hogwash!"

"Wake him up! You'll see how his head sleeps among the stars."

"A wager, from you. Look at his room—he crawls among the stars with his feeble feet, not with his head, as you wish. I like sports, too."

"I should remind you, not all wise ones are flowerless. The spirit of life knows no age."

"Don't try to talk me out of this game."

"You've got a point," the Big Time Believer conceded, intentionally giving Technology a hint that he was hiding something.

Technology wondered about his opponent's motive. "Trying to take me for a ride, you golden bard. But this won't work. I see, you think governments are the most unprofitable organizations in any world. They're parasites to any healthy organism. Well, you don't need secret agents to discover their lies and fraud. Natural resources, everyone knows the owner—they belong to everyone, not to any private organization. Is that it, Big Time Believer? You think I've played all my cards, and I'm at a deficit. You give them freedom, only for me to take away."

"I have hope in the young. They can easily contract and market an entire government to competitors. And every five years or so, anyone in the world and underworld will be able to apply for your presidential office. The post will be filled, leaving you as a runner up. Yes, Technology, some people can be much more evil than your little mind could ever imagine. They're a threat to your own kingdom. They could easily privatize your armies and police force. Your universities, colleges, and hospitals already underwent privatization. Your weak opposition to the most powerful in the underworld couldn't influence the private armies that you had created. Trying to really destroy the human world definitely implies your own destruction. Is this what you want?"

"Bluff! But, you still have a point. To destroy your world, I must make someone more evil and powerful than me. You're not so bad, reminding me of my own house. You're not practicing a hideous deception on me. It'd go against your own nature. A complete destruction would imply my own disaster. But, the last answer is still mine. How do you want your most faithful servants to dream about you, Big Time Believer? I always think of myself as having a clear conscience because everyone is welcome in my domain—Hell. But now, you ask me to question my own armies. My own creation!"

"For all these years, you've been telling me goodness doesn't grow. Now, I'm telling you, evils flourish wild with ever increasing power. You've undermined your own security terribly."

"You've taught people how privatization works: the fittest will enjoy everlasting life. You know the art of creating competition among people, competing to enter your kingdom. You teach them about the glory of being the best. Now, you've got their everlasting rat race. Struggling to be the best at everything. You also tell them each person is a complete individual—everyone must cherish his own fat ego in your holy name. But their egos have swallowed up your holiness. Though we can't see things alike, I've opened their eyes. Everyone had an equal share in this realm. Can't you see? Each person had a fair dose of pollution, nuclear waste, depletion of the ozone, environmental dumps, electrosmog—they belonged to everybody. I gave them true equality. Thank you for privatizing your kingdom. Now, nobody owns any of them," said Technology. "Your golden door allows them to enter one after the other like mindless slaves. But my world has countless entrances. Just like pollution—fairness for everyone. Each filthy pig has to chew something up to renew his reflection now and then. That's reality. The lings have short memory of themselves and their belief of immorality."

"Your trumpet of near victory only awakened the sleeping

princes and princesses for another two thousand years of dominance," replied The Big Time Believer.

"Creation is an allegory. Human beings create others so that the first creator could be recreated by their creation."

"The eaten-apple is creating itself out of existence. Crawling prolongs the process. The young can't recreate the created; they still carry your scar."

"Real powers reside with the people!" said Technology.

"But now, the lings will actively participate in the making of their reality. For another two thousand years, the lings will reign," said the Big Time Believer.

"Cheap tricks! Making the cradle dream itself to its own destiny. New vitality becomes stagnated human reality," said Technology.

"The lings inherit no curse. And the fully grown ones are flexible enough to bend without breaking."

"It's too late," cried Technology.

First, Life Struggles, then People Follow

Voices downstairs, the story of spoons, pots, knives, and cups, singing an epoch of human values in the kitchen, chased Chuck's sleep away. He tried to put his hand on something more distinct downstairs; his closed door could not prevent whispering, with razor sharp edges in the virgin morning, from irritating his curiosity. Unsatisfied with himself as an outsider living on echoes, he had forgotten his bed. The image of Lenny clearing the dust before his eyes haunted him. He made his way quickly to the washroom and released his overworked gases. "Now, nothing remains hidden. I'm living, and that counts," he murmured, his toothbrush in his mouth. He stared at himself in the mirror. His image tried to run away from him; he caught it with a strong grip. "Now, you'll serve me," he said between grinding teeth. His mirror reflection panicked, not his mind. He left the washroom and overheard them again. *I don't want to be a slimy spy for bits and pieces,* he thought. *It'll be about me from now on. My book of life is already open. Conversation, conversation on the wall, life will wonder, for somebody is going to fall, and it won't be me.*

Jackie was doing most of the talking while Doris drained an empty coffee cup. The night report kept them together, as they measured each other's activities. Doris wanted to go home to see her family before they greeted the day, and Jackie still had her half-filled glass of orange juice, counting the grams of each sip. At the shift from the screeching of stairs to regular footsteps advancing in the main living room, the voices depreciated to a horizontal line on the cardiac machine. Doris pretended to be busy. Jackie was cresting the edge of her glass with her index finger when the invader appeared, just before the beginning of Doris' day and the last yawn of Jackie's.

"Look at you! You haven't slept a wink. Your eyes are so red. You didn't sleep so well," said Doris, pitying herself, for she did not have any say in this sensitive situation which required more than a sitter's caring and compassion.

"He must have stayed up to finish his schoolwork. They have a lot to do, more than we used to," replied Jackie.

"Oh, it's all right," murmured Chuck, resenting Doris for being here. *Are they going to divorce?* he wondered as he sat down to eat his breakfast.

"You're early this morning," questioned Chuck, "How come?"

"We had a lot to do, so I worked through my break," replied Jackie. "Oh yes, did I tell you yet? I'll be working again tonight. We're very busy, these days."

"Yes, you told me, two weeks ago. I already arranged to come," answered Doris, thinking that the question was intended for her.

"Since tomorrow is Saturday, can Lenny come over then?" he asked, looking at his mother's over-polished circle on the rim of the glass.

"Certainly!" cried Doris.

"Yes—yes, it'll do him good," said Jackie. The empty gap could be filled with friends.

"Then, that is that, he comes!" Chuck cried with a voice of

genuine certainty, giving his mother a penetrating stare. *Parents, they inherit a profound insight into their children's needs without having the slightest clue about the workings of their own head,* he thought. *Yes, look at her miserable life, she lives like the goddess of self-deception. I'm not going to roll on my belly, just because two adults can't communicate. Wait a minute. Am I blaming the persons who breathed life into me, Mom and Dad? Why not blame Doris and Lenny for all this mess? No, it's me, it's my entire fault. Someone has to be blamed for this separation. Why not? No, it couldn't be me. I didn't break them up. I had sweet screw all to do with it. The worst is running out of people to blame. It's the biggest disaster. I can't go about life without the crucifix. I should wear it like a martyr. No, I can't be like this. But, why not? They had a contract, a verbal agreement to have me. Didn't they? I wonder. Even if they didn't, they just can't walk away from it. Oh, no. They can't, but they have. Walking away from their responsibility, it's just too easy for them. This is a life agreement, not a game of hide and seek. Yes, after they had me, each of them grew wings of uniqueness and individuality. All this, they'd hidden from each other before they got married. And heaven knows what more. Denying my happiness, my needs, and my growth. All this, for the price of reinventing freedom. Freedom from me. Oh no, you aren't going to screw me up. Two independent persons still love me. Giving me gifts and occasional visits as though I'm a corpse in the graveyard. This should make me happy, so I could forget everything. And help them to overcome their guilt. Yes, I should refine their dull sensitivity, so they can still pass as humans in society. Killing the third one with their newly discovered freedom and uniqueness. Societal mercy killing, they're practicing on me. No, I'll fight your escaping, your superficial individuality.* He smiled sarcastically as he glanced at the stone face before him, and then to the other one hiding herself in her work in the kitchen. He followed Doris' eyes to the stopping of time on the wall.

"I reckon it's about time, isn't it?" asked Chuck. He didn't really care what their answer would be, anyway.

"Yes, the bus will be here in any second," replied Doris, looking at Chuck as he left the kitchen and started to hum.

"Sweet sweet family
You've somebody
And you can't leave me
For I don't want to be nobody
And if you didn't have me
You wouldn't know destiny
Now that you do
I'm here to stay
With my family."

His song carried him through the door and out of the house into the open morning wetness. He walked backward across the driveway and waited for the rainbow. He knew that the bus would be here as usual; but this time, there would not be any actor for the passengers to look at. From a block away he could hear the approaching tank plowing through the open desert. Maintaining his new selfhood, he climbed the narrow stairs and walked to an empty seat at the rear of the bus.

The bus driver slowed down as he approached the school. "He isn't there," Chuck murmured to himself as he descended from the yellow banana and forced his eyes on the lonely bus stop. He had expected to see Lenny at his usual post.

He decided to walk to the next block. Down the road, he noticed a lonely bike peeling upward. The morning traffic was going toward town, where most factories and offices were located. Chuck waved his hand in an effort to attract Lenny's attention. Silvery sparks in the sun were coming directly toward him to devour the remainder of his life as a helpless moll. Chuck could see Lenny's anger from the night before pouring into the bicycle spokes, with sharp flaming edges to slaughter and split timbers at a sawmill. Headstrong as a bison, Chuck stood his ground as the front wheel stopped about a hairline before him.

"Are you crazy?" yelled Chuck, "riding over the curb like that?"

"It gives you a good scare. It makes life jump into you," Lenny replied, smiling at the ripe fruit in front of him.

"My old lady works tonight. You can come over, only if you want to," Chuck murmured.

"Are you going to bore me? Or give me the folder?" Lenny asked.

Feeling sorry for him, Chuck silently gave him the plastic folder. They briefly made eye contact, and that was sufficient for them. In this glimpse, they recognized their common goal.

"Yeah, I'll see," said Lenny.

"Okay, see you later!"

Without encouraging the eye game any further, Lenny unconsciously reacted to certain unexplained sentiments that they shared. "After the restaurant, I guess," he replied without thinking. He saw his principal's head coming toward him, and it was getting bigger with each flight. "I must hurry!" he cried painfully, for another morning of torture awaited him. His bicycle jumped ninety-degrees and sprinted over the curb into the empty left lane, riding against oncoming traffic. It was better to have a frontal view of what could run him over than to be taken in surprise from behind. He knew that riding against oncoming traffic was daring; if the coming truck was an eighteen-wheeler, it made the rider a hero. Unfortunately, no rewards were given for such heroism.

On his way, Lenny stopped at the Copy Center that was located on his route and ran off ten copies. As he turned to pay for the copies, he noticed Tim at the door, waiting for the merchandise. He handed his agent the entire folder, including the copies.

"Same as usual," said Lenny. "They'll be waiting at the same place." Tim would distribute the ten copies to some other associates, and he would use the original for the database. Lenny did not have enough time to say more as he geared away to school. He used his bike as a dangerous weapon that evoked some anger, and yet pity too, among motorists. Those in their life-protecting tanks knew that two wheelers never had a second chance.

Rats Training Trainers

Lenny's classroom door was closed, keeping out unwelcome ears, and students naturally found that most mysteries happened on the other side of the door. He gently pushed the deceiver open. Eyes gripped the main actor on stage as he confronted the venomous and narrow cliff near the blackboard—too thin to hold any compassion or human understanding against lifeless rules. The utilitarian teacher had already prepared the note of penalty; it was lying on her table. She administered its deterrence to the latecomer.

His grunt of reply short-changed his audience. *I should leave my knapsack in class,* thought Lenny. *No, nothing worthwhile in it anyway, it's better to take it with me. Well, let the note lead me ?* He left without adjusting himself. Softly closing the door as though it was made of smoke, he looked for his eyes' reflection on the foggy floor, as he walked painlessly on his own shadow toward the principal's office.

Now, trainers and rats are molded together, perpetually changing roles to form different kinds of bondage, he thought, reaching in his bag for yesterday evening's detention slip for the secretary. He looked at the half-closed cracker jack box in the bag. A gift in the box could never trick a child, only the quality of the product. And without a well-trained engineer, the pieces could hardly fit together. Lenny put two detention slips on the secretary's desk, and continued to the other door without showing any trace of disappointment on his face. Every little child pushed a hand deeper and deeper into the box for other objects. When nothing hard was in the hand, the empty net was withdrawn slowly. Unsatisfied, Lenny sat on his usual chair with an expression of immeasurable emptiness on his face.

At first, the principal was bemused; he finally saw vagueness in Lenny and preferred to comfort him in privacy with a lengthy explanation of human unfulfilled nature. And yet, the principal could not swallow the courage that this weakling portrayed in projecting himself in such an irregular manner.

Lenny waited, and then waited some more for the principal to warm up. He knew the scream was coming. The principal had no safety valves for excess steam when he noticed the criminal practicing silence as a virtue.

"And, what is it, this time?" he shouted. The rat waited for the trainer to be more attentive by lowering its head and rubbing its front legs together nervously. The trainer immediately recollected and then revised his notes. *Yes, he always gives his answers and excuses without any reward,* he thought. *Positive incentives only could elect the right response.* "Speak up, boy," asked the trainer gently, soliciting a reply with his transparent intention.

I'll put an end to this ordeal, thought the rat. *I'll live in your conscience like a cancerous cell. You'll think twice before selling students to industries. You'll wear your accomplishment as aftershave.* He kept his eyes downward as though hopeless in the maze. The trainer transformed himself into a compassionate and toothless lion that unwillingly inherited its throne, and waited for a little while for the trapped rat to make a learned movement. Seeing that the trainer walked on a thread between patience and frustration, the rat decided to elect responses to maximize the experimenter's happiness.

"You see, sir," whispered Lenny, "our neighbor always fights, every night. Screaming, shouting, breaking things in the house. Really scaring everyone. The father comes home, every night, always drunk. He might kill someone. Scaring everyone up, in the whole building. Nobody can sleep anymore." He stared at the trainer's tie while he rubbed his hands together until both of them became moist with sweat.

The trainer searched his memory and put the pieces together in a coherent whole. The whole was bigger than all the pieces together; it became unmanageable. He realized that he was only a principal, not a psychologist. He picked up the phone and dialed a number "Come over to my office, now!" he tastelessly commanded, not only because the situation was urgent but also because he had an opportunity to remind others who the authority was around here.

He did it for himself, not for me. It's incredible. Poor clown, he is condemned to look busier than he really is. Before you-know-who, Ms. school psychologist, thought Lenny. He knew that his mouth had to deny everything while his body affirmed everything. He tried to work up a severe physical state of drowsiness before she entered.

"Yes, come in!" the principal answered the door from his chair, a pencil in his hand. "This is our school counselor," he told Lenny. "I think you should speak to this student," he told her, failing to notice her long, friendly smile, which was about thirty seconds long and two seconds thick. Lenny eyed the woman.

She comes from a slim culture in which a standardized book becomes an ideal method for explaining human reality and suffering. She's forgotten that attitude-people wrote her Bible. No attitude-person can be classified as an antisocial inhabitant, thought Lenny. *For my life fits my situation. Living in situations is a way of life without crying over truth and lies. And others are only interpreters of my life-situations. A way of life to inspire others, to make them see things my way, to sweep them over to my side. Oh, yes, my life-situations say what the rules are.* He felt better after he had played with the attitude-person reality, for life-situations knew no honesty, no promises, no lying, and no looking back.

"You can come with me," said the counselor, without looking at anyone in particular. Lenny noticed her weaknesses trapped between patience and the sense of authority.

I'll have to convince her, he thought. *I'll be her most faithful experimental rat. And yet, she speaks without referring to anybody specifically. She waited at the door while Lenny remained seated.*

"Will you please come with me?" she politely requested.

Yes, she drives forward and backward without sitting on neutral. I'll allow her to take me forward, as I twist her forward to my own size. Lenny deliberately hesitated, giving them a clear sign that he did not want to speak to a stranger. He waited for some coaxing and sympathetic coaching purely for pleasure and fear.

"Go with her!" shouted the principal, causing a mindless petrified rat to chew itself to death.

That really shows her who wields the power around here. I hope she noticed how frightened I was. Treating her delicate and fragile patient like that. Humiliating the noble integrity of psychology, her profession, her self-identified way of earning a living. I'll wait for my stomach to growl. I have to make it ring in their ears. It was loud enough for everyone. He told them he came to school without eating as he quickly tailed along behind her. He thought that he had to include the principal in this situation, so she could infer that the administrative department did not handle his case properly.

Well, she'll start with the idea that something is wrong with me. She knows that children don't easily give information about themselves. Sometimes they lie. She'll force me to see things realistically, my neighbor becoming my friend. Okay, I'll speak about my friend's life so that she thinks it's mine. He followed her to her office, several doors away from the principal's.

An hour painfully dragged away in the counselor's office. She turned and twisted the same information over and over again until she finally believed. Lenny was stripped to the core—a hard stuff, five feet long and twenty-eight inches thick. And yet, it was colorless and weightless. She did not believe anything less than that Lenny's father was an alcoholic who terrorized everyone in the house. A broken home with scared children and sleepless nights was the logical explanation of Lenny's lateness. The principal, the morning father with a terrible hangover, only intensified the poor child's agony and biscuit self-identity. Lying to the principal was his only way to cover up the truth without losing his fragile self-identity. "Wait outside, please. I have to make a call," requested the counselor. She waited until her patient left and closed the door behind him.

Oh, that was close. I didn't say anything about my family. Dad works during the day and Mom at night. I didn't say that my father drinks, he thought, wondering whom she was phoning. *Business as usual, without the library, now. Well, she can't phone home. She'd be dumb to phone home. She should know some little things about people, by now. No alcoholic would admit it. She isn't a marriage counselor. Mom wouldn't say, oh my dear, you're so perceptive about my life and situation. How charming of you to tell me, I'm unfit for my own family. And worse, even for myself.*

"You can come in now," called the counselor, leaving the door open wide. "I've just spoken to the principal. He was very sympathetic to your unfortunate situation. We aren't here to intensify your psychological suffering. Whenever you're late, you can always come in. You're welcome to speak to me, in complete privacy. My door is always open. I'll notify all your teachers concerning your lateness."

"Thank you, I've got math, it started ten minutes ago,' Lenny reminded her, desperately wanting to escape. *Complete privacy,* he thought. *You miserable snake, you've already used me to pull rank with the principal. Telling him about your fantastic discovery. Selling my privacy, cheap. Very cheap, to the next buyer. It takes much more than power to win my confidence.*

"In that case, I'll come with you," she cried joyfully.

She's rubbing it in too much. Wanting to tell everyone how useful her joy is. She has a belly full of it, vomiting it out all over the place like an over-stuffed reptile. I have to get rid of her; she wants to make me her ideal case. Nothing's going to stop her now, she's having it her way, today. She doesn't know yet that she's already served her function, thought Lenny as they walked to his classroom.

"Here," said Lenny, waiting while she knocked and then entered. The two women greeted each other from a distance.

"You can go to your seat, now," said the counselor in an affirmative voice. She gave the teacher a non-verbal sign that she wanted to speak to her outside of the classroom. The watchful eyes of other students caused Lenny's selfhood to disappear as he went to his regular seat. Some unfortunate students were suspicious of Lenny's terrible crimes and wanted to get the news first. Whispers were floating in the air and the students' ability to recollect someone else's antisocial history was immeasurable.

"Nobody can be late around here with dignity!" cried Lenny, taking everyone by surprise and changing their course of natural inquiry. "Well, they didn't call my folks in, yet. I'm lucky, wouldn't you say?" The class realized how fortunate they were, as they slowly drifted away from Lenny as an appropriate subject for discussion. But this did not stop the noisy shuffling.

The teacher came back in, scrutinizing one of her most outstanding students for physical marks and psychological scars. Her human nature squeezed itself backward to recollect past impressions that she should have questioned more severely. Her unconscious stare quickly abandoned other students who sought attention too and began to talk among themselves.

"Quiet! Class isn't over yet!" she shouted, stopping words in thin air. Her student's traumatic ordeal rendered her even more helpless than before. She was preoccupied with Lenny's long face; she tried to calculate his fear and insecurity. Truth, harmony, none of them had any decimal place.

Finally, you've run your course. Time is mine, now, thought Lenny. *How treacherous, you Hexe—I allow you to paint my world by blaming yourself for being blind and insensitive to my problems. What's worse, I accept all this stinky stuff like a mindless nail. A number becomes a victim of family instability. A Hexe should know, there is no creation, only cloning. Society clones us to be attitude-persons. Fast food alters our genetic make-up.*

The bell rang and the herd bolted through the narrow door without taking it with them, interrupting Lenny's attitude-man self-defiance. He slowly arranged his books and walked to the front where she was gathering her materials. She pretended to ignore his approaching,

"The assignment is worth five percent of your grade, but you can have an extension," murmured the teacher, trying to show that she sympathized with his suffering.

"Thank you," he replied, and continued to the door. *At least she's living out the school psychologist-attitude-person's reality. Well, she must have realized something about herself from all this, taking on a new self-identity to meet my reality.*

The Table

It was already six fifteen when Lenny arrived at All-In-One. The restaurant was nearly empty except for five occupied tables; three of them were pulled together near the kitchen door with a bunch of people eating, drinking, and bellowing. The entrance echoed Belinda's voice. He decided to join her table, for there were also Leslie, Sandy, Martin, and Larry, and the conversation had life and action.

"You're babbling pure nonsense! I have first hand experience," said Belinda. "My sister works at the hospital—day-in, day-out. Everybody has to face these lifeless people. Vegetables is more like it. They're fastened like octopi to machines. Hooking up these dead bears, just to keep them alive. Yes, little children, accident victims, the terminally ill, too. You name it—they've got it. Without these machines, they'd be dead as a stuffed nail. Think about these workers, they have to live with it. It's torturous. I say, yes, Proud City should legalize mercy killing or painless killing. They use a big word for it. I think it's euthanasia. We owe patients this. They have rights. Let them go with honor and mercy. Where is our compassion? Our decency? To stay one afternoon, with these people, you'd want to pull the plug for them. I rest my case." She looked at Leslie, sitting next to her.

"Well done, Belinda! Oh, yes, I really mean it. Especially, playing on others' sympathy and stomachs," cried Leslie sarcastically. "I see it politically. My story's not so nice as Belinda's. It goes like this: Mr. Smith is running for office in town. He offers to decrease the annual deficit. Better medical care for everyone. And equal care for everyone. He promises to create more beds in hospitals… Everyone—grandmothers, grandfathers, sick folks, especially poor people without medical insurance—vote for him. Even medical insurance companies support him. So what happens after Mr. Smith is elected? He quickly makes a law for mercy killing. Most governments work like this. They try to reduce others' expenses, not their own, creating better medical care for everyone by getting rid of terminally ill patients. The means, of course, justifies the end. Well, that's it, you have it. We voted him in. But we didn't ask him for his agenda. Did we? Since he doesn't know his own agenda, we become his puppets."

"Yeah, Leslie," interrupted Lenny. "You hit it on the nose." His sudden outburst took everyone by surprise. "My friend, everything is economics, not politics. Economists make politicians crawl like little babies without diapers. I'm talking about the attitude-world. This must be new to some of you. Economists' work involves making forecasts, predicting the future. Common sense tells us that the future is unknown. But not for economists. Our economist technology rules the world. They tell us who we are. What we'll be. So, our educational institution, using that note, fattens us up with junk food like pigs. You see, we change to attitude-people. Economists make us their attitude-reality. You can bet your last dollar on it! They tell us how to live a successful financial life. And how to be happy doing it. This isn't hard to do. Look at ourselves, we're just teenagers. And we're gearing up for our careers by studying job trends. We don't do it consciously. Our schools have already done it for us. And our retirement saving plans, we have to think about, before we begin our careers. And then we call it all 'life.' Sweet life. To put everything short, face reality—our parents are making our mold."

"Listen Lenny, we're talking about mercy killing," interrupted Leslie. "You can't say it's only an attitude. It's real. We're forced to live with it." She glanced at Lenny.

"Since you put it that way, Leslie, we live in a very competitive world. Parents are advertising and trading their babies for dollars. Everything is commercialized. Pregnant mothers advertise their excess belly for money. People just don't have any personal dignity left. Everything has a price. Business only wants productivity and efficiency as a means of survival. Human resources are their power to stay alive. Without productivity, there are no jobs. And no business. You see how important human beings are! Economists and business managers aren't very intelligent, these days. For a company to survive, customers must have money to buy products and services. Since one company tries to kill another one, and so on, it's killing itself too. Why? Because a dead firm means more people will be out of work. So what happens next? It's like opening a gigantic car-manufacturing plant in the Amazon for the natives. This car plant won't have any competition there. And it won't sell any cars either. This isn't my business, anyway. As I've been saying… All companies need people as their resources to survive. Old people and terminally ill people can't produce. They have zero output. They're stinky parasites to a healthy organism—our work force. Some old ones are filthy rich, hiding their money in banks, everywhere in the world. If others could have this money, they could reinvest it. More jobs. And a better life for everyone. Now, I say, the terminally ill are worthless. And they're a heavy burden on everybody. Their existence defies all economic theories, and it should be terminated."

Nobody commented on Lenny's view. He was Mr. Business; he knew his stuff well. Their pizza and drinks were getting cold, so they took the chance to take a few bites. Everyone was still impressed; eating allowed them to contemplate Lenny's business philosophy. The group of young persons looked at each other for the next speaker. They were quickly distracted when Lenny stood up to have a closer look at Steve, who was coming with an extra large pizza and two extra large Cokes. He did not join the crowded tables, but took an empty one next to them and ignored all of them. "We have enough space here, Steve," said Lenny, thinking of sharing Steve's pizza.

"I don't contaminate my food with words," replied Steve. "It'll give me food poisoning. You get the message, Lenny-boy." He thought it was not necessary to look at him when speaking, but he instinctively sensed Lenny sitting down.

"Here, Lenny," whispered Sandy, giving him two slices of pizza.

"Thanks, Sandy."

"Don't worry, Lenny-boy," said Steve. "I'll get you something as soon as I finish this."

"Steve, remember to buy yourself a dessert, as well," he replied.

"The administrative people of any hospital must work with a lean budget," continued Belinda. "A very tight budget. The government is always cutting their budget. Hospitals have to survive and give excellent up-to-date services. All this is very costly. Terminally ill patients occupy valuable beds. These beds could be used for other patients. Repaired and shipped out—that's how it should be. Dying patients are very costly: doctor costs, medicine costs, administrative costs, labor costs, food costs, laundry costs... Terminally ill patients are waiting to die, so let us speed up the process for them. Euthanasia is the only logical solution. We should think about our population—we're living longer. And they're not only occupying valuable beds, but draining hospitals' financial resources, too. Lean and mean budgets can't open more hospital beds."

"We should consider mercy killing legally. It's a legal issue," cried Martin. "It's killing. The issue is: should we legalize it? That's the question. Civil laws legalizing death would mean that anyone sick could be easily put to death, with a court authorization. It's like having a blank check to kill patients. That's the fear. Why? If patients were unable to give their own authorization, doctors and family members could give their consent to mercy killing. The right to die would be authorized painlessly. If someone has a life threatening gun shot injury, if a doctor believes that there's no way to keep this injured person alive, then the doctor wouldn't even be motivated to treat him. Because the outcome will obviously be death, anyway. There's no need to start the entire machine when policies dictate the result. There isn't any cure for a simple cold, so we shouldn't treat that either. Or, we should wait until a person asks for mercy killing, so he can get rid of his cold. Many poor people have worse pain than terminally ill patients. Their life condition is chronic—endless suffering at the edge of death. What's worse than living without any hope, not knowing where the next meal will come from? Should we put them to sleep too? To put it short, euthanasia can be abused easily. We're making a few people into gods.

"Our adult court system has its own Big Time Believer—the

pleasure in justice is to wield harsh consequences. The whole court system is like a hidden dictator-lover dishing out pain and suffering. Even though terminally ill patients can't suffer any consequences, our court still acts on its natural tendency by dishing out the death penalty without any crime. Legally, we're institutionalizing the killing of sickness, not people. Oh, our legal system is a self-protected institution like a sect. And it doesn't want to lose any power. And it thinks that it is scandalous to give doctors and family members such a dignified responsibility of saying who should die by mercy killing."

"Mercy killing is a social problem," Larry remarked. "Suicide is a non-natural death. And everybody knows this. You don't have to study the Bible, or any other book. Teenagers, adults and old people commit suicide for all sorts of reasons. Broken marriages, work stress, unemployment... All these suicides are violent deaths: cutting wrists, jumping off high buildings and bridges, jumping in front of a subway, blowing your head off. The people in social sciences want to explain why someone commits suicide. We want to know why too. Does he have a drug problem? An alcohol problem? A work related stress? Financial problems? A suicide attempt is the ultimate cry for help. It's used for identifying severe problems in society, our neglected problems. Too bad life is the cost. Mercy killing is like suicide. It tells us about conflicting values. Technology represents a significant human value—the promise of eternal life and the cure of all sicknesses. Yes folks, people never getting old. Human free choice is another value. The promise of eternal youth can't be fulfilled. You see the conflict—terminal patients cry for their right to death. And if we give them this right, we'll be denying the promises of technology. With technology, it's like playing lottery. You continuously throw away so much money with the hope that you'll win.

"At least this problem doesn't exist in my neighborhood. For life expectancy there is about sixty-eight. People are frozen in their own apartments. Nobody sees it. Nobody wants to know about it. This isn't suicide; it's an international issue—a minor evil compared to brutal and bloody death. For society, it's a natural death. Now, you've got a solution of how to practice natural death without assigning guilt. Young people from the slums never get old enough to be terminally ill. They're just assassinated and murdered. Most people never get old enough to complain about the their illness; they die before it. We live, without any illusion, in our slums. Life listens to our prayers, no debt to society before death." Although his mood changed frequently like a yo-yo, his temperament drove the point clearly, and it was difficult to misunderstand Larry.

"I thought you'd say something religious. Your father, isn't he a priest, Larry?" Sam remarked.

"Yes, Sam, I follow him every weekend to his service. Going to the old, the sick and the homeless to distribute food. Whenever someone dies, mostly during the night, the first person there is my father. And then some other friends come along. Giving the dead the last dignity. We clean them up, and give them clean clothes. This, the most my father can do, is the least for mankind. Giving them cleanliness, warmth, and respect. After this preparation, the police usually come to make their report, to update their list. They make sure the dead go straight to the morgue. They play it safe, no mass media. And no public awareness." His tone was monotonous, but his face showed profound reflection. "Sam, your father owns most of these run-down buildings. From a block away, these buildings cry out 'death.' I've seen more death here than in a graveyard. We have to beat the roaches and rats to the corpse. This is easy to do during the frozen winter months. In summer, my father and some other people around the block have to count heads, each morning," he replied, without any malice.

"You're always so sensitive," Sam replied. "Sensationalizing everything. There may be changes—but there's no guarantee. I'll teach my father to see things differently. But it'll be a slow process, not an overnight job. Since I put myself in the spotlight, I have a religious point of view of—" Sam abruptly stopped speaking, as he and the others traced the newcomer who pulled a chair from another table and tried to put it near Belinda. "So Virus, you're here, without the computer. This is incredible," cried Sam.

"Your mother told me you were here. So, what was it you were about to say about religion," Virus said, indirectly informing his friends that he did not want to be the object of discussion at the moment.

"I'll make it sweet and short," said Sam. "According to most religions, killing is immoral. If anyone intentionally contributes to someone else's death, he is morally guilty of killing. He commits a hideous crime. And it's a sin. Sinners go to hell. Euthanasia isn't a Christian thing to do. Christianity teaches us that life is precious. And that's it."

"You're absolutely correct Sam," cried Leslie, "it's a sticky matter, especially when we really think about a society in which there are several different cultures. In most countries, there are Christians, Hindus, Moslems, Jews, Buddhists, Mormons, Taoists, atheists, and what not. Not everyone has the same belief about death. Should we simply ignore people's cultural values and uniqueness? The answer is no. Mercy killing should never be legalized. If it were, we'd be telling people from other cultures off. To make the matter a bit gluier, hospital employees all have different religions. A Jewish doctor or nurse, for example, could refuse to participate in our ceremonial killing. What would happen if each doctor refused to do it because of religion or cultural values? What next? We'd have a special death squad going from one hospital to another. We would have lawyers and judges to do it, too. We might as well go to a country where capital punishment is practiced and hire a lynching squad for hospitals. Hospitals would be into the lynching business! Fantastic—we'd have hospitals to execute convicts sentenced with the death penalty. Oh, it only tells you how sick some surgeons are. They spend their entire lives making themselves intelligent and specialized. All this overworking of their brain drains their common sense and integrity, leaving only filth."

"I'm not too sure about the exact wording of Hippocratic medical oath which binds each medical practitioner," murmured Martin. "But one thing is for sure, it says doctors should try to save lives. If doctors assisted in killing, it would be contradictory to their codes of conduct. Doctors ought to think about their patients' opinions and trust, instead of their own self-interests, blindly following hospital policies. You wouldn't want to go to a doctor who also practices mercy killing. If he doesn't like rich patients, for example, they're gone. The problem is much more fundamental than this."

"We want doctors to be much more than people. But they're really just another Joe with a specialization. People continuously deceive themselves by thinking that medical doctors are moral agents. It's sick to think that a degree makes people moral. Doctors are just technicians like any engineer wearing a businessperson's hat, telling us smoking is dangerous for our health."

"My view is slightly different from yours," cried Sandy hesitantly, "but it's not so bad. I really don't know what to call it. Let see. It's a rational argument. It goes like this: a person may argue that patients have the freedom to have or not to have medical treatment. But it isn't only patients who have rights. Everyone does, equally. If we want to assign rights to patients, they must be able to act and to fulfill their right without any assistance from others. That means, they should be allowed to kill themselves if they want to. But with no extra help from us. It's dangerous to say that everyone has the responsibility to assist others to die. If this were true, our population would be quickly reduced. A population control through mercy killing is too cheap. Yes, I know this, too well. Egoists may argue that dying can be regulated and highly supervised by qualified personnel. Then, we must still redefine human right, choice, and responsibility. It'd be unfair to say that terminally ill patients have more rights than others. And more choices than others, and less responsibilities than others."

"Sandy, thank you, for leaving something for me to say," Martin said humbly, with a smile. "The phrase "terminally ill"—relating to an end—is a blank check. If 'terminally ill' means near death, how near is near? Is it one week? One month? Six months? One year? Twenty years? We shouldn't fool ourselves about 'near death or incurable sickness.' It is only after a person's death that we can accurately say that he or she was terminally ill or near death. If we diagnose someone as terminally ill, but we forget to kill him, and if he continues to live for another five years, and finally recovers from his illness, then we see that the chances for recovery and the development of new medications are eliminated by easy death."

"If a person has an unknown deadly contagious disease that could wipe out a few billion people, should we put that person to death, so we can save humanity? If he doesn't want to die? What should we do? Any sensible person would roast him like a chicken," Belinda began. "But let us change the situation a little. Now, without knowing it, this fellow has infected one billion people including himself. But he can help discover the cure for this contagious disease. Unfortunately, he demands to die because he is in a lot of pain. Should we respect his free choice? You wouldn't. But, we should. The point is, everyone should be given a free choice regardless of his situation. This means we shouldn't allow a fictitious situation to affect our judgments."

"Most people who have experienced an accident, divorce, or loss of a loved one, have, at some time in their life, said to themselves or close friends that they wish they were dead," Martin put in. "So should a doctor act quickly on that person's verbal request? Why not? He has the right to put those buggers to death. They said themselves, they wanted to die. We can't say that these people aren't rational. The problem is not so much about terminally illness and old age—it's about losing hope."

"The question about mercy killing is, would you do it?" interrupted Sandy. "Would you pull the plug out from your loved ones? Think about the psychological problems that may arise from your active contribution to killing! We always want someone else to do our dirty jobs! Only recently we've been studying the long-term effects on those who pulled the plug because their job had demanded it. I say, this has unforeseeable consequences. And they're immeasurable! It's nice to speak about the suffering of patients. But what about the people who had to do the pulling!"

"I'm not a weakling!" Steve suddenly cried, food in his mouth. "I'll pull it, all the plugs away from everyone, if you wish.

You all sound like mindless wimps who have missed the issue. Meatball with euthanasia! You're crying out like little children but there'll be over eight billion people in the world in a few years. We're worried about having enough food for everyone; living space for everyone. Look, in certain countries, they have baby regulations. Each family can have only one child. We always find it easier to regulate birth. But, we should seek ways to speed up death. Most westerners abandon their parents, anyway. To hell with guilt and bad conscience! After sixty-five years of enjoying the earth and life, they should be put to death. I'd be the first one to surrender my parents, but they still have another fifteen years to go. It's nice and crunchy when you put your teeth in cold pizza.

"If we really want to go forward in this world, there's only one solution to most problems. First and foremost is, each family should have only one child. And each family should be four individuals—two separate pairs. Two mothers and two fathers. Both parents have to work to support a child. Neither of them has sufficient time to be with their child. Two pairs of married couples should get together and plan for a single child. It'd be like applying for a car loan. They'd have to submit a detailed application contract, covering all relevant points. Like who would conceive the child, and so on. When our childbearing board accepted a four-family's application-contract for having a child, then, and only then, a single father could impregnate one of the members. The point is quality of life for the child without being dependent on any government support. Then, and only then, could we fully appreciate our own lives. I'll let someone else continue. This really makes me hungry."

"Steve doesn't want utopia. But to bring a child into the world must be well thought of beforehand. Perhaps he's right," said Virus, glancing at Steve, who was going to the front counter to order some more food. "In this way, one can really feel euthanasia in the blood. Old people can perform valuable functions and services in society. For instance, we can request that they retire from the work force at the age of sixty. Retirement should be after so many years of services, not only at a certain age. Or after thirty years of service, bang! Retirement. Nonetheless, from that age onward until death, they can occupy a position in the military. They can defend our country and protect our economic interests all around the world. We can send them whenever and wherever there are problems and conflicts in the world as warriors and peace officers. The benefits would be immeasurable. We'd save the young men and women from needless death, and from bad faith. I'm sounding like Lenny now. They should be given an opportunity to enjoy their adult life fully. After we've done this, we can address the issue of easygoing death."

"Is that all? If it is," remarked Larry, "we should send your father, head of Bishop International Private Investigations! An over-wealthy roasted pig. We'll change his profession, so that other people can become as fat as he is! Oh yeah, we should also take away his wealth. Virus, you may have some of it, if you like. And we shouldn't forget Sam's old man! He's practicing slow killing, and nobody's complaining. And yet you'll find young people in this world, struggling to protect their lives. Nothing will stop that, but adults can chip in. You may think that I'm against richness. No, I'm not. But no honest person gets fat without bending the laws. And if they're caught, they get a tap on their hand—naughty boys, for being careless."

"Look at western businesses. They're lobbying international humanitarian organizations to support them. These charities sit on our sentiment like parasites, telling everybody to ban third world countries' products, because these countries use child labor. These businesses just don't want any competition. Humanitarian organizations are speaking about the rights of children. They cry out, 'children have rights!' The right to have an education only. Filthy lies to turn poor children into good capitalists. And product-dependent consumers. It's not honest, but treacherous! Most of these children don't have fathers. They have to support their families. Their younger brothers and sisters depend on them. The alternative is a worse condemnation. If you take them out of the work force, how will they afford to go to school? Buy books? Get food? Get clothing? Taking them away from work puts them in the street, where they can die much quicker. These stinky organizations should be abolished. They never start with preparing the infrastructure of a family before they prevent children from working. The basic survival needs come first. Why spend money on children who don't have any physical or psychological security in their environment? Give them free schooling, free books, free medical services. And pocket money to spend. Then, an education will attract them like flies. But no, western companies engineer this trend through humanitarian clubs, so they drive away competing companies in third world countries from the western market. These clubs are flaunting a handful of kids from poor countries around the world. Paying them, well behind the scenes, to be martyrs against child labor. And they're telling us to boycott those companies that use child labor. Nobody ever tells us that these kids would kill for a job. They don't have to prostitute themselves to western visitors. They don't have to join a gang. Sell drugs. Or steal. Or sleep in the street. Boycotting these companies starves millions of half-dead people."

"Let's get our facts straight. Life expectancy in those countries is very low. Most adults are either sick from hopelessness, drugs or illness. In most cases, a mother is left alone with a handful of kids. She fights against her own heart—the reality is, some of her kids may die before adulthood. But the one who is working has a greater chance to survive. And the younger ones' chances to live are improved. Why should we go so far? It's happening right here, in lower town. Sociologists and social workers came to study delinquent behavior in our neighborhood. After a few years or so, they've given kids baseballs, basketballs, and a run-down shack with a handful of ping-pong tables, not books. This should keep them away from the streets."

"These jerks also go to underdeveloped countries without having a clue about the culture. And they give every resident a toilet bucket. A toilet bucket, to shit in! Just because they don't want to get it on their shoes. They never stop crying out for more funds, in the name of their hygiene program. These charitable organizations are the biggest polluters in poor countries. Giving away everything in plastic and metal containers. And these poor people don't have garbage dumps like us. They use the rivers and farmlands to throw away these containers. It'd take them about fifty years to clean up all this pollution. The biggest danger is pollution. And they're dying because of donors' pollution. I'm not finished yet!"

"You know why they want children to go to school. It's because western businesses are cultivating a whole generation of new consumers. Their plastic wrapped customers! Now, they're not having many business deals in poor countries. The reason is simple. Most people are illiterate. They can't read what is displayed on a store's shelves. For us, when we see a bottle with a fat and chubby baby on the label, we know it contains food products for baby. But the majority of illiterate people in poor countries think it contains babies' meat. For the rich boys and girls here, let your parents wear your hearts in their business-decisions. Ours already have theirs on."

"You're going to school, Larry!" replied Sandy. "And yet, you deny that right to everyone. I really don't understand you. We have to start somewhere. The most obvious place is human health and education."

"Very nice speech. Let's start with the entire family, Sandy. And then school. But no! They want to cripple families to have economic globalization. Can't you get it? It's quite simple. A single mother with three children, perhaps, two of them are still babies. And they're still tied to her apron. She can't work. If the older one works, it is not only for himself, but to assist his mother too. It's a sacrifice. It's noble. In our fat society, it rarely exists."

"Perhaps, you're correct, Larry. The lesser evil is the biggest monster," she answered. "But don't get me wrong! I'm talking about the principle of everyone having an equal and fair chance to go to school. But you're talking about the entire context. And it tells us to undress our nice principle."

The Chair

"Aren't we going to hear about Middledale Technical College, Belinda? I'm planning to go there next year," asked Sam.

"It's a long story. It all started in my first semester when they introduced bilingualism to attract students," replied Belinda.

"It's still your first semester at college," said Virus. "Well, I might as well check the computer out." Virus left the group.

"Honestly, I don't think my baby pizza is ready for this stuff," cried Steve. "You see Juliane, over there? Her back is toward us. They're talking about when two atoms will make a happy marriage. That's not all. They're peeling over sex too. It's real scientific. Like how many upward strokes would make an enjoyable and satisfying sexual intercourse between both partners. Throwing in orgasms and ejaculations into the hot pot, as well." He passed a small Coke and fries to Lenny, and hurried to the table near the stairs.

"That's Steve for you," said Belinda. "Since everybody else wants to hear about Middledale, then, this is how it goes. Middledale teaches everything in two official languages: English and Business Language. This school is completely bilingual—fifty-fifty." She looked around the noiseless table. "But bilingualism means one thing for students and another thing for teachers. For students, it means separate classes. But for teachers, bilingualism is about time. Time is important and has priority. Week one is a unit of time. The teacher should be teaching in English. Week two is another unit of time. He will be teaching in Business Language. Each unit of time must be equal: week one equals two hours; week two equals two hours. If each unit of time is unequal, it's not fifty-fifty. Week one and week two must rotate like Newton's mass until the course is finished."

"Oh! This is fantastic—I love it. I can always miss week two lectures without missing anything. Oh, I can sleep in," cried Sam.

"Get a hold of yourself, Sam! It's not a train, or an airport, where you hear the same message repeated in two different languages—once in English, and then in Business Language.

Teachers' bilingualism as fifty-fifty has a new meaning. It's related to time without repeating the same message in another language. You don't want to make them parrots, do you?"

"The trouble is, all theories, important concepts, formulae, interpretations, are presented in Business Language. In week one, we had to do exercises and experiments from week two lectures. Even the exam is in Business Language—nothing about week one. Some kind of fifty-fifty. No justice! Poetry, philosophy, arts, religion, everything is given in only Business Language."

"Perfect bilingualism equals a fifty-fifty distribution of both semantic and syntactic division. Yes sir, the same gift with a different package. A model of bilingualism should be based on a hundred/hundred distribution of information without affecting the dignity, sensitivity, and responsibility of any teacher. What do you say to this, Sam?"

"Now you're talking nonsense! Where did you learn arithmetic? Bilingualism is like an object, an apple. If we divide an apple into two equal pieces, we'll have two halves. Each piece is fifty percent. Yahoo, fifty-fifty! Now, what are you doing? Are you hungry?"

"No Sam, I'm not hungry. By chance, I have two apples in my bag. Here, have one. And one for me. No, don't eat it! Thanks. You cut your apple into equal halves. And I'll cut mine. Here, you can give me a half of your apple. Thank you. I'll give you half of mine. Do you have a whole apple?"

"Do I have a whole apple? Of course I do!"

"You have two halves, and I have two. You have a whole apple, and I have one. Bilingualism is like the two apples, which we've just divided. English equals one hundred percent like your whole apple. And Business Language is one hundred too, my apple. Now, we've two hundred percent. We can't divide a language into fifty-fifty. Do you think we should call English a half language? I'd really like to see how you could write and speak a half language. Now, Sam—in week one, English equals one hundred percent. In week two, Business Language equals another hundred percent. Week one plus week two equals four hours of class time. Divide four by two gives us two hours of course time. Two hours is a fifty-fifty time split of a hundred/hundred information distribution in English and Business Language."

"I get it, Belinda. Time is a fifty-fifty. But teaching is a hundred/hundred in both languages. Can I eat the apple now? It'd have been something, if you'd said that English is a banana. And Business Language is a nice juicy orange."

"I still don't understand your rambling about Business Language!" cried Sandy. "I understand something about English. If you're saying bilingualism is the solution for the generation gap, it's a neat way of putting it. In this way adults and young adults could understand each other."

"German, French, Spanish, and the likes of them, don't attract newcomers," Belinda said. "People are not interested in learning these languages. They're too complicated. People don't have the time to enjoy classical forms anymore. We don't need a guru to tell us that these languages are burning themselves out of existence. They have to be simplified a lot. Make them easier to learn. You can't sell a dead language to living people. Of course, we'll have only native speakers of Business Language today. Parents and governments' martial laws enforce these dead-end languages for children. If you gave children a choice of languages, nothing would stop them—parents and grandparents would be reduced to artifacts. So Proud City's language has to be integrated into all languages."

"All this business stuff," interrupted Sandy, "business having its own proper language, isn't totally hogwash. A teacher has to sell everything. To attract customers, to hold customers' interest. Show them the business aspect of literature, history, philosophy, art. Each course has a financial benefit for students. Here we go again, arts versus sciences, business versus poetry. And the artists are losing the life-influences to technology. It's more like westerners speaking Business Language and third world countries howling in English." Everyone looked at Lenny for a reply. He stared back at them for a moment without answering.

"Ah, my stomach! My stomach!" cried Lenny. He held his

stomach with both hands, and his head was about to touch the table before him. "You know it by now!" replied Lenny. "That's Business Language. It's the attitude-man reality today. It's rhetoric from which people infer attitudes as positive or negative; it evokes people's attitudes. Just like how you thought I was in pain. I should tell you something about the trend of applied knowledge. All educational institutions want to be in business, to attract the best students. Professors have to sell their recipe to students. Each of them has to carry a crystal ball and to sell his subject. They have to explain to each student why he's learning a poem, how it could be used during a business lunch to impress your colleagues. To show other businesspeople that you know other things besides business."

"You stinky son of a dog! Fooling everyone in here. How could you do it to us?" Sam asked angrily. Everyone smiled at Sam as though nothing had happened.

Forks and Spoons

"In that case, I'll go to the next table," replied Lenny, moving toward an empty table near the window.

Sandy and Larry quickly followed and joined Lenny. "Excuse me, I can wait. But my bladder can't," murmured Lenny. He headed downstairs to the toilet. *You have to be a metaphysical being to live two different sets of reality, an attitude-man and me. You always have to be ten thousand times more alert than anyone else is. Oh, it's so fatiguing,* he thought, washing his face with warm water until he felt regenerated. After exchanging a few words with Virus in the basement, he went straight to the counter and ordered an extra large Coke. To his surprise, when he turned around he noticed that Virus was upstairs, sitting in his spot. *He moves very quickly, even when he's not connected to his computer,* thought Lenny. He walked slowly, as though he was attempting to prevent the uncontrollable waves in his glass, and then drifted near Virus without interfering with the harmony at his table.

"Applying censorship to our own comedy and tragedy," said

Virus, summarizing their present chattering.

"That's sweet and nice for you to say! Who in their right mind can censor politicians? Everyone obviously knows that they're overpaid for their function," complained Larry. "We give them free luxurious houses, all expenses paid, authority, power—all this to screw us up some more. We make them like gods, so they can return the favor by making us more meaningless and insignificant. Look at our brown nose!"

"I see your point, Larry. If they love their country so much, they should perform their function for the same salary as any unskilled laborer," added Sandy.

"We even allow these lame ducks to occupy the highest office in a country—without any job experience. No formal training. It's amazing, what people can do. We make them heroes. And what's more, they turn their backs on all their pre-election promises. They'd throw the keys away if some ordinary person had told those treacherous and deceptive lies!" said Larry.

"Cool it, Larry. It's getting to you," Sandy murmured calmly. Her comment could not quench a deep flame.

"Those rotten oversized public parasites get away with the most vicious and reckless crimes against humanity! It takes only one of them to cripple an entire nation. All history books should be condemned to the flame for being so kind to those worthless hogs. Winners always write history, not losers. What's worse, all kids must learn about these bloated figures at school as though they were saints. You don't find history books telling us how many lies and promises weren't kept. How many homeless people starved during their time in office. No, we're ashamed to tell the truth. We can't swallow it whole. We've been overfed with trash for too long; it's our reality. We don't want others to know about the dirt of our government. We want to hide ourselves with icons. This feeling of helplessness, I say, it's gone too far without any check. Yes, you Virus! You think I'm mad! I should be censored! Don't you? We're supposed to be unfit for anything else other than chasing drugs until they catch us. We're victims of teenage crises, running after sex and bottles, searching for idols, stealing and robbing. To put it nice and short for you, we're society's outcasts, potential delinquents before becoming terrifying and horrible criminals. We're just waiting to be hardened some more, so we can take up our career as criminals. Nobody can think anymore! Can't you see, we're the world? They're corrupted. We can control these old bags. They only accumulate security and cheap pride. Tell me, Lenny, am I an idiot? I don't see things like Virus," cried Larry. Everyone was silent and glanced at each other. Even Virus was choked.

"Today, I gave them their own book—the book of the attitude-man's reality," said Lenny, breaking the silence that hung over the table. "An ontology, with no real entities. You may call it lying. But, I say, it's playing without losing. It couldn't be anything less than logical. Deducing one attitude from another without any contradiction. Principal, school psychologist, and all, taking an image as representing reality. It's their reality… Well then, they can chew on that for a while. It's strange, how people look for meaning and joyfully give meaning to just rambling. We believe that everything means something else, so we don't trust ourselves anymore. Our natural tendency to infer an image from spoken words makes us image-makers. Our educators inferred that I was talking about myself. But speaking their Business Language isn't expected from me. Of course, we have an advantage."

"Is this going to be our new reality?" remarked Sandy. "Imitating gruesome images of lies and broken promises! Praising lies as our norms! Stuck in our parents' quicksand. The more effort we put into it, the deeper we are driven."

"Why not start with yourself, first," commented Virus.

"Oh, how profound," objected Sandy. "I've finished with myself. So who's next, you? Should I rework myself until I crack? Sometimes I ask myself, what are human beings for? We're like matryoshka dolls, with an empty core and an over-blown body. As Lenny would say, an attitude-person without any real substance. And Chuck calls it the image-man existence—a way of living without any bones. A rational pig becomes so rational it leaves nothing to be rational about. For Juliane, a bundle of atoms repairing unhappy marriages. We're only greedy carnivores eating ourselves away. The head is already gone. How about the next feast? Only insignificant beings seek out self-definition? And renewal of self-identity? We do it as though we're not sure whether or not we really exist."

"How about self-amusing animals? Aren't we the only creatures that feed on self-amusement?" Virus whispered softly, surprising everyone.

"Piss on all these definitions of ourselves!" said Larry. "Nobody will define me out of existence. I don't have to kick myself in the ass to assure myself that I'm here! And here to stay! I don't have anything to prove to a mouse or a rambling monkey! I don't need anybody to explain who Larry is! Just go to lower town, if you want to learn how people live with nothing. You'll see how people recycle food from nothing!"

"I really don't know which war you're fighting, Larry," interrupted Sandy. "You're just wasting your anger, picking on Virus. You haven't heard a word he said. Nobody is reinventing human beings. And nobody is placing things on an ivory tower. But to have a clear view of human beings, let's look at amusement."

"All the same, can't you get it? We're here. What is it, Sandy? You want to know more about the graveyard, so you can find out about my life. You want to look at fossils to explain the poor who are alive right now. All you have to do is open your eyes! Look around you! I bet you'll have more answers than questions."

"Listen Larry, I don't know what's eating you. Every one of us has a life. It's real like a rock; and yet, weak like a glass. We could be shattered anytime," cried Virus. "Changing the entire window would give people a new way of looking at themselves."

"Here again, you're shooting your mouth off. The church fails to change people. You're more than naïve to think you can bend an old tree without breaking it. I say, you must live now to change here. You have another five hundred years to live, but I don't. Let us use our technology to organize ourselves. And start with little things. That's the most sensible way," cried Larry.

"Larry, there are little Proud Cities all around the world," said

Lenny. "Young people realize they have something to say and do in this order. Until now, we've been passively contributing to where we are. Without cooperating with our own parents, their jobs and daily activities, we just can't make any significant progress. Let our parents start to take us more seriously. We must work with them, not against them, work together as if there's no end. They're going to listen to their children, about morality, ecology, and employment… Kids our age used to take parents as their sparring partners. Confrontations were our path, not partnership. We often allowed our parents to worry about our future. They became grey, because of our developmental stages. We ignored our responsibilities. If we behave like babies, parents have to be ruthless to protect our future. Let life be our age. Let's help our parents. Let us be on their side, for once."

"Lenny, I've always had some respect for you. Mostly because of your cunning. But now, I don't know who is speaking. So, what should I tell my father? Dad, come on, let's go to another block. Some more empty houses down the street cry out for us. Let's go see how spacious their fridge is. How huge the cupboards are. Let's go greet their sweet loving little animals on the sofa, behind the stove, on the carpet. Let's count the running noses, today! Measuring their crying on a Richter scale. Dad, go give them the word of God. Tell them the truth. 'You've chosen your own life with your own hand. Man and God are your witnesses. Now, perish! You worthless hogs—in both Worlds!' Parasites can't pass the Golden Gate, without passing the human world with a dignified and noble life."

"Larry, you can do things. Say things without telling the truth, but without lying. You remember the attitude-man's reality," Lenny murmured.

"What do you mean, Lenny? I can help them without helping them—this is pure nonsense!"

"I think Lenny is right. They need food and clothing to survive. But you give them hope, integrity, respect, caring, and kindness," interrupted Sandy.

"It's clear, you're helping them without helping them. But

they're helping you to help them, like now. We're helping you to help them without helping you," said Lenny.

"Is this supposed to be amusing? But I get your drift. But your expensive sport car, Virus, would surely make a lot of poor people..." Larry began.

"You think people have an on/off button. Switching them on/off whenever you like," Sandy cried sarcastically.

"No need for this, Sandy. I can manage for myself," said Virus. He knew very well that Larry's presence had affected his concentration, but still tried to respond. "Human beings can be nothing more than a self-amusing lot," said Virus. "You may wonder what this means. A self-amusing creature has two sides—comedy and tragedy. Man intentionally creates these two attributes, because he wants to hide his own weaknesses. Don't get me wrong, I'm not saying it's bad to hide oneself. But it's terrifying, not admitting our own weaknesses as a fact. All human beings are helpless. Larry, you're absolutely correct to think that I'm off beat from the orchestra. But the orchestra is playing a different tune.

"As I said, comedy and tragedy have evolved in human beings. Let us face it squarely. Our ancestors, primitive man, observed accidents in nature—animals being struck by a sharp branch, falling off a cliff, falling into holes, injuring themselves fighting, and what not. They imitated these tragic events. Throwing rocks and sharp sticks at their food, chasing their food off cliffs. They reused tragedy to overwhelm other creatures."

"Meanwhile the sick and old members of the tribe made paintings in caves. Why? Because they were left behind, all along, and had nothing else to do for food but be the entertainers of the tribe. All this tells us how human beings hide their weaknesses. Our work hides and protects our meaninglessness. Of course, this is a kind of self-amusement, creating an image-identity for others to perceive. That's how comedy becomes inherent in man."

"The tragedy of adopting animals' techniques for survival—the hunt—they washed down with the cave philosophy. They rewarded the tragedy with comedy. Since then, the imitation of the cave has never left us. It'd be terrible to think that hunters don't have any hope before hitting the terrain. We, as a matter of fact, still have the hunting hope. It lives in us. The kill stays in us. Even our language originated from copying natural events. Imitation furnished our ancestors with a language. And this is all we do with our languages nowadays."

"Really, Virus," said Sandy.

"When going for a hunt, Sandy, one hunter snorted to others. *Pig* is the first verbal sign. Members arrived at the cave, and then repeated their hunting experience with grunts, physical movements, queer sounds and motions to represent getting the fallen prey. Language started from imitation and remained with it. And the imitation in the cave was nothing more than entertainment."

"Abstract thinking and casual talking about our language are much more than imitation, Virus," remarked Sandy.

"Human beings are self-amusing-beings. People laugh at their own follies, or someone else's mishaps. The tragedy is about our survival techniques coming from our ancestors and staying with us."

"Virus, I don't find it funny! I'm not amusing myself, a bit!" cried Larry. "What do you expect us to do? You want us to give people something else to entertain themselves with? No! You take us for banana brains! Instead of doing something, hard and solid, and here and now, you must look in the jungle for trees! How can you tell us that? Some people look at our situation with a disguised smile on their face. And then cry out, pity! It isn't funny! Three percent of them amuse themselves while ninety-seven percent of the population submit themselves to highbrow irresponsibility. If this is what you're saying, I don't want it. You don't live in lower town. Man as comedy/tragedy, won't roll!"

"Hold yourself, Larry! You're smoking yourself up, just because you want to," cried Virus. "Can't you see, a whole lot of people want to be someone else's tool and technology. They want to be tragic heroes and heroines. Look at yourself! All you do is count empty houses rather than trying to change things. No, you want handouts from rich people to change your condition. You must carry your weight, too."

"Larry, we're attitude-people," cried Lenny. "Aren't we, Larry?"

Larry was calmed for a moment. "Virus, even though you may disagree, you can't take Christianity away from people," he replied.

"Of course, Larry, You're surely correct. Adam and Eve were both intelligent. And redundant in their day-to-day life, too. They were searching for true amusement. All the other trees and animals couldn't have satisfied their longing for new experiences and discoveries. Till the birth of comedy and tragedy in the Garden of Eden struck us. With the image of God as a comical figure and with a monocular eye, He was becoming tired of continuously controlling Adam and Eve. He allowed boredom to crawl into creation. Perhaps, Adam and Eve were perfected with boredom and loneliness. They couldn't entertain the Creator anymore. So, He ordained the forbidden tree to take some drastic initiatives to persuade those two mindless square creatures. Bang, tragedy was born. Everyone, including God—the first originator of comedy—wanted to escape the assembly line. Tragedy was born like an unmovable shadow in our life.

"I think, Larry, your question is about important and smart stuff. But, imitation is natural in human beings. Look at us—we're masters of cloning, altering the environment to fulfill our comedy. People are cloning themselves without making any commitment towards their children's needs and wants. And we even train pets to understand our motives. Yes, primates couldn't break away from man's invisible claws; we're stringing up nature together like a brass monkey. Isn't it part of our comedy, wanting to snuggle everything in a tight net? In our one-eyed net, everything must fit. Then we cry out, we see it all. If a rock could imitate, we'd say it were rational. It'd be foolish to think that cats and dogs don't dream. We allow them to sleep next to us. So, they have to dream if they truly want to be man's companion. Imitating is like having a reproduction machine in our head. We want and long for copies. We experience only copies of our own dream in a jungle of images. Image-makers too, are what we call rational animals.

Those animals that can't have any image of us, we call them the beasts. When we realize our own tragedy, we secretly hide ourselves behind comedy. Some pieces of our comedy have been neglected in our world of images, so tragedy creeps in the middle of the night like a toothless hog to show how talented human beings are at cruelty. This should satisfy you, Larry. There're countless examples of human self-created tragedy. Any thing or person that is dissimilar is condemned to the flame."

"Well, Virus. You're saying a lot of things," Sandy replied. "To get you straight, you're saying because man wants and continuously seeks comedy, tragedy creeps in. But, we praise the results. And we minimize the consequences. These consequences are tomorrow's poison."

"Our government secretly pays scientists to study cloning with our money," cried Larry. "It obviously wants something out of it. Trying to convince the public that genetically engineered foods is necessary. We're forced to swallow it. Cloning animals, making animals that grow human parts—isn't for the sake of knowledge, but of demoralizing the starving half of our population some more. Cloning humans tells the poor that a copy is much preferable. The comedy is that we'll be marrying pigs, sheep, cows… You won't be surprised when we legally take pigs and chimps for our sexual partners, because we've given up on making ourselves human. The big show begins when we mistakenly eat pigs with human organs. Eating our own babies would be a tragedy. Businesses and governments are cloning us in a less radical way. Telling us how to think, what to eat, when to eat what, what to wear. All these whatty-whatties make us their entertainers. We make ourselves dummies, lifeless, and disgusting. We're unworthy to hide behind common sense. Comedy and tragedy are like Lenny's attitude-person reality. Lenny is enjoying all the fun while he adds to the tragic state of the world. If we don't organize ourselves soon with a grain of common sense, we'll never be able to discard our predecessor's images. I'm not hitting knowledge. Gaining knowledge is great. But, manipulating our partial understanding of nature for profit is very dangerous. It's too risky and reckless, especially when all the consequences remain hidden from us. My friend, we can do what we can do to change what's changeable. Remember, we belong to this nature. So, we must change ourselves. Our wants and our desires first. Help our parents to see our world transcending with life."

"I've got to run over to Chuck's place," said Virus, growing tired of the argument. He stood up.

"Me too," cried Lenny.

"It's nine already. I might as well come along," said Sandy. The trio left Larry alone at the table with his thoughts.

The Kitchen

"Here we are," Virus cried as he pulled in near the curb in front of Chuck's house. The drive was fast—seven minutes, including finding the car in the hive.

"Thanks," said Sandy, "I'm going, it's not so far from here. Just a few houses down the road." Lenny stood near Virus as they watched Sandy quickly widen the darkness between them. They went up to Chuck's house. The light was on in the living room and in Chuck's room. Both Chuck and Doris answered the door as soon as the bell rang.

"Hello guys, I thought you wouldn't come," Chuck cried, delighted, as they entered and Doris closed the door behind them. The television was running without anyone admiring the frames.

"Yes, we're here!" replied Virus, giving Chuck a look as though he was in a hurry.

"Self-amused beings, we are! Aren't we?" Lenny commented, as he looked at Virus for a way to break the ice.

"No, some people's comedy is a third person's tragedy," he corrected.

"Yes, I see," interjected Chuck. "I better get the disk before we have a tragedy."

"Aren't you going to offer your friends something?" Doris reminded Chuck.

"No thanks! I have to run, before the restaurant closes. It might take some time to test this program," answered Virus politely. Chuck hurried upstairs for the disk while they waited in the living room.

"You boys should get something to drink," Doris insisted, and headed to the kitchen to search for some glasses.

"No, thanks anyway," they replied.

"Here you go," Chuck said, placing the disk in Virus' hand.

Virus examined the disk. "We'll have the answer soon," he said as he left. Virus had already calculated how to use the disk from its weight alone.

Doris returned to the living room and keenly watched Chuck and Lenny as they mounted the stairs. She felt content and proud in a situation that called for her caring duties as a mother. She definitely knew where her son was tonight. She nodded her head and then returned to the overworked television.

"Be careful, I've just cleaned up!" instructed Chuck, giving the warning before reaching for the knob. Lenny kept his eyes on his feet and moved more gracefully than a puppet. The air holes in his shoes kept his sanity and sensibility alerted. He was much more occupied with how to say sorry without doing it.

"Look Chuck, even if I felt like mud for last night, I'm not sorry for anything. Only feeling sorryish. This doesn't give you the right to think I'm a rotten low-down sucker on sale. You get it all wrong, if you think I'm an object without a heart. I don't want your sentiment, either. Keep it for yourself. You get it. Don't you?" He glanced at Chuck to see whether or not he got the drift. Lenny counted to five, waiting for a reply. Chuck walked around, rearranging objects. He went to his desk. Lenny knew something was coming or else there would be an explosion.

"Me too," murmured Chuck, "I couldn't sleep all night. How can anyone swallow the inevitable conclusion? You didn't do much to help it. Barking your head off in the restaurant! How could you do that, Lenny? Does it really matter, if she sees someone? I really don't know." He walked around the room without breaking any glitter on the floor, thinking that someone had to show that there was a sense of responsibility in the world.

"What does Virus mean about getting the answer soon," interrupted Lenny, knowing very well that Virus would enter into someone else's database without permission.

"It's complicated. With the disk, you get access to any computer's database. He can find out if my mom has really been at work. I tried it out last night. It didn't work." Chuck felt that he should have been the first person to have access to the data. "He's also getting his dad's private detective agency to do an investigation."

"You are scared, aren't you?" asked Lenny. He looked at Chuck; it was obvious enough that they were sitting on a shaky fence that wobbled with the breeze. They checked each other out malevolently and realized that the only way out would be to do something drastic and vicious. "Virus surely knows his way around the system," whispered Lenny.

The knocking at the door took them by surprise. Jackie forced her head in. "Hello, see you all, have a good night," she said as her body magnetically pulled the door closed. They kept their freedom under control until the car started, and then rushed downstairs. Doris drifted away from the front door and followed them to the kitchen.

"We're starving!" cried Chuck.

"A horse wouldn't be enough," commented Lenny, as he slipped a twenty-dollar note into Chuck's hand.

"What can we have for twenty dollars?" cried Chuck.

"She'll be going shopping tomorrow—let's see," said Doris, closing the half-empty fridge. She examined the fridge door, a bulletin board with magnetic buttons. "Here, we go, a take-out pizza place, with free delivery. Tell me what you want," she asked, for ordering out was taken much more seriously with an adult's voice on the phone. She phoned and then turned the house's front light on.

Within ten minutes the doorbell rang. "I bet you can't get them any faster," praised Chuck. The three of them went to answer the door, as Chuck gave Doris the money to pay for the pizza. Instead, Chuck saw some more of his friends at the door. "I didn't know you made house calls too!" Chuck cried, surprised.

"Belinda saw the front light on when she was coming to my place," said Sandy. "Belinda is staying over for the night." She looked at Doris and Lenny for approval.

"Come on in!" cried Doris naturally, opening the door wider to allow the guests. She closed the door after them and tagged along to the kitchen, seeing everyone looking at the empty fridge for something quick to drink. Doris did not mind having them over, and prepared the table. "We're having pizza, the best in Proud City," she remarked. They remained seated, sizing each other up until the doorbell rang again. This time, it was the delivery boy.

"I'll get it," Doris said, leaving them seated as she hurried to the door. She looked at the bill in her hand and the young man in front of her. "Keep the change!" she said. It was less than two dollars.

"Thank you!" cried the young man happily.

Doris put the warm, flat box on the table. They opened it before the vapor had a chance to touch the ceiling and served themselves. Doris went to the basement for a huge bottle of Coke and gave everyone a glassful. It was imperative for her to grab a piece before it was all gone. She took one and sat awkwardly near Sandy.

"Only the best!" she remarked.

"Oh yes, they really know how to cook for a group of people. It really has a group taste," answered Sandy. "You must have known we were coming over to help you eat all this pizza."

"No, it wasn't me, Chuck bought it," she replied.

"Who cares! If you keep on yapping like this, all the taste will disappear," interrupted Lenny. He did not want Chuck to say anything about the essay money.

It did not take long before they devoured the entire pizza. Belinda looked at the empty box. "Human history is infested with everything to have and nothing to share," she said abruptly, changing the silent subject around the table. She knew that Lenny's mother had studied history without being able to complete her studies at the university.

"They carved out western history from the Neolithic age on a piece of baked clay the size of your palm. The worst part is, we still practice it today. We still live like Mesopotamians in 2100 BC without King Hammurabi's laws," said Doris, pleased with herself, for certain cues could trigger precious fragments of knowledge. "Slavery is the penalty for lying and abusing one's position. Stealing and bearing false charges against others could carry the death penalty. Yes, the Hammurabian laws penalized negligence, excess richness and human exploitation. Oh, I can go on forever." Everyone was taken in but Lenny, who was bitterly angry with his mother for taking an attitude-reality among his friends.

"I didn't know you ever went to school. Speaking of historians, they're a bunch of gravediggers, living for the rotten past, not for the future. They should all be burnt like wretched witches. Why are you digging up graves for useless junk?" cried Lenny, hiding his joy in his remark.

"Nothing has really changed, only our techniques. We haven't made any progress in friendship, love, caring, trust, freedom," cried Doris, attempting to apologize for her son's rudeness. She would remain here to protect her son's silliness some more until everyone forgot why she was being so kind to him. She struggled again to put the pieces together. "The Paleolithic family transformed to the Neolithic family, it took only three thousand years. In less than two hundred years, what do we have now, the single family? Tomorrow, what will it be? I say, the famine family."

"Mom, you're out of touch. Your night job is mixing you up. Famine means starvation and hunger. Not family!" He knew his mother; she would not reply. She smiled at him; he looked bad among his friends. She had never seen her son in this manner, for they never had time to speak to each other.

"Lenny, your mother doesn't want to hurt your feelings," said Belinda, taking a reckless route into the family dispute, "but she's absolutely right, by saying famine family."

"Stop! Right now," cried Lenny angrily. "The corporate family is the answer! Can't you see beyond your belly? What's the matter with you people? In this world, each organization breeds it own employees. Giving them a huge building to live in. Having a special doctor to check them up. Having private teachers to teach their children. Companies are running their own daycares for workers. They even have their own grocery stores, banks, and what not. There's no need to step out of a company's living quarters. That's it, the answer to life with no more family problems, no drug problems, nothing. Everyone would have a good night's sleep, just to be on par the next morning for work. Everybody would know each other, playing together, and thinking alike. Oh, yeah, all living for one thing, the corporation." He paused for a while, rechecking his abruptness. He did not want to frighten Belinda, but to put some sense into his mother. Belinda had denied him the only chance he had so far. "I only want to stop you, not to scare anybody."

"You want to stop me. So, you have! With your collective family with no diversity," cried Belinda. She recognized that Doris was uncomfortable with their way of speaking, so she came to a calculated stop.

Sandy stared at Chuck. The non-verbal message was clear—everything was under control. She knew that nothing could stop Belinda from continuing to deliver her comments.

"Look at what we're doing to ourselves, Lenny. Nothing romantic, I say. Even famine family is near. I believe it's already here, but hidden. Our body is polluted with every chemical substance that exists—contaminated food, air, drinking water. To put it short and sweet, our body is a chemical dump. It's a reservoir, a rotten storage tank. And with electro-smog eating us up, the gene-baby isn't far away. The human body is useless to carry and to bear children. It can't carry a healthy baby anymore. It can only manufacture deformed worms. Our way of life echoes back to us, Ooh, George and Mary! I'm terribly sorry, you're not allowed to have any children. Sorry folks, your body can only create monsters, nowadays. Like how mentally retarded people and AIDS patients aren't allowed to have children, it'll be like that. Even young couple will be horrified with fear by what faces them ahead. The horror of their own creation will be greater than any nightmare. We already have the famine family. People want children, but too bad, you can't have them. This isn't so bad. But, what's next? The gene-babies will pour into society like acid rain. Government offices will control the supply and demand equilibrium to meet market requirements. We'll need two hundred laborers. Five thousand computer programmers. The government will take over reproduction and give training programs to workers."

"The famine family is about hungry people wanting to test the functioning of their own bodies, using the output of their own natural reproductive organs to hide their problems. The famine family will be compensated royally. Yeah, free services will be given for stuffed pets. We'll make them our permanent companions. And even if we get the opportunity to have a live one, we'll mold her to be like the stuffed one. Well, I should confess, our generation is still safe. But if we don't do something now, who will?"

"Look at Lenny's Mom, she spends her life on the chase. Making herself a prey for some, and a predator for others. She leaves her house to crumble in reality. But she believes that God makes a direct effort to keep her family together. She'll be the last person to know that the foundation under her feet has completely vanished. Well, it's true for all parents. We shouldn't think that two thousand years of old magic binds family together. Daily life tears everyone apart. Living in a civilized world means technology, from which a single person is reduced to an insignificant polluter. We'll never stop blaming others, especially the rich part of society. All this, because we're gutless. We want someone else to do it for us. Someone to stand and fight for us, while we go about our daily lives. No, we don't have doubles; I'm not talking to you now, while my spirit is in the street protesting hideous forms of injustice. It'd be nice, but it isn't so. Put the flame back where it belongs." She turned to Lenny. "I guess your Mom wouldn't agree with me."

"No Belinda, I don't have anything to enlighten anyone with," said Doris. "You must remember all the demands that life places on parents. To live happily, to have food, to have clothes, to work, to please your children, to educate your children, to keep them busy, to participate in their activities, to have time for your husband, to have time for the whole family, to be with friends, to cook, to have time for yourself... you can never put a limit on what is demanded of us as parents and human beings. As you said, we have so much trash around us. We don't know what is truly genuine anymore. To find what is good amongst the trash is like looking for a needle in a haystack. Look at you young adults, you're still so young. You can see the difference, not us. We are born into blindness, hoping that our children will do better than us."

Lenny was fascinated to hear his mother speaking, instead of screaming and shouting. But an inner bitterness finally swept over his secret. "A charismatic preacher among my friends, really impressing everyone. Your imitation of a sane human being could fool everyone, but not me. How could you? You know darn well that Sara is all alone with Dad. He walks around the house like a chicken without a head. But what the dirty do you care? You don't. You just run away from everything. You expect Dad to come home every day. Don't you? But one day, he'll just go. To hell with everything! So much for your job, putting food on the table! And giving us an education. Face it, whatever you're doing, it's only for yourself. Did you ever ask me what I want? Or Sara? Struggling for food with a spear and axe in your hand doesn't give you the right to turn these weapons against us! Throw them at your political representatives, not at us. It's the duty of those slimy snakes to give you a job. And the choice of jobs. To let you live in dignity, meaningfully, with your family. All your fatigue, stress, anxiety—you should wear it like a crown in public. But you shed them in your own house, on us. Unscrew yourself somewhere else, not at home! I don't feel bad, talking like this in front of anyone. Even in front of my friends. But you feel embarrassed. I should keep it for home, so you can yell me down to my place. Here, you can't. You don't want my friends to see who you are. Nobody from outside could see how weak and nervous you are. Don't worry, I won't go on anymore."

The table was silent; everyone could feel the warm air from Lenny's liquid bones and muscles, melting into a pile of wax. Doris felt sorry and hurt to see her anti-Aesopian son become the ungrateful sort who bit the hand that fed him. She barely held the tears back; the dosage was indeed very powerful for her. She sorrowfully left the table and drifted upstairs to Chuck's room, leaving them to throw darts at each other.

"Well, I see we're still here, talking at least," Sandy hoarsely grumbled, "just trying to say something, anything. And I'm not doing so good. Well, I don't think anybody really wants to hurt someone. But it always comes out this way. I have to hold myself together, it's trying to burst out in all directions at once. My life is fighting to burst out." She had failed to mount the morale of everyone else, who were all occupied in peeling the inner layers of self-identity with a surgical knife.

Belinda saw what was happening. Lenny's attitude-man was like a lightning bolt, hitting a bare house on a barren hill. "Yelling your head off, throwing fireballs at people. Just because they've misplaced their courage and hindsight. That makes you a barbarian," cried Belinda, believing that howling at the hidden moon would not make anybody more receptive. "Trying to find your own place in this mess, only close ones get hurt. Even when pain can't be hidden behind walls, hurting others isn't the solution, Lenny. There's no need to say you're sorry. Your barrier says there isn't anything to feel regretful about. But Lenny, we can't make ourselves merely trash, like worthless creatures running after the Believer's destiny. Even our own parents must be treated with tenderness and respect."

"Okay, there's no need to rub it in. There isn't anything to feel sorry about, as you said. For sure, I can only change myself. We're also growing and need psychological nourishment too, not only tasteless food," said Lenny.

"You can always tell your friends and family how you see things. How a little grain of sand is meaningful to a hill. The worst is that nobody is ever around to worry about family members because the family is taken for granted these days. Even growing up, in itself, is a contradiction, like nature killing itself to renew itself, wearing a bigger shoe to throw away old ones, killing history to grow for the future, parents living for us and forgetting what we want," replied Belinda.

Chuck wanted to say something without making a confession of his sentiment; he believed that everyone had already known his predicament in the restaurant, wanting his parents to live together without possessing him, cherishing their counsel, not control.

"I really don't get it," Sandy nosed in. "You mean to say, without joking, that life is a contradiction. So there isn't anything genuine to live for. How about my love, my principles? You mean to say that all of them will become tasteless. What horror awaits us!"

"Sandy, Belinda is talking about how we evolve. We change. We have new values. We have a better understanding of our own love-principles, wanting to be free from our parents without them giving up their obligation," murmured Chuck unenthusiastically. "People must be open to grow, to understand without any prejudice and to be free for change."

"Well said, Chuck. Lenny, don't look, your mother is coming back," whispered Sandy. The congregation was silent, waiting for the monumental sermon to begin. The priestess gracefully mounted the altar and surveyed heads like psychologists and economists. She hesitated a little for their heated breath to rush out, reducing the pressure on their clothes. Her deep look kept their repentance down, making them afraid to reveal their bare and unprotected faces to a sage who could transform their feelings to public knowledge.

"Worldlings," she broke the silence. "If you think I wiped my sorrow away upstairs, you're wrong. I'm hurt, yes, not venomous. Not angry at all, only taken in without any warning. Our old way takes too much for granted. Nothing changes for us. We struggle to stay out of trouble, to make ends meet, to accept our situations without capsizing the boat like how everybody else does it. We're ashamed to cry out. I've seen my life, like a powerless old woman.

I'm grasping for security as though I have to live another horrible life with less. But there's only one life, here and now. Our reality is day-in-day-out. We have to see it as a phase, like a teenager's bile. You're right, Lenny. I phoned home. Sara and your Dad are doing okay. I told your Dad that things would be different. Starting tomorrow, Jackie will have to find herself another person. I'm finished here. If I can't get the job I want, I'll be a lonely protestor, standing against our representatives. It's about time I did something real. I have to direct my anger to the cause, not look for helpless victims. The system must serve the people, and we're the people. I still can't believe it! All this time, I've been sleeping in someone else's bed. And dreaming their dreams, not mine." The long faces at the table seemed to be hypnotized for a moment.

"It's about time parents actually listened to us," cried Belinda. "Not only occupying us with school, and not seeing us as a valuable part in anything. Parents never have any time to see what we want, and what we value. No parent in this world can stop me from doing what I want to, even living in the street. They have the responsibility to guide the young, not make them their humble and idolized pets. But when parents can't do their duty, they want public institutions—teachers, social workers, police, firms—to do it for them." She saw Chuck rounding his mouth but he was too slow to get a word in.

"I didn't want to say anything," Sandy said to Doris, "because you may think we're all against you. This isn't true. To look at things squarely, our parents have less than five friends. They have one or two good colleagues at work. And maybe a few childhood friends. Look at us! How should we have friends? We have to do it ourselves. To join a group in our neighborhood, we must be like them. If we want to be acceptable and normal, we go to parties to meet people. For us to count in most situations, we must do what others do. All this because we value friendship. I don't know if you get my drift, Mrs. Holden. Have you even seen our parents going to our neighborhood and introducing us to people of our own age group? How often do our friends' parents ever have a picnic together? Never! A lot of problems would have been avoided if our parents had introduced us around. They don't even give us any place to meet others of our own age. If it weren't for All-In-One, you wouldn't have known me. Belinda is right, we must speak our parents' dead language and suffer their insecurity and anti-social attitudes. So you see. We have all the tools to do things wrong. Actually, none of us mind taking the most adventurous path of meeting friends. But when it doesn't work out, it's good to have a dear friend at home."

"Yes, Sandy, sometimes in the morning, I've seen you riding your bike to school. Besides that, I can't even answer for myself. And can't say anything about what you just said. Each person has to look within herself. But I can't prove you wrong. We're not helping out a lot, are we?" said Doris, as she turned her attention to Belinda. "You're from Mayfair, aren't you?"

"Yes, not so far from where you live. If you're thinking about me getting home, I'm staying over at Sandy's," she replied. Belinda did not wear the uniform of the last unicorn roaming among rose bushes; she neither wanted anyone to search for her nor model her free spirit.

"So, you're not coming over, anymore," Chuck said sadly, wondering whether his mother would be able to find someone else in time. "So, she didn't tell you anything yet? Nothing about changing her shift?"

"Sorry Chuck, I've only just decided to quit. I've had my senses knocked into me, tonight. I really don't know your mother's plan. She doesn't talk to me about her business. You should talk to her."

Thank you, thought Chuck. *When one person puts the left foot first, others blindly follow. There are people waiting for this opportunity, to have her job. It's like turning over a mountain without touching its rocks. Nobody, with a little sense, can afford to put principles before paying bills. Now, I'm really pushing square rocks up a mountain. Oh, my will to live is nowhere.* Chuck's courage disappeared, for it was likely her replacement would be Florence Nightingale without her white overalls. He imagined several children playing with his vertical line of life:

Mary goes around the jingle ring, as they're laughing at him, for they had the last laugh. Well, poor Jack thumbed and broke his skull, and his imaginary rocks lost their sharp edges and couldn't make an indent on their downward path. Life is doing time, now, isn't it? I'm buried alive without being able to reconcile my conscience of fairness. My parents' unwritten responsibilities are binding. All this is unbearable. Doris quitting, things arranging themselves with someone else's magical hands, not mine.

"Do you know if Mom has another sitter?" he unconsciously echoed, glancing at Doris for hints.

"You shouldn't think about this. There isn't any problem in finding someone for you. It's important to have some confidence in your mother. She wouldn't do anything to hurt you. She wants the best," she assured him. The others could see that she did not feel comfortable with this subject matter, burning an old bridge that she intended to never cross again.

"So you think we're worldlings without any direction? And lost too," said Sandy. "We have to be understood and taken seriously. Politics and economics simply don't offer us an intellectual outlet. We aren't Tychean stuffed pigs. We're searching for something permanent, something meaningful that doesn't change with the changing world. I don't want my tombstone to carry a Tychean inscription—'Sandy is perfectly molded by her society.' We've never had a chance to say what we want. Our world is full of adults' pre-selected choices for us." She watched Doris from the corner of her eye for enlightenment.

"I'm really taken by surprise, Sandy. You're provoking me to say something. But, I'll take it as teasing. You may think I'm a Hellenistic Tychean worshiper. But no, the mass out there has overwhelming power. Let me show you worldlings how a simple structure grows to insanity. The Neolithic people started off with little kingdoms. Several thousand settlers with one king. Other kingdoms grew nearby. They fought against one another. And then alliances were formed. They got bigger. And fought again, just to get bigger. Everything for wealth and power. Kings, priests, and aristocrats were official citizens of any kingdom, owning all the land. They had commoners and slaves to work for them. A handful of aristocrats were politician-traders. They even controlled and administrated the Persian Empire and Alexander's kingdom. They protected their interests by re-stamping soldiers as true citizens, stamping out the herd's revolts, protecting trade routes. And making sure that commoners and slaves worshipped Tyche. I'll not bore you anymore with this over-ripe human renewal."

"The moral is," cried Sandy, "that we're worshipers of Tyche's elected people, a handful of high priests. The rich in society elect true citizens, police, soldiers, the justice department, to protect their monasteries. Being rich is like a religion today, so the poor have to worship their gods. And the slight trace of a circle around the capital, 'A'and we're condemned as misfits and outcasts. All this, because others have collected lavish rewards from their goddess. I'm talking about immortal gifts, like the secret of out-living workers. So we're workers of Tyche's selected people. What will it be, fate? Change? Or doom?" She saw herself walking in a realm of perplexity. Neither Chuck nor Lenny were able to shed some light, since Lenny did not want to reveal anything more about himself to his mother, and Chuck was still troubled by his new dreadful situation.

"Cynicism, my dear Sandy. I prefer Diogenes," cried Belinda, "telling Alexander the Great to get out of his sunlight. And giving him his contribution to the war effort by rolling in an empty barrel in the acropolis, the town square. A pack of sheep could be poisonous. I don't hold any alliance with any government. Let them take their pollution, genetic engineering, taxes, and wealth. But leave me, my air, my sun, and my plants alone. We can grow and harden ourselves into genuine cynics. But leave our natural world alone. I want to enjoy it when I'm older. I'm not worried about anything. Some young people will turn out to be harder cynics. And society doesn't have a choice about it, for nothing worthwhile is offered to them. But again, we can turn to quietism.

"Yes, Epicureans, the lovers of mixed pleasure as the good. Our virtual world is pleasant with the absence of pain. We should be drunkards and stoned addicts, prowling the streets for another dose to put ourselves beyond the level of addiction. How charming everything would be! After Chuck popped out, his parents woke up and found individuality from their blind collective fate. But the magic of Chuckhood quickly wore off; he couldn't overcome his parents' boredom and insecurity. Now, what do we have? Parental individuality without responsibility. Yes, paying for child support is like electro-smog binding human collectivity and family relationship. There's no need to hire a secret agent to spy on life. For freedom is only in the head. I didn't say anything about the stoics, yet. Did I?"

"No," answered Doris.

"Well, I should, then. Everything obeys natural laws. We're a part of this natural order, a harmonious whole. It can be measured mathematically without using numbers or fractions. The stoics tell us that we're like Shakespeare's clowns on the stage, acting out our roles without being able to change the play's course. We can only transform ourselves into our own self-made clowns. And then we cry out, 'Are we coming or going?' How sickening!

"I'm here. And here I'll stay. Permanent like smog. Were Zeno and Shakespeare walking now, their works would have condemned them to the flame. It's not a question of anarchy, as Sandy said. Adults carve out our course. Fate, chance, or doom, I guess. All in all, can we escape the goddess, Tyche? Everyone is against everything—nobody is happy! We don't need any metaphysician to tell us that we all have one thing in common—life. We must put life where it belongs. We don't need others to entertain us. We don't want to change the world—only to change ourselves. Learn to say no. Be proud to say it's too much! Be strong enough to refuse trash on the golden spoon."

"We've unfortunately made a beautiful mess of our own life. We deceive ourselves, telling ourselves we have individuality. All this makes us strong egoists," Doris agreed. "I'm telling you, it will get worse. You haven't seen anything yet. The barrier of exclusion is becoming wider and wider. Nobody has any work, anymore. We're starving the have-nots out of existence. Still, all the atomic bombs together, all the armies in the world, can't match the ultimate power of the will to live. Technology isn't the last enemy of humanity; our trash is. You're correct, Belinda. We still allow ourselves to be easily manipulated by others. We trust the wrong people. We mistakenly believe they are doing their best to help us. We follow them like a mule on a single harness. We're just sitting around while others exclude us from our means of survival. It's not only shocking, it awakens my extinguished flame." She crested the imaginary flame on her chest until the sharp edges rounded themselves off. She looked for dancing thorns on her chest, but there were none; they were burning inside, as she glanced at Chuck and her son.

Both Belinda and Sandy noticed her queer behavior as they were transformed to clay with a single message. Lenny was much more occupied with his mother's decision of quitting—it was too quick without any plan. This was too easy; he was trying to figure out her motive.

Doris fully acknowledged her predicament, for she had long ago been robbed of the pleasure of paying her bills. Only mad people would accept paying taxes twice, once from the earnings, and then again on merchandise. She remembered that Lenny once mentioned it while they were having supper at the table. Many people were getting business licenses; they were marketing their services. They took themselves as real businesses. Every single cost, including food, outfits, shoes, etc. could be tax-free. One could buy anything at a business price. The relation was one business buying directly from another. People had to conduct themselves as a real business when dealing with other institutions. And a business could not pay any tax without making a profit. New capitalism for each individual could be a slight hope against bigger institutions.

"Tell me, girls," Doris cried, "do you speak to your parents the same way? I mean to say, do you talk to them like how we're talking? You don't have to answer if you don't want to."

"Come on, I wouldn't be able to come to Chuck's place if you didn't know his mother."

"Right, Lenny!" interrupted Sandy, cutting him short before

he could put his mother on a guilt trip. “Yes, our parents know each other. During the summer, we went picnicking together. We trust them. They know they have to be united and strong to follow us.”

“Wait Sandy—speak for yourself!” cried Belinda, noticing that Sandy had poked Chuck with a rusty nail. “To put it bluntly, they made us, for us to remodel them. You can meet our parents. We’ll be having another outing together this summer. You’ll have an excellent time.” She checked her watch and then showed it to Sandy; it was after twelve. “I don’t think you want to hear that, Mrs. Holden. You want to know if we drink, smoke, take drugs, enjoy sex. In this world, when you have true friends, there’s no need to conquer, impress, or search for acceptance. We don’t have enough time to be ourselves; how can we have habits? Mrs. Holden, we don’t have any time to take a drink, for the effect lasts too long. With drugs, it’s even longer. For smoking, the world is already divided. One half doesn’t even eat smoked salmon, meat and cooked food. For sex, the risks outweigh the pleasure at the moment. To put it short, you’ve misunderstood worldlings; it’s about genuine friendship, acceptance, trust. But adults did everything to take our world away from us.”

“Sorry, we’ve got to go now. We have to get up early tomorrow,” murmured Sandy as both girls prepared themselves to leave.

Doris felt alone because of the parting of such wonderful company, especially when she had an opportunity to gain more insight into the young, her son’s friends. “Yes, I’d be more than happy for an outing in the summer. It’s good to have a change of breath. I’ll make sure I don’t stand in your air, Belinda,” she said to the girls as the boys followed them to the door. Doris stayed back in the kitchen to clean up with fresh pleasure; the joy remained in the smog for others to take. “Wonderful kids carving out life,” she murmured to herself.

“We’re going up, too,” said Lenny. ‘Good night!’ they both echoed, and she quickly saluted them in return.

“You’re not going to bed, are you?” asked Lenny, who appeared to have a lot of things on his mind that had to be unloaded.

"No, your room is already prepared, down the hall," he replied.

"You've missed it all this evening, Virus said man is self-amusing. Who will buy it? No intelligent person would like to be known as self-amusing. It's degrading, reducing people to pigs. Defining man by his weakness." He glanced at Chuck, wanting him to say what he had kept from everyone. After waiting for a moment, he believed that Chuck could not hold himself any longer, and he did not.

"Yes, of course I believe Virus. Rational beings can't justify their slimy hopes and beliefs. You can take a pig away from the sty, but you can't take his nature away. I know this." He ran out of words and stopped abruptly, as though everything in his room became invisible to his thoughts.

"If you think any deeper, you'll hurt your backbone," Lenny interrupted. "Look, Virus will get us something tomorrow. I have to see him at the restaurant. Are you free tomorrow?"

"I don't have anything to do, other than sit around."

"So you come with me," said Lenny. "You saw my Mom's exhibition. She can be a perfect machine before my friends. Wait and see, when we get home. Her beast will devour me mercilessly. At least, I don't know where she stands now. I'm okay. You know my little sister, Sara—she is ten now; she needs them. But what do we have these days? Parents practicing their separation career. They don't want to stir the water in society, even if they remain together. Oh, it's all too simple: parents still believe in the deterioration of our intelligence and values without their participation in it."

"She'll fight for a better life, but the goddess of society will intervene, creating and paying off another group to oppose her. If not, they'll plant their agents to disrupt our parents' reincarnation and handcuff their milky hands of life. Yes, Chuck, be yourself. No goddess people could detect you. I hope we're not creating another ism or ideology like building our house for someone else to destroy. Well, we can't wait for society to see us without its steel bars. Give ourselves our own rights and tell society's followers of their duties. Society would be nothing without worshipers. If you don't believe in yourself, Chuck, you'll never know how meaningful life is. We must sweat for the golden spoon of everlasting life and a trace of infinite happiness. I'd have picked its fruit already, were it growing on trees. But again, nobody could satisfy my inner craving—only me. This tells you something for sure, you have to do what you can do for yourself, first."

"Sometimes, I can't help it," Chuck replied. "All this goddess stuff is like talking about my mother. A few people like you know how to use the system. You get what you want. A great majority of us, from executives to the unemployed, are victims. We have to dance to everyone else's secret tune. We can easily be smacked like flies. Yes, thank you. Now, you're dead—smack! That's reality! A mother hiding from her shadow, a father creating a castle with smoke. A son fighting not to be a smoky shadow. Yodeling all night until morning changes nothing. They think the world would be a better place for adults without children. They should be banned from having children. Then, they'd know how absurd their life would be, meaningless like death. They'd surely give up on immortality. If the highest bidder had the right to have children, others would have something special to live for. If each family were allowed to have only one little kid, there would be only boys! Every parent would want his child to carry the name of his deflated image. Responsibility before birth is the answer. Don't go to sleep on me now, Lenny! You brought it up, not me! It doesn't matter how you cut it, self-centered people would sacrifice a good portion of their life to feed on others. Well, all isn't lost, our rights surpass parents' rights."

Lenny finally nodded his head in agreement as the window became foggy with his exhalation. "So, we meet tomorrow," Lenny said as he held himself up and stretched his arm toward the ceiling.

"Okay, we go to bed, then. What do you say?" said Chuck, feeling like a balloon blown up in the sleeping wind.

"Yes, you're right, we'll be up early. See you then," Lenny

said as he walked toward his room, glancing into the darkness downstairs.

They hardly had any sleep before they were awakened; it was already morning. Their tiredness and fatigue followed them for a while, as though their world would pass by without any conscientious observers.

Doris believed Lenny should go home with her by taxi; she definitely had things to work out with her family, picking up the pieces that could hardly be added up to a whole. Charged with courage to confront her situation, she intended to harmonize a weak thread that bound her family together. She believed that past episodes of her life got washed up in the rain. They got themselves lost on the riverbank and then clamped themselves together to form new banks to obstruct her path. Though she believed that the tide made an advancing stride, she saw the old Doris being left behind. The new Doris had to go against the flow until she found a path. And with each stride, the path would be widened before her.

As the boys ate their breakfast, she glanced at the broken clock on the kitchen wall, pacing back and forth, rechecking the order of the kitchen without pondering the idea of her last visit to this place. "What's keeping her? She should have been here an hour ago!" She was talking to herself, for the boys had much more important things to do than to be her spectators. She looked at her watch; it was already eight thirty. She habitually compared it again with the clock on the wall. "She isn't here, yet!"

After Lenny and Chuck had eaten, they went to the front door. They remained there for a while, observing her restless behavior in the kitchen. "Chuck and I can go to the restaurant while you wait," he suggested to his mother, hoping not to be here when she spoke to Jackie.

Chuck already felt that everyone was abandoning the sinking ship.

"Oh, waiting! There's no end in sight!" she said angrily.

"I heard something outside," said Chuck in a dry voice, showing no interest, for his puppet arms were not long enough to pull their own strings.

Lenny looked at the taxi as it pulled up in front of the house. The passenger double checked the house and finally decided to approach it. "Mary goes around the mingle rings—dingle-dangle, today," Chuck sang for Lenny and Doris as Lenny swiftly walked away from the window and then took a seat near him in the kitchen.

"She came by cab," Lenny whispered.

"She never takes a taxi!" Doris said. "I thought we'd be getting a ride home." She stopped herself before she said something undesirable. They were automatically drawn to counting Jackie's footsteps along the driveway, the front door, more steps, the cupboard door, jacket, shoes, house shoes… "Would you like something else to drink?" she asked the boys who had eaten all their breakfast. The echo of the advancing steps was getting too lonely, as Jackie's aroma swept the kitchen.

"Someone stole my car!" Jackie protested. "Of all the places in the world, from a hospital. How low could they get?" She went to the fridge for something, and closed it without removing anything.

"Didn't you lock it?" asked Doris.

"Of course, I did! The police believe it's an amateur job. Taking it for a joy ride and dumping it when the gas ran out. They left it in the middle of the road. The CD-player and telephone were gone," she cried, going to the fridge again where no gin and tonic could be found.

"Thank God, nothing else!" Doris replied sympathetically.

"I have to go to the police station today; I couldn't prove my ownership. It must be still in his name. Yes, the insurance papers are gone, too. I don't know what else. It'll be crazy today." Jackie finally sat at the table, and Doris gave her a glass of orange juice.

"Well then, you don't need me around," cried Doris. "We'll get a cab." She went to the living room to help herself with the phone. Lenny had flashes of the security guard, and Slade, who knew the plate number.

"If you don't mind, Doris, can Chuck be at your place today? It'll be crazy, running around and all this. I'd really appreciate it, if you don't mind," Jackie insisted.

"By all means!" replied Doris, making Lenny smile, a perfectly fashioned counterfeit without showing any trace of the prototype. He fought against himself, for he felt sorry about her car, and yet he was angry, for it could have been more interesting if the car had been stolen yesterday night.

"You're thinking about Thursday night, aren't you?" asked Chuck, walking toward the waiting taxi without exchanging glances.

"There's nothing to deny or feel guilty about," answered Lenny. They were far ahead of Doris, who was dangling behind them with some hesitation. The boys sat in the back seat and looked at her new shoes, reflecting the sunlight of a new era. Lenny knew all the answers could be found today, and Virus had them.

Doris stopped and waited for a few seconds, and then she returned to the house. Her decision already made, now she had to go through the motions.

9: Guilt and Revenge

The following morning, Alex and Cathy had faithfully returned to the building that hated people, not sickness. The north wind had passed and preserved its lifelessness; trees covered with sheets of silvery zinc had been snatched away from the ice age. The maiden dew overcast a handful of lonely cars that were thrown about here and there. The frozen openness scared the visitors more than the tomb that awaited them straight ahead.

They passed the unscrewed guard behind his desk, waiting to be replaced like the living imitating the dead. A janitor's floor sterilization products left them dizzy as the visitors passed the admission office with a sign, "Closed," hanging on the door. As they fought their way furiously toward the other end of the foggy corridor for an elevator, Cathy watched their footprints behind them. Some seemed to linger on while others disappeared, marking their passage in a familiar world that waited for everyone to pass through, at least once. She walked close to Alex, who kept a steady speed. They were going straight to the psychiatric clinic. Occupied with the vivid memory of the night before, the thought of whether or not they would be allowed access to the clinic did not pop up to them. Habit led them onward like riding a bicycle; the road toward answers sparkled like scattered pebbles. Their strides were cloned symmetrically; other motions were synchronized without music.

There was nothing spectacular about a psychiatric hospital—people still had one head, two feet, two hands—but several ghosts on a single head were invented. The door could be opened from outside and from inside with a key. Huge windows, which could be partly opened, were protected with steel bars to keep symptoms and side effects together. Morning sweat polished the floor and hid the naked feet that moved about without going anywhere.

Narcotized patients clamped on a dried up lemon with twisted mouths, and shuffled with heavy feet and paralyzed limbs. Nothing had really changed in here, only a little identification tag separating doctor-tranquilizers from patient-tranquilizees until tranquilizers found the compatibility between symptoms and textbooks. In this high kingdom, patients did not act out their unconscious desires because staff prevented them from hurting themselves or others. Instead, medical staff were responsible for causing intentional symptoms. When they were tired of playing this little game, they fed the patients to reality. A ravishing two-way dependency was strengthened; the influence of psychiatric hospitals followed staff home, and the hospital reality of experimental drugs trailed behind patients. It was a world that flourished without any winner, for patients had to carry their doctors' narcotic habits home to face reality.

Cathy was amazed to confront trembling hands, mental fatigue, and staggering feet prowling around. Though everyone looked the same to her, each patient belonged to a complex mental world. But conventional dog-tagging reduced them to commoners. Some patients stood around the newcomers and sniffed, for they were not tribe members.

A man with a distinguishable characteristic had seen them and was coming. He wore his identity on his belt strap, and it dangled with every step he made. "Can I help you?" asked the nursing assistant, dressed all in white.

"We're looking for Elizabeth Brown. She was admitted here last night. We're very close friends of hers," Cathy replied. The assistant turned his head and grinned as he walked away, seeing that all family members and friends said the same thing about patients. This tune was too old to evoke a new response. Alex felt stupid, waiting at the barren corridor with a bunch of loonies getting closer to them, as though they were an appetizing pizza. One of the patients took Cathy's hand, but she slapped it away furiously, driving an electric shock to the patient. Because of her insecurity, she completely misinterpreted the helpful patient who pointed out for them the direction of the nursing station.

"Much obliged!" said Alex, rushing toward the station.

Two nurses could be easily seen from the station's transparent plastic glass; they were yapping their heads away without noticing the intruders. Alex tapped at the glass window. They turned habitually, as though they expected to see a few regular patients who always disturbed them. They replied by wiping their smiles away and donning the professional mask.

"Police!" said Alex. "Do you have Mrs. Brown here?" he asked, showing his badge and placing it back in his pocket without allowing it to be cold and lonely.

"Yes, we do," the nurse replied. "Follow me, please." She passed between them and walked toward the assistant who was now standing near a slightly open door. She pushed the door open fully to allow the visitors.

A woman who was partly covered was lying on her belly on a single bed with her face toward the inner wall. The visitors quickly noticed that both of her hands were strapped, one to each side of the bed. Hoping that the nurse was mistaken, they also saw that each leg was tied. The practice of binding people on their belly reduced them to a tiger or a bear skin on the floor. For the belly would have been too vulgar to satisfy expensive taste.

"Hello, Mrs. Brown, you have visitors," whispered the nurse into the patient's ear. She repeated her greeting without getting any response.

"You better untie her, right now!" ordered Alex, for he could hardly restrain his beast. "How could you treat people so inhumanely? Without any dignity? Without any respect?" he questioned.

His questions triggered a stream of flame in the nursing assistant, who took another look at the hypocrite with his police uniform. *His self-gratification in handcuffing suspects doesn't only show the deterioration of intelligence and common sense. It's the worst type of psychological brutality known to humanity. Our scientific achievements and developments are alienated from basic common sense. Techniques and technicians are the rulers of the world. But blind followers are the most dangerous; they could commit atrocities. Look at this bloated hippo. He's crying out for the innocent against inhumane treatments without questioning his own double standard in the name of society. A blunt knife has no conflicts,* he thought. The assistant could not see his own holiness, for only society could pay people to strip others naked.

After living with oneself for an eternity, it took a doctor about twenty minutes to tell a person: "Sorry, you are dangerous to yourself and others." Soon after this diagnosis, therapeutic treatments followed a rigorous course in which patients had to convince themselves that they were really a threat to society. The black magic of self-realization turned patients to believers of their own self-destructiveness until it became their elongated shadow. Psychiatrists did not change the circumstances and society that caused mental sicknesses, they changed patients' images.

"Get her free!" shouted Alex.

The nurse jumped out of her clothes with fear, and then into them again for a bigger fear of not being able to pay her bills. "Yes-yes, the doctor has to give the order," she answered.

"Go get him! Don't stand here!" he commanded, screaming louder than his bullets did at the degenerates of society. She left; she was not paid for taking out the garbage. Her business was patients, not the lucky ones still roaming the streets.

Cathy attended Elizabeth, moving the hairs one by one away from her face. Elizabeth showed the signs of being burned out from an overdose of tranquilizers; slime ran out of her crooked mouth to the bed.

"This is incredible! Insane! Inhuman, violating every decent rule," Cathy cried. She looked at Alex for an explanation.

"Yes," he replied, searching for the right sentiment. He turned away from the bed and hurried to the door. "Where's the phone?" he asked the assistant at the doorway.

"It's in the corner, near the entrance," he replied, pointing to the door. "Wait, you can't leave without the key." Alex turned back abruptly and then hesitated, telling the assistant to open the bloody door for him with his body movements. They went to the entrance that could not be seen from the nursing station.

The assistant quickly returned to his duties. He closed the door enough so that he could still have a view of both women in the room, maintaining the transcendent qualities of Elizabeth's integrity in the air.

The squeaking rubber soles on the floor gradually increased in volume like a headhunter drum in the assistant's ears, until he heard only the pounding of his own heart. The patients in the hallway sensed the coming feast, as they followed the tribal call of the jungle beat that increased its tempo in its victims. The assistant consulted his watch: *Two minutes ago, my shift finished. Oh, it went by pretty fast,* he thought, as he refused to acknowledge the queer character that attempted to put fear in them. From the corner of his eye, he noticed Alex taking his wife's hand, and she followed him without missing a stroke of the marital harmony between partners. They came to the door and then closed it behind them, as they were waiting for the tribal priest.

"Sorry, I have to keep this door slightly open," politely requested the assistant, as he pushed it half open. "Regulations, you know," he affirmed with a friendly tone. Neither Alex nor his wife returned his politeness. They just stood near the door without speaking to each other. Some patients were still looking on when the assistant told them again to go to the dining room. He hoped for the nurse to release him; he wanted to go home. He sensed the struggle for survival with tax payers' resources, and he could not determine his own role in this Roman arena.

Alex moved smoothly to the right of the assistant, leaving enough room for Cathy to stand on his left—a tactical move, freeing his gun arm. He reached in his pants pocket and took his identity and pinned it up on his jacket. He freed his jacket buttons, exposing his superiority over others. His uniform, a permission to horrify and arrest others, was fully exposed for lookers.

"Go to the dining room!" yelled the assistant, but some of the patients were too impressed. Two of them panicked and started to shout, all the way to the nursing station. "Police! Gun, gun!" they anxiously screamed as they ran into the nursing station for protection. "Gun, gun!" They sweated and trembled in a corner in a desperate attempt to hide their fear. One of the nurses was still on the phone, trying to get hold of the psychiatrist who was on call; the other one was trying to comfort the two mindless weaklings in the office. The assistant took the other patients who were standing in front of them to the dining room. Next, he went slowly to the nursing station to the nurse on the phone.

"It's more than you can chew," he remarked. "The nursing office would be interested," he murmured.

"I don't need your advice!" bitterly remarked the nurse on the phone, bewildered about the current development concerning her patient. "Get to your duties!" she screamed at the assistant. The chain of command worked everywhere.

"She won't go anywhere," he murmured. "Excuse me, my shift is over. That means I'm off," he reminded the nurse. But he could not leave, for it was getting too interesting. He wanted to see the outcome. He was ambivalent toward the nurses, feeling sorry for them on the one hand, but also wanting to teach them a good lesson because they thought of themselves as immune to society's symptoms. He hesitated near the nursing station now, and eyed the entrance. He obviously expected more action. As soon as he got sight of two long-coated men approaching, he rushed to his post.

The two men in trench coats entered and looked around for a sign. Ignoring the nursing station, they noticed Alex's uniform and went directly to it. Following them were ten more police officers and a cameraman who was filming every symptom and capturing every crack on the walls and floor. The nurses tried to intervene without any success, for the visitors knew what they wanted and how to get it. Images meant much more than words as the camera went in the room and registered Elizabeth's helpless state and the depressing pale walls crying out for pity and compassion. One of the men in the long-coats was questioning the attendant, who appeared to be acting out his Shakespearean role well: uneducated, ignorant, and just doing what others had told him to do without being able to dream up any question concerning others' decisions. The other detective was busy with Elizabeth's nurse in the room; she freely divulged information about the patient's physical, pharmaceutical, and medical state without violating medical secrecy. She explained her legal limitations to the detective; she could neither make diagnoses nor prescribe medications. While the other nurse was administering patients' morning medications in the dining room, the camera sneaked into the nursing station and filmed room twenty-two's medical files.

"Look, what is coming our way?" cried Cathy to herself. The female nursing director of the hospital and two security guards were coming. Behind them, an albino pigeon with an oversized white coat, hiding humanity and yet passing as a doctor, was dangling along toward the scene.

"What's the meaning of all this?" asked the director firmly. "We have no visiting hours, now! We have rules and regulations in this place!"

"We're removing Mrs. Brown to a private clinic for control. You'll hear from our lawyers," said one of the detectives. "Take her out of restraints now," he ordered with a frozen face that had just been pulled out of the arctic, leaving the icebergs completely intact.

The director quickly glanced at the assistant, who was standing near the door like a costly incompetent fool. "Do as he said! We hold no responsibility for Mrs. Brown now." She recognized the fact that there was no need to blow the situation out of proportion. She could not admit any misunderstanding on behalf of the hospital, for she had realized her own image: a chief before her subordinates could be stubborn and authoritative like a dinosaur. Bad publicity and legal costs could destroy any dignified place with a high public reputation.

A noise at the entrance shifted everyone's attention. Two ambulance medics were rolling a stretcher toward them. Another police officer accompanied them as they entered Elizabeth's room. One security guard was busy talking with some of the police officers he had known over the years through business cooperation. Cathy noticed one of the nurses, who had briefly escaped the ordeal, returning to the nursing station with the doctor and a guard to protect medical secrets. The nurse then returned with a paper in her hand and gave it to the director, who knew the contents from the heading alone. "Here is a release form. You have to sign it, before removing our patient," said the director.

"Sorry, lady! You've misunderstood us. We-are-removing-her. Her life is threatened here," the chief officer clearly articulated. "We'll sign nothing! This-is-a-police-investigation, get it! Our lawyers are gonna contact you." The director's face changed, and she moved away to allow the stretcher to pass with Elizabeth. She followed for a short distance like a sour mourner.

"Excuse me, we're trying to locate her husband. He was injured last night. And he was admitted to your hospital," Cathy asked the director politely. The director looked at her and counted her words carefully.

"He's on the ninth floor, medical wing. Ask the nurse in charge there, before seeing him. I think they're expecting visitors," she replied.

"We thank you once again. Bye," said Cathy, and then quickly followed her husband's team, which was about to reach the door. Alex kept himself a little behind for his wife to catch up with him. While the other officers used the main door to exit the psychiatric clinic, Alex and Cathy used the inside entrance that led to the main hospital building. "Do you think Elizabeth will be better off?" asked Cathy, thinking that all this extra show of force wasn't really necessary.

"Of course, you've got to teach these people a good lesson. They can't do whatever they want," cried Alex, sure of himself and his methods. "They're taking Elizabeth to Fairdale. She'll be better off there. It's private."

"I hope Charles is doing better than his wife," she mumbled. She knew the pattern—twenty clans on each side to determine what's legal or illegal, costing each side a huge hole in the taxpayers' pocket.

They finally reached the ninth floor, which was divided into a surgical wing and a medical wing. All room doors were open wide, for human interaction with passers-by in the hallway could help the healing process.

Charles was lying in bed. He was amazed to see his partner and Cathy entering, He hopelessly searched for his wife near them.

The visitors were more shocked to see two fully dressed police officers near him, sitting on each side of his bed. "Hello Charles, how are you doing?" asked Alex, tapping his partner's shoulder with a strong touch of courage and sympathy.

"It takes more than one shot to bring me down," Charles grinned, rubbing his injuries.

"We couldn't sleep all night, hoping you're doing well," whispered Cathy.

"Well, it's nothing really," he answered jokingly, as the screeching of rubber on the floor drew Charles' attention to the door. He was disappointed once again, as he saw the chief of the police department entering.

"I thought you'd gone with them," muttered Alex to the man in the long grey coat.

"Happy to see you're getting well, Charles. See you soon at the grind," he assured Charles with authoritative intonation.

"Happy to see everyone, sir. Thanks, for coming," Charles murmured. He was really amazed to see all of his colleagues being so friendly and compassionate toward him.

"Mind you! Before I go," cried the chief, "don't sign any papers unless I see them first!"

"Okay, if you say so," the patient replied.

"In that case, get well soon," the chief commanded, and turned away without wanting any thank you note from anyone. The room was silent for a while, for no suspicion existed between the patient and his superior.

"We've got to be on the road," said the two policemen, as they tapped Charles on the foot. "Bye."

"Thanks again for coming," murmured the patient.

"See you guys, later," called Alex as they were leaving.

Alex and Cathy occupied the only two chairs in the room, sitting on each side of the bed without having any intention to confuse, to distract, or to put strain on Charles' neck from turning side to side. "How are you doing, old buddy?" asked Alex, thinking that more details of his situation would be scattered on the floor like little marbles.

"The doctor was here, early in the morning, waking me up and all. He said, it looks good," he answered, glancing at Cathy, and silently telling her to kindly excuse them.

She intuitively got the message. "I'll be back in a few minutes. I have to use the washroom," she said, disappearing from the scene.

"To put it short, pal. I was hit in the groin area, penis and nuts, belly and inner legs. Other than that, everything seems all right." He stopped for a few seconds to take another deep breath, as he saw Alex changing colors. "They want me to come back for another operation in a couple of months or so. If I want to have kids, I don't have a choice. Do I? Other than that, I'm still a stud, roaming the plain. If you want to know, next week, I should be out. Hopping around like a kangaroo with his tail up. But with no milk." He painfully stressed the last phrase.

"I really don't know what to say," murmured Alex. "I should tell you, but you won't believe it. They thought the little rascal was also injured, and took him to the hospital, right here," he giggled, without noticing how Charles felt about the kid.

"The kid was scared stiff, he just threw the gun down. And it went off... It wasn't the kid, it was an accident," he explained.

Alex had already entered in his report that the kid had shot him, deliberately.

"How do you think Elizabeth will take it?" asked the patient, who believed that she had been working hard, come home tired and gone straight to bed without thinking about him. Probably she had thought that he came in later, slept on the couch and left earlier than she did. Sometimes he worked a double shift without coming home, especially after a quarrel. Now, he was a little bit happy that his wife was not here, for he had a chance to speak about his medical problems with his best friend.

Alex did not know how to answer Charles' question, so he looked at the door for help. "You should ask Cathy, women together, they're better at this. I'll go see if I can find her. She must be right outside." He quickly departed, not wanting to hear Charles' reaction and comment. Cathy was waiting near the door, and she came in with Alex.

"Don't worry Alex, I can ask her myself," Charles said, trying to change the subject.

"Tell him about Elizabeth!" Alex told his wife.

She glanced at Charles and then at Alex to sniff out other information floating in the thin air. "Well, she felt very sick. Yes, sick. She couldn't come," she replied, without causing Charles any extra suffering.

"Yes, as she said," affirmed Alex, agreeing with his wife's attitudinal logic.

"Yes, as I'm telling you. It was really an accident. That little moron, he was crying near me, those tearing eyes. All he was trying to do was to comfort me," murmured Charles. Being all alone with his suffering was much worse than his physical injury. *Die alone. Just fooling myself that others love and care for me. They couldn't go with me to the grave, or for me. Pain and suffering—couldn't be scattered on the floor, without having people stumbling over it. And sending them back to their origin,* he thought.

"I have to go see Elizabeth," said Cathy.

"I'll have to go in soon. Hang on, pal!" said Alex.

"Tomorrow, Elizabeth and I are coming over. See you then," Cathy finally concluded, as love held hands together and walked toward the open door.

"Don't close it, please! It's good to see people walking by. It makes the day pass by faster. I appreciate it, you coming." He watched the couple as they walked away from him and disappeared in their own sunset.

He felt sorry for himself and hoped to make his pain a self-fulfilling prophecy. He wanted to be a fatalist; he obstinately believed that he must be reminded for the rest of his life of what could have been. For him, people had only one true choice, one golden chance, and it had already been made. Now, the consequences had to be lived. *There's no second chance, no mercy in life. Not choos-*

ing is a choice. This essence of life, we've forgotten, he thought. *Everything was written on stone. Quit your job, first, Charles. And then we'll have children. Now, my balls have rolled away. Children can't come. Another operation, and then my own nature is sure. And it's guaranteed. I've got a choice, a real choice. Am I sure about it? There's always someone to stop me. What do I have for a choice? Compromise, compromise, and more compromises. Oh, I can't even live my own life for a bloody second!*

Damn everything, let misery take its course, let suffering unite us. Let us eat each other with guilt. I'm in the right, my revenge will torment her and me, too. It was she! Yes, she refused to have a child. How can anyone put a lousy condition on life? Who does she think she is—God? Yes, God? So God, you've foreseen my suffering? She wants stinky security, not a child! I'll live for revenge! Punishment! And how about early retirement. A big fat handicapped-pension, life insurance, too. And I could remain at home, always reminding her like a scar.

She can overcome all this, like a God. Yes, quit the situation. But dumping me is the worst thing to do. It'll feed on her conscience. Walking away from it all isn't so easy. Oh, a compassionate image for society, everybody would feel sorry for me. Am I going out of my mind? It must be the medication. Oh, no, I can't believe my own thought. I want to escape it—all. He reached for a glass of water on his night table and continued to look at the regular drops pouring out from the intravenous bag. "Drop by drop," he murmured to himself. "Did you hear that? Drop, drop, drop, in my head, on my bone, dropping-drops. Who'll sing my song of dropping, no more?" He closed his eyes for a while, but he could not sleep, for the music was still playing.

Life doesn't mean very much anymore, he thought. Ideas were floating around as though some were his and others did not have any owner. *She denies me. And now, I'm denying myself. Society will condemn me less harshly. Even if people think of me as taking revenge, there's no penalty for breaking this law. Penalty and revenge depend on who's doing the defining.*

The old Charles stops here. I wanted a child, and she refused.

Now, my essence wants to come out, to be me with or without a family. There's no escape from the big ME. And the me is more permanent than my ego.

I spent two long years in the service. Controlling over ninety-five percent of the population as suspects and potential criminals, and the other five percent, I protected as our ideal civilized inhabitants, who wouldn't give up their seat for a cripple. He shook his head in disgust, for he could not believe himself for wasting his precious time, controlling people and things that finally rubbed into the controller, mixing up his life because unofficial lords had to be protected.

As the days in the hospital dragged away, his thought became hardened as though serfdom had transformed his destiny. After a few months at home, his wife received fifty thousand dollars from the hospital—an out-of-court settlement. Including her money and his accident pension and insurance, he voluntarily allowed himself to be encouraged into a new direction of life, rooting from Charles' Big Time Believer. He quit his job and opened a restaurant in the new shopping center. Though he followed Elizabeth's advice, he had his own notion of what sort of restaurant he wanted, and whom he wanted to serve. A restaurant for the young, and for them alone.

People wanted work so they could feed their children and send them to school… It was honorable to educate children. Parents sold their children's natural development to buy a societal Big Time Believer: dignity, identity, and most importantly, their children's intellectual honor. They denied the young from parks, playgrounds, and public buildings, and affirmed their new entertainment—business education. Third World countries believed in children as natural resources, for the probability of life and death could be calculated. At least, one young adult could take care of their parents when old age and sickness rolled in. But industrial societies reduced the young to the level of household objects; pets had more freedom and liberty outside than they had.

Since Charles was an ex-policeman, he had certain privileges.

He found a business location quickly, and the proprietors of Fairview Mall were thrilled to rent him a place, thinking that the entire location would be more secure, for Charles' friends would be regular customers with their uniforms on. Blind trust in public officials ruled the world, for the profession was mostly used to assess character and integrity, by stamping out lowbrow indignation. In acquiring a license for a public establishment, nepotism overruled objectivism. Because of his career, Charles had a license on a silver platter. Lords granted privileges, serfdom had a moral duty to serve lords. They supposed that Charles had fully understood his role and his inheritance as a businessman. Yet his reality was fashioned from his new, unchangeable self-identity. He realized that he had chosen to stay with his situation; now, he had to be ready to live in contradiction: the unspoken universal law of human nature.

Elizabeth kept her job, contributing to her own self-satisfaction; she used her talents to see present social situations as a hint to people's future conditions. Social workers had to correctly predict the future as though it was knowable. Despite office policies, she honestly cared for people and wanted to help them to overcome their economic and social situations.

Though work separated them, an idealized relationship emerged in their minds when they were apart. The secret of a happy marriage had not been invented yet, so life had other things to carry people over to the next day.

He wanted to open a pizza restaurant called All-In-One, a name that had nothing to do with food. Something common ran through all human beings. A degree of regret and guilt could be overwhelmed with a drop of happiness; a tragic human history justified current decisions and choices in life. Removing children's stigma would be a way of life for a couple of millennia. Hope found itself in children. Since affirming and denying co-existed in all things—enjoying carnal pleasure versus denying children, milk versus guns, school versus street—All-In-One satisfied the meeting and exchanging of ideas without emptying worldlings' pockets. It would be a place to be and to feel acceptable without being controlled and influenced by adults. The time to evolve with the development of children, to separate two conceptually distinguishable worlds, and to remove the stereotypes of children, had come. Children were always rational human beings, but parents did not want to see this in them because they wanted to be amused and to act out their suppressed beast by projecting themselves through the young.

10: Virus

Information is knowledge. And knowledge makes you powerful, thought Virus, spreading himself on the table like an overworked rug. *Knowledge without responsibility could be dangerous, too. Luckily, pigs aren't bearers of knowledge. We'd laugh until we died with pleasure. Gosh, maybe we need it today. Responsibility without knowledge isn't any better, and the homeless would admit it. How charming everything is. All this raw data in front of me about the hospital, and Bishop International, we eat tasty barbecue steaks, not like raw meat. For sure, we have a standard; cooked meats as a rule for us, with ingredients to color our meat. I'll balance them out and tie them together as a bundle of delicacies. It should be very delicious. As soon as I put my tongue into it, zooms—evidence.*

He moved about in the computer room in a peculiar manner, stretching his body like a hungry carnivore before hitting the terrain. He ended up crossing his arms on the computer desk and leaning sideways on the right with his head against the concrete wall. He looked at the half open door. *A boy looks out from the window into the street, wearing his new clothes, thinking of obeying the call from the street. As a slight drizzle drifts in, he is responsible for getting his clothes wet. Responsibility cries loud, but others cry louder. He should just take his nice clothes and go to bed and forget being here. Well, procrastination is a decision. There's no need to think about my responsibility as sitting around like a sage next to me. Oh, no, Belinda would really have a belly full when she hears about freedom and knowledge. The weight is too heavy for everything I do and say, and when I don't do and say anything—I must be accountable. If I have knowledge of my freedom, I'm doomed. I'm responsible for my act. I'm not progressing very much. Am I?*

I've chosen the lesser evil in this delicate situation. Just because some possible situations must be realized in the future. But I still have some doubts—prison is like a nightmare. If I'm ignorant about my own freedom, I'm still doomed. In prison, they'll use me to scare off other potential offenders. So, what is the point, here? It's freedom, maybe it's too much to handle. Our knowledge of being free is a parasite. It forces me to be responsible for my actions. That's it! Our own responsibility takes precedence over civil laws. And laws were intended in the first place to remind people of their responsibilities. And everyone should act on his highest responsibility. This is what I want. Now, I'll go ahead, I can tolerate a common cold, if it violates bad laws. I'm not looking for any chronic illness. I have to be on top of this little thorn. If not, it can become an ideology, another ism. Yes, do what I can do, is the motto. This would wake up all passive participants in the continuous process of life. The footsteps on the stairs alerted him, and his consciousness subsided to the noise.

Larry peered through the door. "It looks as though you haven't hit the sack for ages. Now that you've sold your car, what's next? Taxi. You've got fifteen thousand bucks for it."

Virus knew that Larry was asking for money. "I hope you'll put it to some practical use. You've got one month to spend it. Whatever you can't spend, you have to return. Well, what do you say? It isn't a bad deal," Virus offered.

"I get your point, Virus. You distrust charitable organizations because they spend about sixty percent of their income on logistics—paying personnel, transportation costs, paper costs, telephone costs, and so on. Within one month, we can have minimal logistical costs. Virus, you can assist us to spend your money. You're really welcome to see how people live with nothing, standing on the edge," invited Larry.

"The garage is expecting the car before four this afternoon. Next week, I'll give you the check. I know this will not solve their problems—giving them jobs would. Giving them a means to make it by themselves is the answer." He cautiously glanced at Larry, who felt sorry, but still happy to have something concrete besides religion.

"How about your parents? What did they think?"

"I spoke to my father, a week ago, in his office,and during school hours too. He was shocked to see me and knew it was important. We agreed about the car. He believes in me, and that a person ought to do what gives his life meaning. I told him about the Mayfair area; he couldn't believe that such awful conditions really existed in lower town… He asked me how he could help. I told him how. His company had to hire some people who were below the poverty line from lower town. Instantaneously, he called a board meeting. I was in it, too. He asked me to tell the board about Mayfair area. Fifteen minutes after my account, he asked everyone for a solution. After agreeing and disagreeing for a while, they started to vote. The result is—they can currently take ten people from lower town in his company. But there are strict criteria. The first one is, they will see about fifteen candidates and select ten. The second is, the people in the worst conditions will be chosen to work. The next is, if any of them lies about his situation, he'll be booted out. The contract is for five years. After that, they'll be transferred to another company of their choice. There are other rules for all employees, but I'm not interested in them. Their jobs will just be ordinary functions—cleaning, doing routine duties and tasks in the warehouse and shipping and receiving department. Generally, it's helping out wherever they're needed. Before I forget, they'll have the title, 'Priority Employees.' And only management has access to their files. You can send about fifteen people who want to work next week. Here is the company contract. You can read it later. It's about company policies and regulations."

Larry was amazed at Virus's involvement. "I really don't know what to say. Well, we've known each other for a long time, it finally gets to you," Larry said.

"That's not all. My old man will have a meeting with other owners. They'll do something about Mayfair. They'll also contact our local representatives, here. It'll depend on the result of their meeting, but the way things look now, instead of companies paying taxes, they'll use that money to provide direct social services in Proud City. Local government will have to do some, too," he murmured to Larry hesitantly.

"All this stuff in the right direction. I like the name, 'Priority Employees.' It really creates a new standard for recruiting employees. I guess most of these rules and conditions are yours, not your father's," remarked Larry, now rethinking what he had always believed—that Virus had his feet a foot below the ground and his head beyond the sky. "Virus, I'm impressed. But, I hate charity, too. Charity from the rich. We need opportunities to help ourselves. All this means one thing. We'll repay you for your donation. This has to be arranged with residents and new workers. We'll create a pool to reimburse you. Now, your charity is like a loan without taxes. Giving jobs, not exploitation, is everybody's business, not only the rich." He looked at Virus, who appeared to expect Larry's bluntness. "But still, you didn't call me to tell me this. Why didn't you say this last night? There's something more happening around here. What are these computer disks doing here? And piles of loose pages all over the place," he asked. Larry knew Virus. He always gave you the most obvious reply and information, leaving the most important one hidden somewhere in the dark, until it popped out in front of you, Eureka! And then, you started to blame yourself for not figuring it out earlier, for it was so simple.

To kill some time, Virus decided to be redundant: "Two things. The first is simple, just routine. For a while now, I've been manually deleting web sites that have subliminal messages. Last night, I let loose the automatic killer. It's quite harmless. It detects and destroys only bad web sites. By now, I guess the killer has entered all the web sites in the world. It's really undetectable. The first thing it does is destroy its origin. So, you have it. Nothing could detect the killer in any system. It stays in the logical perimeter of a bit. A person has one choice—changing his hard drive. And this stuff here is just junk. The terrible thing for me, Larry, is I have to explain myself to everyone."

"Why don't we get to the point, Virus? What's the matter?

Aren't you sure of yourself, anymore? What I do know is, you're scared to talk about it. Is it so terrible? Let's face it, I'm the last person you'd want to call for something important, or for advice."

"Why call you?" Virus raised his head from his arms and faced Larry squarely. "You're aware of Chuck's situation. Aren't you?"

"I have no kindness or compassion!" cried Larry, without really being angry. "You better keep me out of this! You can buy your way out, not me. Society ordains my reality. One foot dangling outside and the other one losing its grip. They're just waiting to confirm their prediction."

He saw that there was no need to convince Larry. Arguing with him could stir him up even more, so Virus changed the subject. "Soon, Belinda, Sandy, and Lenny will be here," he remarked. Virus glanced at the computer, searching for protocol access files on the database to modify its contents, so an external or unauthorized user could not be registered.

"I guess your computer has been really working overtime. Mating with others," he hesitantly uttered, unable to find the necessary energy to leave.

"Yes, they're coming, all right!" replied Virus, waiting for them to take off the excess pressure of being with Larry. They were like incompatible substances harboring the same tube, about to explode. Stretching himself like a tiger, he made himself ready to confront the fruitful world, breathing pleasure into himself, forgetting his tiredness. The screeching stairs became joyful music for him.

Virus's joy was short lived, as he noticed Chuck leading the procession. Virus had told the others not to bring Chuck, wanting to protect him from the truth.

The computer running was the only thing hissing in the air at this instant. Everyone was meditating; solid thoughts ran downstream and vanished, and new ones raced in.

"I have the right to be here, too," said Chuck.

Without making any comment, Virus went quickly to the printer and took a stock of printed pages. From the pile of papers, he handed Lenny about twenty pages from the bottom.

"Well, this is her employment record for the last six months from the hospital. You know what to do with it, Lenny. She officially works only three nights per week. Each working night, you'll find on these sheets. With your mother's calendar, Lenny, you can circle those nights your mother came over, but Mrs. Crawford didn't work," said Virus. "Well, since he's here, you can ask Chuck to help you." They went to the other computer and started to work at once.

"Larry, if you're still in with us, then you've got a special duty. Nick and Peggy Peterson—husband and wife—work on the same ward as Mrs. Crawford. It seems that Nick and Jackie are having an affair without Peggy knowing about it. So, their liaison must be stopped. With these pages, you'll find out which nights he didn't work, but she did," he clearly expressed, hiding any sign of hesitation, as though he had already checked all these possibilities.

"Virus, how stupid do I look?" cried Larry. "You know very well the answer. Rechecking what you already know condemns me to recycling smoke." He remained still without any intention of moving. He gave Virus the eagle eye as though he wanted to cook him alive.

Virus glanced at Belinda and Sandy: "Belinda, Mr. Scott Crawford is living in High Town, probably with his secretary, according to Bishop International's detective report. But the company's investigation did not suggest any course of action. Recommendation was left blank, too. So, it's a blank check." He was hoping that Belinda would not challenge him now, for his tiredness was crying out for his bed.

"Just say, 'immediately transferred to home base,' is good enough," she said. " 'Head office prefers company integrity to be intact.' "

"We can create a new post in hell for him," interjected Larry.

"Larry, cross-checking your data with Lenny and Chuck has to be done, too," cried Virus. Larry smiled and went to his job without lighting a short fuse.

"Create a new job for him!" said Sandy. "We should keep damages to a minimum. This is much more delicate than I thought.

I don't think his girlfriend will follow him, especially a married man. This might give her the strength to finally leave her miserable condition."

"Sandy, nobody could know the outcome," said Belinda.

"I bet you, Belinda. These business folks are programmed to see human relationship as a ravishing investment. Look at him! He's really enjoying his return, low costs with high benefits, our market principle of human nature," cried Sandy. She took another moment to realize her thought; the sour milk in her mouth twisted her jaw, freezing every muscle.

"Fire him!" shouted Larry from the other table.

"Putting the trader out of business doesn't guarantee he'll crawl home with a white flag!" cried Belinda, loud enough for Larry's graveyard temptation to rest peacefully for a while.

"How terrible, if Jackie or his girlfriend still want him. We can't pull them apart. What's next? Let Chuck decide, it's his father and mother. And it's his family. If we put them together, they might eat at each other till everyone has to escape for safety," murmured Sandy, knowing that Chuck was listening to everything without commenting on any course of action.

"Here Belinda," cried Virus, "I'm bushed." He handed her a page before he made his way upstairs.

"Belinda, now you know," said Larry, "why he wants you here. You've got the codes for the company and the hospital."

"Yes, double trouble," exclaimed Belinda. "We're in it up to our necks, we're stuck between the Dead Sea and quicksand. He drags us all the way in."

"I didn't know you were as crazy as he is," said Larry.

"Larry, do your stuff!" said Sandy. "This calls for affirmative action. Go Belinda!" Belinda led the way to the computer and took her seat while Sandy looked over her shoulder. "Bingo! You nailed it. There, the recommendation section," she happily instructed, witnessing how easily Belinda got around on a computer. She started to read what Belinda wrote. "After intense reflection, I recommend an immediate transfer to Head Office. His knowledge of the company is a costly investment, and it should be highly guarded. He should be promoted to Director of Marketing." Next, Belinda drifted to the title of the report and wrote, "Top Priority!" and underlined the word "Confidential!" As soon as she finished, she sent a copy to each board member, including the president and vice-president, via the company's internal electronic mail system. To close, she changed the company computer's internal date to the correct date and time.

Before Belinda could exit Sandy asked, "Are you sure about this? Doesn't he have to be a shareholder for that job?" Belinda, nonetheless, closed the file.

"Sandy, if you want to know, businesses accept benefits, not losses," she replied carefully.

"Where is Virus?" asked Chuck, pretending to be unaware of the fact that Virus had left. "We've got a correlation. He has the same nights off as my Mom. Nick's wife works when he's off. Virus even gave us their schedule for next month."

"So?" asked Larry, as he turned his full attention to the conversation as usual. "You guys are just too kind. We should roast him. Send him to the unemployment office. No! Take his employment record, and write 'terminated.' His act is incompatible with hospital ethical codes of conduct between colleagues. Oh, that's too kind. Just condemn all of them to hell, cheating on their wives, I don't care too much for adultery. How low can you get? They're all working in the same department. For adults, their world is smaller their crotch. Shame, guilt, bad conscience are out of favor these days in the real world." He cocked his head and glanced at Lenny for some remark, but none was coming from his hidden face.

"Of course, Larry, it's better if I handle the situation. You can go have yourself a Coke upstairs," said Belinda. "You too," she told Lenny and Chuck.

"Here then, I've circled the days when he was off and his wife worked," said Larry, returning the pages to Sandy. Sandy knew that she could remain downstairs.

"Should I get you all a Coke?" asked Larry, hoping to have a positive answer. But none came from the girls.

"What are they up to?" questioned Chuck, eager to be there like Larry.

"You should be happy, your old man has a transfer. And your old lady will be working day shifts, I figure," said Larry, as they were climbing the stairs.

"Larry, what makes you think she'll have day shifts next month?" questioned Lenny.

"Virus, he got us here for that reason. Didn't he?" he replied, thinking that with several ideas floating around, the lesser evil could have its course. "Look, the Buddha is sleeping with his eyes open, checking us with his mind." While Larry and Lenny sat on the same side of the table, Chuck went to the counter. They waited until he returned with something to drink and eat, and he squeezed himself near Virus. They rewarded themselves with a dozen donuts. "Fresh," murmured Larry. "You're content, now, Chuck. I guess things are fixed. It's funny!" he said with a huge smile on his face. "I just want to see your Dad and Mom facing each other. I wonder who will spit it out in the open first? To say something about egoism, the first one to confess would be the first one to be condemned, while the second one plays the innocent game, the untouchable." Nobody at the table was amused, for this had already crossed everyone's mind.

"Look! There they are!" cried Larry. "Well, tigresses, have you started eating your own tails?" The girls ignored him and pulled themselves two chairs, helping themselves with the remaining food on the table. The wind was turning to a storm, the young had hatched like eggs frying in the desert. Giant lizards had been playing with their food but the young did not know any games. Now, paradise was available to those who stood with both feet on the ground.

"Lenny, your mother is with the hospital payroll. We found her application for general cleaning duties. The hospital offered a part-time job, three days per week. Starting next month, she'll have a confirmation letter from the personnel office," said Sandy. Everyone was amazed, but hiring and firing were computer activities, and finding a match between job descriptions and human skills did not require human intervention. Larry took Lenny's pocket phone and went to the computer room.

"She'd really applied there. I didn't know that," said Lenny, trying to feel happy, seeing his mother as a person. "Fantastic, I don't know what to say. Her common sense, after a long struggle, happens to have an outlet. What's next? Wait and see, I guess."

"To put the final touch on everything, Chuck's father was in for a transfer, the director of marketing, in town. We couldn't do much about your mother, Chuck. Other than changing her working hours, and switching her to a different ward. We put the Petersons together for the next six months to work the same shift," said Belinda. She knew everything was done, and she could contemplate her actions, now. Except for Virus, everyone was stagnant and speechless as though a revelation had come to life.

"Well, this day has never occurred, in reality," cried Larry as he mounted the stairs. "I did it, imitating an old man with a sore throat!" he continued, causing Virus's head to slowly raise above the table, exposing his sleepy eyes and incredible tiredness. Larry took a sip of Coke to relocate the germs in his mouth. "I wore the hat of Mrs. Peterson's private detective. I told him I'd been observing his disgusting and deceptive relationship with Mrs. Crawford for several months. I told him I had to give his wife a report next week concerning his whereabouts and his activities. He was hysterical. And he took an oath with me, to live honestly with his wife who loves him the most. In turn, I'd destroy the file without anybody knowing anything, not even Peggy. And he shouldn't ever mention this to her. It was really funny, when I told him about the joke they'd play on him at his work place. Nobody would ever trust him, not even with a dog, let alone with a female patient. To polish his taste a little bit more, I told him I have over twenty years of experience in this matter. And he should phone Jackie and discuss the end of their relationship, like two mature people, today. It's incredible, for the first time, I forgot to get angry." He tried to control his laughter. Nobody else was rolling on the floor.

"Larry, your day isn't over yet," said Chuck.

"I know, I know," said Larry. "Whenever we turn a corner,

we'll be looking out for police. We'll wonder whether or not it's our turn. It'll become unbearable. Until we want to go ask him for mercy and compassion, and beg him not to take us. We're sorry, sir. We won't do it again. Never, never again, we promise. But we won't do this. And worse, there'll be no escape from our own consciousness and fear. I see, things will get bad, unbearable, until our great minds create a rationalization. We'll start to hate police, wanting to exterminate them, wishing them away. But, we can't. They're here to stay. So, the only escape is hardening ourselves some more, committing some more illegal acts. It's the only way to confuse ourselves about which offences they're coming to get us for. Soon, before we know it, our mind is like Jell-O. Now, we're running away from our own shadow. And next, the laws shadow us to our graves. We'll try to hide ourselves, staying in the dark, without a shadow."

"Laws are for everyone to obey," cried Lenny. "But survival surpasses any institution, any community's rules and laws. The drive to survival knows no borders, my friends. We shouldn't feel good, when everyone feels sorry for us. We did what we think is right only in a non-repeatable situation. Let's face it, man is a weakling. And laws disguise his fragility like children hiding themselves under their mother's dress. That's human beings. Look at you, Virus, Larry, Belinda, Sandy, and Chuck, we're the nimble. We merely violate our own nature, we don't have anything sensible and permanent to paint ourselves with. Everything we did is utterly innocent. If it must be known, our judicial system rewards and punishes people's weaknesses with its own disgusting, fallible, and inherited wickedness. Listen, guys, we're guilty under adult laws. But to apply them to us, it's uncivilized." Lenny needed to justify his own actions, for he had to live with himself first, and then with society. The others waited for the magic word, which would enlighten them, elevate them, and remove this weight from their shoulders.

"Some people have a few notions about others and even fewer about themselves," said Sandy. "Mixing ourselves with others is a fact of life. Without thinking, two individuals have deliberately decided to undertake a certain course of action, to be together, to have children, and what not. The having of children implies a tacit consent, from both of them. Parents are held responsible for the third person. And they're responsible for their act from which a baby is conceived. Nobody is ignorant about the consequence of having sex. Sex is a responsible act; both persons agree to it. Children are conceived from responsibility. I'm not talking about exceptional cases like rape. Some laws protect children from sexual abuse from adults, and even from other children. This shows you there's a responsibility in mating. Chuck only fights for his right. And parents can't escape so easily from sacrificing themselves for the third person, for us."

"What we have today is an entire institution telling people that divorce and separation are alternatives, benefiting both parents. This may be so for parents, but not for Chuck. Chuck's parents surrender their right and individuality for their son's existence. How meaningless would adults' lives be without children around? They wouldn't have anything to hold them together, eternally. Without us, their own little lives would depreciate quicker than their expensive new cars. We don't want their wealth, only their caring, love and guidance. Just their spirit and strength, we need as nourishment. Our act has an eternal value, Chuck's life has an eternal meaning to him, and we must tell his parents that. We attempt to preserve life, the only eternal essence in human beings. Life taps us on our shoulder, my friends. At least, the Christian God—as a matter of fact, any God—would suspend His judgment, for He knows we've just started. Even God said we are created in His image, and we're still creating this image. We're image-makers. So, we're not the Big-Time-Believer of the Golden Apple anymore." She pulled herself back from her viewpoint to take a deep breath.

"Everybody wants a good argument for what we've done," exclaimed Belinda. "I've done it, and I'll do it again."

"We all want the best possible world. Since we're living in the actual one, we can change the actual one by fashioning a possible world. I hope you're following me. We've just done it, placing a possible world that must be actualized," cried Chuck, as Virus finally gave him an approving smile.

"I didn't sleep so well last night, and that's that," Virus said, continuing to smile. "I guess everyone is waiting for me, because I called you here. I confess, if worse comes to worst, I did it," whispered Virus. For him everything had already been done before they arrived this morning. "So, let's go home, and grow in our own way. Before I go, here Lenny, you can make as many copies as you wish. You can sell as much cocaine as you wish. There's no limitation. If I don't go home now, someone will have to drive me home." He took off, leaving the world standing with only a few people to dictate its faith.

In each generation, some people held the faith of others in their hands. Lenny held humanity in his hand. Would he protect them as a sacred species? Or use his power for his own advantage? With Virus' departure, they saw tomorrow as an unfinished product; it had to be continuously worked upon and reshaped.

11: People Arranged Themselves

It was already October; the summer had brought its fruit and was closing in, with new roots gathering soil around themselves to overcome seasons. Two months before, thirty-five offices had been opened around the world, and each carried the name "Proud City."

Proud City had become infested with adults' reality—unemployment, pollution, materialism. But to the young, Proud City was their home, their way of life, their future, their active role in society to shape their future. Proud City was becoming more than just a place, but a symbol of the high spirit of the young, overcoming the low spirit of the old. Proud City could be any city in the world—in Japan, Canada, the U.S., Peru, Cuba. Proud City could be found in each family, in the relationships between mother and son, father and daughter. And Proud City could be found in each person, in his values, interests, habits, and feelings.

Mostly Belinda, Sandy, Sam, and Tim were responsible for organizing and synchronizing the opening of all the offices at once—making it the most sophisticated organization in human history. From the local office here, each office was connected, using the most modern communication technology. Through this network, other offices sent and distributed important information concerning the direction of Proud City, creating a workable standard for each party.

Sam's family had donated and renovated the office building in the middle of town, and Sandy's family had supplied all the necessary office furniture and stationary free. The community participated by picking up the phone, heating, water, and electric bills. Tim was in charge of the database and the general maintenance of the office, including reinvesting one third of Lenny's remaining funds in local businesses in Proud City. Everyone was on salary until the age of twenty; salary workers were encouraged to change their office after a few years. Most high school students wanted to be volunteers, and adults from all socio-economic sectors offered their free services. Proud City had to remind the mob of volunteers that it was a reality, not a God. It selected volunteers pragmatically; the first choice was children, then adults without families, and so on.

Together they created a manifesto, outlining their demands and expectations for the future. A constitutional policy concerning anyone below the age of twenty, and judicial systems with similar laws to cover all participants around the world, were established. Because of Martin's technical training in jurisprudence, he was occupied with drafting legal codes for Proud City's inhabitants. Except for victims of rape and incest, abortion would be considered legal only on the grounds that aborters completely gave up their right to bear or to adopt another child in their life. This article applied to both parents, biological or legal. Concerning putting up a child for adoption, both parents, biological or legal, surrendered the right to ever have another child by birth or adoption in the future. Concerning divorce when that marriage or any prior marriage act had conceived a child or children, both legal and biological parents surrendered their right to have another child. Moreover, in the case of divorce, the third party, a biological or legal child or children, legally owned all the property of their parents. In single-parent cases, Proud City would become the other parent with respect to the general welfare of the child, without taking any financial responsibility.

If military services were obligatory in a country, anyone would have the right to postpone his or her service until he or she was sixty-five years old. Members of Proud City would have fifty-one percent of the voting right in any government,because decision-making in one country directly and indirectly affected other countries. If anyone below the age of twenty years committed an offence or offences, then that person would be tried according to Proud City's judicial system. If any adult committed an offence against Proud City's inhabitants, then Proud City's laws would take precedence over any other legal systems.

They realized that for Proud City to enforce its laws, it would have to be connected to the adult legal system, which had all the necessary resources to apprehend and penalize criminals. The court would be held in the adult court building. Unlike the adult court, lawyers, judges, and juries would be Proud City inhabitants, below twenty. Since Proud City would not dish out the death penalty for any crime, if an adult had raped or sexually abused a youngster, then the judge and juries would be rape and abuse victims. And if it were not possible to find any victims in a national sweep, then ordinary members would have to occupy the aforementioned posts as lawyers, judges, and juries. In most legal proceedings, there would be ten juries, and each jury would vote on a point basis by pressing a button in his jury box. There were ten buttons, numbering one to ten. Near the end of a legal proceeding, a jury would just press a number, and if the total points were fifty or more, the accused was guilty. The judge would pronounce penalty, when guilt was proven, on a mathematical calculation. If the juries' total points were ten, then the judge would dish out the minimum penalty to the accused—suspiciously free but never completely free from guilt.

An open door policy concerning admission to any university and college would be guaranteed—regardless of high school grades. Each high school student would have the right to be taught the laws of Proud City at any academic institution of his or her choice. This course could be completed in about one school year, and it took precedence over learning mathematics and science courses.

Proud City's inhabitants could buy anything without paying taxes. Unemployed people would be allowed to have free public transportation and all purchases for them would be tax-free, too. A special card, like a credit card, would be given to both the unemployed and youngsters.

The idea of Proud City was growing and there was no stopping it; the eternal flame had found its furnace; life could walk again without being threatened by a two thousand year old expired correlation between age and rationality. During this warm summer day, seven hundred families had been invited to Victoria Park for a picnic, getting to know one another, bringing in all the different worlds together, and removing all the mysteries about the other. Proud City assumed the charges for all the food and drinks. There were more than nineteen hundred people at the park. Some came from other cities and nearby suburbs, and others were from the local community. Most invited guests had to freely transform themselves into hosts for the uninvited ones; they had to raid their own fridges for more food and drinks. Some local vendors had to open their back doors on a Sunday to meet the demand.

Among the invited were Virus's father, Mr. Bishop, and some of his business colleagues. He attempted to explain to non-businesspeople that they had never meant to hurt anybody. Because business was still in a pre-scientific stage, business people had believed that to get ahead, they had to eliminate competition. In doing so, they put businesses on a fatalistic course with no gain; with no competitors, no suppliers, and no customers, everybody suffers. They inherited primitive business practices; they mostly thought about the investors and shareholders as the backbone of it all, without whom they would crawl on their bellies. But Mr. Bishop was learning that the most important investors were customers. Without them, stockholders could not exist; they were nothing without buyers. Customers should see the direct profit of what businesses produced, including the income generated to purchase goods. If people could not, they failed, and shareholders crumbled, too.

The objective of business was to create jobs. If they were successful with that, other things like profits would follow. Lean and mean business practices meant top managers had a secure place as idols, while others had to beg. Mr. Bishop realized that instead, every year companies should think about creating ten more jobs,

All this meant that workers in companies would have to work smarter, not harder, to create more work for others to do.

Mr. Bishop recognized his son as his tutor, opening his eyes to the reality of the young: consumers as beggars could not support any business. Every business was necessary to enhance survival, and the continuation of businesses depended on the trust of people from different classes. For everyone had to be humble and to share each other's reality, because a single person could not survive very long without others.

Scott, crawling home, and Jackie, enjoying her new job, were also among the invited. They came to their senses, realizing there was, at least, one thing they could be absolutely certain of. They had a son, and to be reliable guardians for their son was their objective. Neither Scott nor Jackie had mentioned anything about their insignificant adventures.

The man of the good book, Larry's father, was here as well, thanking the businesspeople and community leaders for being able to recognize their own feet without any shoes on.

Some young men and women were extremely busy with their parents—getting them to feel comfortable in their new situation, introducing them to other visitors, guiding their conversations, breaking their rigidity, removing their tightened masks—so trust and understanding were established among them. Since it was the first grand meeting, some worldlings guided their parents and other family members into a world that surpassed their parents' one. Worldlings introduced themselves.

Though Doris had found her new joy at the hospital, and though she already knew a lot of people here, Lenny had to introduce his parents around and stay near them continuously. His parents and Slade's parents grew up on the same block, and they were fused together.

Lenny did not really mind that, but after several hours he was sick of seeing Slade tailing along. Slade had been invited to the picnic, but he had invited his entire gang as well. Though some of his gang members brought their parents along, others just came for the big free meal and to check out the scene. Slade's gang was very radical against business. They phoned businesses around the country to fill their computer voicemails with triviality, electro-smog, recordings of a truck engine, etc. They also sent email messages to a company until its memory was exhausted. Their gang was also getting bigger, with several hundred members. Slade was particularly jealous because Lenny had the antimatter programs, which he did not want to share with anyone. And Lenny knew this very well. A Lenny or a Slade could challenge any world order: one of them, at least, could be easily found in any epoch. Utopia resided with dead people; in contrast, institutions and people had to modify themselves to accommodate new situations constructively.

As the picnic was enjoying its climax, several police cars arrived unexpectedly. The entire police department came, Charles and Alex leading the way. Though many people were unaccustomed to friendly police visits, they were at ease after they noticed that the officers were served some food and were mingling without searching for criminals. People were friendlier toward them without digging into their unconsciousness for ghosts, and found that the sweetness of life hung on a tiny bit of trust and tolerance. There was no need to shape oneself into the Big Time Believer of greatness and success, for life had it all in the worldlings' destiny.

About the author

Amo Sulaiman

Born in Guyana and continuing his education in Canada, Amo Sulaiman received a B.A. degree in Philosophy and Psychology at the University of Guelph in Ontario. He then completed his Master's degree in Philosophy in Montreal. Shortly after this, he went to Switzerland where he did his Doctorate in Philosophy at the University of Bern. He has been living in Switzerland ever since.

Besides publishing two books on philosophy, one on English literature, and several academic articles, Proud City is his first novel.

Other titles available through Picasso Publications:

The Carnevalis of Eusebius Asch
Peter Gimpel
(Red Heifer Press)

Beethoven and Schoenberg, Schumann and Hesse, Levi-Strauss and Vico, each has a role in this seagoing carnival of platonic lust and manic scholarship - a role as Protean and unpredictable as that of "Zeebee" himself, as he struggles to recreate the world in his own fuzzy image - a world in which the erudition of Faust, the wisdom of the Rabbis, the music of the spheres, and the angelic charms of a forbidden coed, all succumb to his miscalculated advances.

ISBN: 0-9631478-1-1
$7.95 US
paperback

The Final Warning
Kathleen A. Keating
(Picasso Publications)

A worldwide disaster is approaching and you won't be able to escape it! Wherever you are - in a plane, at the office, or doing laundry - it will find you!

The Final Warning can prepare you in the final minutes of the era. It is your survival guide and your beacon of hope in the darkness of chaos.

ISBN: 1-55279-030-4
$22.95 US, $24.95 CAN
hardcover

Chinese Encounter
William Steeb
(AGBE Publishing)

As professor Tim Bennison, international aid advisor, travels to China on government business, he uncovers with wit and insight the real face of China – a country fighting with itself and its deep-rooted feudal nature as it searches for new economic paradigms and moral standards.

ISBN: 9810430183
$15.00 (US), $19.95 (CAN)
softcover

Wisdom of One
Thomas C. Kelly
(Hara Publishing)

Wisdom of One is an exceptional new book of quotes unlike any that have been before. Author Thomas E. Kelly chose each of the 1400 plus quotes, from a wide range of thinkers who span two millennia, for their existential-1st point of view. The result is not a depressing, fatalistic work that reflects the popular misconception of the existentialist ideal. Instead, Wisdom of One provokes thought, offers insight, promotes self-determination, and celebrates living life in the present.

ISBN: 1-883697-42-5
$12.95 (US), $16.95 (CAN)
paperback

Available at your local bookstore, online at Picasso's web site, or mail/fax your order to:

Picasso Publications
10548 – 115 Street
Edmonton, AB
Canada
T5H 3K6

Tel: 1-877-737-2665
Fax: 1-877-250-2665

Or order online at: www.picassopublications.com